P9-ELT-054

For Tony
Fernandez

Advance Praise for The Agenda

"A recipe for winning in today's fast-moving, hypercompetitive world."
    —**Dave Pottruck**, president and co-CEO, The Charles Schwab Corporation

"I've long admired Michael Hammer's insights into what's wrong with businesses and his prescription for improvement. Dr. Hammer is absolutely on the mark about how growth has to be created, not just harvested, and that makes management among the most difficult, risky, and precarious of human endeavors. Today with dot-coms turning into dot-bombs and even long-established businesses being upset by upstarts, *The Agenda* provides a series of valuable lessons for anyone seeking success in the consumer-dominated economy. Read this book—and hope your competitors do not."
    —**Joseph Nacchio**, chairman and CEO, Qwest Communications

"Investing even just a few hours in *The Agenda* can help set your agenda for outexecuting the competition. Hammer has written an anatomy of execution, revealing the key processes that drive customer value and consistently superior performance. His principles certainly resonate with EMC—aka the Execution Machine Company."
    —**Joe Tucci**, president and CEO, EMC Corporation

"Michael Hammer has once again forged ahead of the pack with a practical, specific, easily understood, and prophetic view of what's ahead. As world business competition continues to intensify, CEOs will do well to listen to Hammer."
    —**Larry Bossidy**, chairman and CEO of Honeywell International

"As usual, Mike Hammer brings the reality of the emerging and demanding game of business to the forefront. Winning customers and retaining them is the real game of business. At the same time, creating shareholder value is what counts. This is the book of how. It is remarkably clear, easy to understand, and enables the reader to take action and execute. It's devoid of jargon and platitudes. Simplicity is its virtue. And practicality is its value."
    —**Ram Charan**, author of *Boards at Work* and *What the CEO Wants You to Know*

"*The Agenda* addresses two critical and timeless leadership imperatives: focusing on the customer and fostering teamwork. Michael Hammer's tool kit for addressing the agenda of the future is clear, inspiring, and practical."
    —**David A. Spina**, chairman and CEO, State Street Corporation

"Like Dr. Hammer's previous books, *The Agenda* articulates a new and important business sea change, the emergence of a customer-centric economy. His practical road map—for those who are willing to rise to the challenge—is a wake-up call rallying business leaders to start thinking like customers. From the boardroom to middle management, this is a must-read for every company executive. Your company's future depends on it."
    —**Mackey J. McDonald**, CEO, chairman, and president, VF Corporation

"All you can ask of any business book is for it to make you think about how your organization performs. In *The Agenda* Mike Hammer gives us a lot to think about."
    —**Mike Eskew**, vice chairman, United Parcel Service

ALSO BY MICHAEL HAMMER

Reengineering the Corporation:
A Manifesto for Business Revolution

The Reengineering Revolution:
A Handbook

Beyond Reengineering:
How the Processed-Centered Organization
Is Changing Our Work and Our Lives

The Agenda

*What Every Business
Must Do to Dominate
the Decade*

MICHAEL
HAMMER

CROWN
BUSINESS
NEW YORK

Copyright © 2001 by Michael Hammer

All rights reserved. No part of this book may be reproduced or transmitted in any form or by any means, electronic or mechanical, including photocopying, record-ing, or by any information storage and retrieval system, without permission in writ-ing from the publisher.

Published by Crown Business, New York, New York.
Member of the Crown Publishing Group.

Random House, Inc. New York, Toronto, London, Sydney, Auckland
www.randomhouse.com

Crown Business is a trademark and the Rising Sun colophon is a registered trademark of Random House, Inc.

Printed in the United States of America

Library of Congress Cataloging-in-Publication Data
Hammer, Michael, 1948–
    The agenda : what every business must do to dominate the decade /
Michael Hammer.—1st ed.
    1. Organizational change.   2. Organizational effectiveness.   3. Consumer
satisfaction.   4. Competition.   I. Title: What every business must do to
dominate the decade.   II. Title.
    HD58.8 .H3548   2001
    658—dc21   2001028954

ISBN 0-609-60966-1

10 9 8 7 6 5 4 3 2 1

First Edition

In memory of my mother

Helen Gartner Hammer

1919–1997

A woman of extraordinary intelligence, great humor,

and unfathomable courage.

She taught me more than I could ever learn.

Acknowledgments

Some books seem to write themselves; this one most assuredly did not. Fortunately, others lent their shoulders to the task of pushing this boulder up its hill. Jeff Goding and John Hughes made major contributions to the research and learning that underlie this book. Hannah Beal Will and Lindsay Field made sure that neither the book nor I fell between the cracks that kept opening beneath our feet. I owe a special debt to Donna Sammons Carpenter, who urged me to undertake this project in the first place and provided invaluable and insightful advice along the way. Bob Barnett did everything and more that one can expect from a literary agent. John Mahaney, my editor at Crown, has been a forceful and articulate champion for this book, and his critiques and suggestions have been flawless. Above all, my wife, Phyllis, with her wisdom and her optimism, kept me from falling off the rails more than once, and she and our four children tolerated with good humor the side effects of a seemingly infinite number of drafts. To all these and more, I offer my deepest appreciation.

Contents

Contents

Preface

In reflecting on how this book came to be, I am reminded of a line from the Grateful Dead's 1970 anthem "Truckin'": "Lately it occurs to me, what a long strange trip it's been." My own journey to this book has been very long and more than a little strange.

I arrived at MIT in 1964 with some nine hundred other freshmen. Though we didn't know it at the time, we were about to witness—and in some cases, contribute to—the dawn of the computer age. At that time, computing was still an obscure and peripheral phenomenon. Out of the public eye, and principally employed for scientific and accounting applications, computers of the 1960s were, by modern standards, extremely weak. Yet something about the computer fascinated many of my generation. We were attracted by its exactitude and its clarity, and perhaps by the ability it afforded us to control a machine that could even then outperform the human mind. Many of us followed its siren call, abandoning more traditional fields of study to push the envelope on hardware and (especially) software technology. We became software engineers and computer scientists before these terms were coined. Silicon Valley may be its contemporary center, but the modern computer industry was forged in the crucible of Cambridge in the 60s and 70s. Among my professors and classmates and (later) my colleagues and students were the inventor of the Ethernet, the builder of Lotus 123, and the architects of the Internet. Caught up in the heady atmosphere of creativity and invention that defined the Cambridge *zeitgeist*, I continued at MIT to earn a Ph.D. in computer science, and then joined the faculty in that field.

But over time, it became apparent to me that I did not share my colleagues' intense passion for and exclusive preoccupation with computing technology. I was also curious about the applications of computers, the purposes for which people actually employed our inventions, and about how this technology was changing the ways in which people did their work and lived their lives. So in 1982, I resigned my tenured position at MIT (an act that some thought bordered on madness) and set off to explore the "real world" of business.

In this endeavor, I had the great advantage of never having attended business school. As a result, I did not perceive the business world filtered through the theories and expectations transmitted in the classroom. Rather, I saw it unencumbered, unmediated, and as it really was. And what I saw appalled me.

As a naïve academic, I had assumed that sophisticated business-people were exploiting the power of the computer in imaginative ways. Instead, I discovered that the vast majority of companies were simply overlaying computer technology on antiquated business practices: "paving the cowpaths." Where was the imagination, the creativity, the elegance? Even worse, as I looked more closely, I found that the operations of supposedly great corporations, automated or otherwise, were largely haphazard and undesigned, cobbled together in the crudest of ad hoc fashions, and rife with inefficiency and waste. Pampered by buoyant economic conditions and pliant customers, companies were wasting the business opportunities that computer technology was offering them. They were operating as they always had, using the new devices without thinking deeply about them, and squandering the ability to harness the power of the computer to truly innovative ways of doing business. To an engineer like myself, this was an outrage bordering on the sinful.

There were some bright spots in this bleak landscape. In my peregrinations, I had the good fortune to come across a few companies that were actually starting to do things differently. Usually because they were in desperate straits, these companies were forced to make truly fundamental changes. They rethought how they worked and created unprecedented methods of operation. They reinvented their old ways instead of merely automating them, and they deployed technology in support of these innovations. The results these companies achieved were breathtaking, and more than justified the bold risks they had taken. Here was something new and exciting.

While I was thrilled to encounter this work, it felt incomplete to me. My training in the disciplines of mathematics and engineering pushed me to look for the theory that underlay these innovations, the axioms and first principles that these companies had applied. Unfortunately, there were none to be found. These companies had been improvising, not following a textbook. They had their hands full creating new ways of working; developing ideologies to support them was a luxury they could not afford. That responsibility fell to me. Starting with the raw material of their experiences, I worked to synthesize an explanatory theory of what they had done, as well as a methodology for others to emulate. Thus was born reengineering.

Reengineering was the term I coined to describe these innovative ways of doing business. During the 1990s many other companies joined the pioneers that I had found, and reengineering evolved from experimental construct into serious business practice, employed by hundreds of major companies and countless smaller ones. Throughout the decade, I continued to study these companies, their new ways of doing business, and the challenges they encountered in implementation; I documented my findings in two further books.

While I learned many things from my studies, the most important one was that Curly was very, and even dangerously, wrong. I refer not to the Curly of Three Stooges fame, but rather to the taciturn cowpoke in the film *City Slickers,* played by Jack Palance. In the film, Curly offers a bit of Zen-like counsel to Billy Crystal's character, a seeker after life's purpose: "It's just one thing," meaning that everyone should focus on just a single goal. Perhaps that is good advice in private life, but following it in business leads to disasters even worse than cattle stampedes. In reality, as opposed to the movies, there is no one grand solution to the problems of business, no one technique or single idea that brings salvation and success.

One of the (inadvertent) sins for which I may one day be called to account is having caused to be unleashed on an unsuspecting world a flood of "big idea" business books. *Reengineering the Corporation* had one central notion, that dramatic performance improvements could be achieved through radical changes in business operations. While I did not claim that reengineering was all that companies needed to do to defeat their competitors, the popularity of the book and success of the concept led some to see it as a panacea, which in turn encouraged others to promote their favorite silver bullets. For nearly a decade, businesspeople have been deluged with books promising simple recipes for eternal victory. Perhaps part of my atonement for this unintentional transgression has been to write *The Agenda.*

For Curly indeed was very wrong. There are no silver bullets. In my studies of the past decade, I have found that the best companies have been innovating on a broad front: reengineering their business processes, to be sure, but doing much else as well. Leaders of these organizations have been questioning and reshaping virtually everything about them, from the roles of managers to the structure of measurement systems to relationships with suppliers and customers. Again, as was the case with reengineering, these innovations were not applications of some previously developed theory or set of principles. They were tactical battlefield responses to the challenges of a new business environment. The power and success of these innovations demanded that they be chronicled and explained. *The Agenda* is the result.

The goal of *The Agenda* is to illuminate a set of nine emerging business concepts that underlie how the best companies around are mastering today's turbulent environment. While a number of motifs—the power of process, evaporating boundaries, profound cultural change—recur throughout the book, each of these nine ideas, presented in its own chapter, stands largely on its own. By highlighting them, I hope to make them explicit and accessible to the entire business community. For companies to survive and thrive, everyone from the front lines to the boardroom needs to understand and act upon these themes.

They capture what is happening right now at the business frontier, and they will shape management discourse of the coming decade, much as reengineering shaped that of the last one.

Long and strange though the trip to *The Agenda* may have been, it was also fascinating and exciting. I hope that the book captures some of the thrills of that journey, and that you have as much fun at the destination as I did along the way.

The Agenda

1

Get Serious About Business Again

Welcome to the Customer Economy

S uddenly, business is not so easy anymore.

For a very brief period in the late 1990s, it seemed that all the problems of business had been solved. Everywhere one turned, enterprises were booming. Established companies were racking up record sales and earnings. Start-ups were deluged with capital. Everyone was doing well, and everyone was making money. Growth and success were taken for granted. Confidence was high. Customers were spending. The stock market was moving in one direction only—up.

Anyone seemed to be able to win at business. Knowledge, technique, and experience were not needed, only energy, gumption, and attitude. The new American dream had nothing to do with working hard and long to build a business but featured instead hanging out with some buddies, coming up with a cool idea, and "going public" in a year or so. The business *zeitgeist,* as promoted by self-proclaimed visionaries, was that we were in a "New Economy," in which the business cycle had become a thing of the past. The Internet had changed everything, and mundane issues like cost and quality and inventory had become irrelevant.

Not anymore. The longest economic expansion in U.S. history is winding down, and the giddy days of the 1990s are now mere memories. As of this writing, the business media are no longer reporting on plants running over capacity, on companies scrambling to fill positions, or on venture-funded start-ups revolutionizing this industry or that. Instead, we are hearing about layoffs and store closings, energy shortages and soaring costs, decreased advertising and lower profits, missed earnings expectations and steep stock market declines. Business school applications are up, and IPOs are down.

Businesspeople's smugness has given way to anxiety. They can no longer take growth for granted or assume that this year will be better than last. Now they must worry whether customers will buy, costs will rise, or competitors will overtake them. They lie awake wondering if the fundamental premises of their businesses will remain valid. They are shocked to find that markets go down as well as up and that growth has to be created, not just harvested. Managers are learning again that most new ideas do not succeed, that many companies fail, that resources are always scarce, and that above all, business is not a game for amateurs.

Managers are rediscovering that business is about execution. It is not about having the right "business model" or capturing eyeballs, about creating a really cool work space or planning a launch party. Suddenly bereft of inflated stock market evaluations—a cushion that on the one hand allowed companies to make acquisitions for free and to pay their people with options instead of money, and that on the other made customers feel rich and free-spending—businesspeople are back to watching every penny. They have been reminded that it's not enough to get the order, you have to fill it; that having an idea for a product does you no good if you can't develop it; and that even Wall Street analysts will be fooled by a hot concept only for so long. Business today is no longer about grand visions and the arrogance of youth. The time is past for frivolous notions and flights of fancy. Business today is about nuts and bolts, the mechanics of making companies work. It is serious stuff.

Even if the current downturn proves to be brief, even if fiscal and monetary policymakers pull more rabbits out of their hats, there will be no return to the state of innocence of the 1990s. Just as a generation of investors was permanently scarred by the Great Depression, a generation of managers has been transformed by the collapse of the bubble of the late 1990s. They have become modest and serious, fearful of their environment and uncertain about their futures.

This is as it should be. The halcyon days of the 1990s were an aberration. Tough times are the norm. Only rarely do external events conspire to give us an environment in which businesses can operate nearly effortlessly. The 1950s were one such period, when the United States alone had an intact economy with which to take advantage of the postwar expansion. The late 1990s was another. But between such occasional interludes, business is very difficult indeed. In ordinary times, businesspeople must wrest market share from their competitors, motivate customers to part with scarce cash, earn success instead of having it handed to them, and wake up each morning knowing that all of yesterday's accomplishments count for nothing today. This was what we faced in the 1970s, in the aftermath of the energy crisis, and in the 1980s, when we confronted the onslaught of Japanese imports. It is what we encounter today and will continue to face in the future.

In short, today's managers have rediscovered that business is not easy. Management has always been and continues to be among the most complex, risky, and uncertain of all human endeavors. Indeed, how could anyone have ever thought otherwise?

If managing were simple, why do the majority of new businesses fail? If physicians had the same success rate as executives, the medical schools would have been shuttered long ago.

If managing were simple, why do so many new products founder in the marketplace? From the Ford Edsel to the Apple Newton and New Coke, the business landscape is littered with the remains of can't-miss products that did.

If managing were simple, why do even companies that become successful stay that way for such short periods of time? Why did Pan Am go out of business, why is Xerox near bankruptcy, why did Digital Equipment fall victim to acquisition? Why have such former industry titans as Lucent and General Motors, Levi Strauss and Rubbermaid, become mere shadows of their former selves?

If managing were simple, how do leading companies allow themselves to be overtaken by upstarts? How could Nokia have stolen a march on Motorola? Why do giant banks now stand in awe of GE Capital?

If managing were simple, why do so many successful managers have trouble replicating their success when they change companies? Why did AT&T come to the brink under Michael Armstrong, who had been so effective at Hughes?

If managing were simple, why do so many managers fall prey to the nostrums of hucksters? Why are they such suckers for fads? If they were not overwhelmed by the complexities of their responsibilities, they would never be taken in by superficial and simplistic remedies. They would not be tempted to believe that all they had to do to tame the beast of business was to run their companies like Silicon Valley startups, or set outrageous goals, or embrace the Internet.

The challenges of management are eternal and extraordinarily difficult. How can a company devise products and services that satisfy customers, and at the same time deliver them in a profitable way that satisfies shareholders? How can a company retain customers in the face of new competitors, and respond to new needs without sacrificing its existing position? How does a company distinguish itself from other companies with similar offerings and identical goals, and maintain its success as times change? Devising the answers to these questions is the eternal task of management.

Periodically, the answers to these questions are codified, written down in management compendia, taught at business schools, and enshrined in the folklore of working managers. Peter Drucker's 1973 magnum opus, *Management,* was one such compendium. Tom Peters and Bob Waterman's 1982 *In Search of Excellence* was another. But although the problems are eternal, the solutions are not. Each generation of managers faces a world different from that faced by its predecessors, and so each must find its own direction.

It is told that Albert Einstein once handed his secretary an exam to be distributed to his graduate students. The secretary scanned the paper and objected, "But Professor Einstein, these are the same questions you used last year. Won't the students already know the answers?" "It's all right, you see," replied Einstein, "the questions are the same, but the answers are different." What is true of physics is true of business. Today's business world is not that of Drucker or of Peters and Waterman, and it calls for a new edition of the management agenda. The mission of this book is to set it forth.

Today's managers need a new agenda because they are doing business in the aftermath of an epochal shift. In the fourth quarter of the twentieth century, suppliers, who until then had dominated industrialized economies and set the terms for how business was done, lost their position of dominance to their customers. Over the past twenty-five years, customers in virtually all industries have revolted against the suppliers who previously held them in thrall. Consumers abandoned the companies to whose brands they had long been loyal and embraced generics, house brands, international competitors, and anyone else who offered a better deal. They did this in cars and household products, in banking services and TV stations. Corporate customers stopped tolerating abuse from suppliers who condescended to fill their orders. They refused to accept high prices, low quality, and dreadful service just to get what they needed. Instead, corporate customers now instruct their suppliers regarding the prices they will pay, the level of quality they require, and even the times at which they will accept delivery. Suppliers who don't meet these expectations become ex-suppliers.

Executives of the most powerful companies in the world now tremble before their independent and demanding customers. They know customers have the power and that they will use it. Welcome to the customer economy.

How did this customer power arise? Like most "sudden" changes, it resulted from the convergence of several long-developing trends. First, scarcity gave way to abundance, as supply overtook and exceeded demand. In the late twentieth century, capacity increased enormously in virtually every industry. Whether companies were selling steel, insurance, or toothpaste, they became able to make much more than customers were buying. For instance, today's worldwide automobile industry has the ability to produce nearly 20 million vehicles a year more than what the world market demands. A key reason for this remarkable development is that advancing technology has dramatically increased manufacturing productivity and thereby reduced the costs of entry to and expansion in many industries. Simultaneously, driven by Wall Street's demands for growth, companies expanded capacity in order to build market share. The trend was magnified when globalization led to more competitors pursuing the same customers. This increase in supply inevitably put customers in the driver's seat. Customers are no longer supplicants for scarce goods; roles have changed, and sellers have become supplicants for scarce buyers.

At the same time, customers have become more sophisticated and informed buyers. In theory, customers have always had choices, but until recently those choices were more theoretical than real. Consumers did not have time to run all over town comparison shopping, while corporate purchasing agents could not plow through the spec sheets and price books of every possible supplier. As a result, customers stayed with familiar vendors because that was easier, and that gave these vendors the upper hand. But customers' servitude ended when it became practical for them to take advantage of the alternatives that other vendors offered. Information technology (including, most recently, the Internet) enabled them to find and analyze competing products and to make intelligent choices. Customers discovered they had options and the power to exploit them. As both consumers and corporations increasingly came under pressure to save money, the inertia of staying with old suppliers became a luxury few could afford. As a result, customers now aggressively seek alternatives, compare offers, and hold out for the best option.

Customer power surged even more as many products became virtual commodities. It used to be that technology evolved slowly enough that products remained different from each other for long periods of time. I sold my product, you sold yours; each had strengths and weaknesses that made it the best choice for some customers and a poor choice for others. Now rapid changes in technology have dramatically shortened product life cycles. No sooner do I introduce a new product than either it becomes obsolete or you imitate it. The result is a lot of similar offerings that make it very difficult for me to differentiate myself from you; this further empowers our customers.

As an illustration, compare what it is like to buy a car today with the same experience fifty years ago. In the early 1950s, your choices were limited to the Big Three. Unless you were a car aficionado, you learned everything you knew about the car from the dealer, who held all the cards in your negotiations. By contrast, today, some twenty-five car companies compete for your business. A host of information sources, from *Consumer Reports* to Web sites, prepare you to bargain with the dealer from a position of knowledge and strength. Now you have the upper hand, and the automakers and their dealers know it.

In combination, these phenomena transformed supplier-dominated economies into ones ruled by customers. This then is the real "new economy." It did not begin in 1995, it has little to do with the Internet, and it certainly does not require pretentious capitalization. It is the customer economy, which has been growing and gathering steam for the last twenty-five years. The circumstances that have driven the customer economy are not yet played out; indeed, they are accelerating. There is no foreseeable end to increases in global competition, overcapacity, commoditization, or customer knowledge, or to the customer power that flows from them.

Managers did not sit still as the new customer economy began to displace the old supplier economies in which they had been reared and trained. Throughout the 1980s and early 1990s, they undertook an unprecedented program of managerial innovation. Behind the scenes and largely out of public view, American managers created and deployed dramatically new ways of operating their businesses. A new arsenal of management strategies was built to replace the assumptions and techniques that had prevailed at least since the days of Henry Ford and Alfred Sloan.

Even a minimal list of the business innovations of the 1980s and 1990s would have to include just-in-time inventory management; total quality management and its avatar, six sigma quality; cross-functional teams; the use of portfolio management and stage gates in product development; supply chain integration, including vendor-managed inventories and collaborative planning and forecasting; performance-linked compensation; competency profiling in human resources; measurement systems based on EVA (economic value added) or balanced scorecards; customer-supplier partnerships; business process reengineering; and many more. It is difficult to overstate the extent and impact of these changes. A Rip Van Winkle who had fallen asleep in the 1970s and awoke today would not recognize the business world

Not surprisingly, these innovations were first deployed in the industries that felt the brunt of the new customer economy the earliest—automobiles, electronics, computers—and then spread to virtually every other sector of the economy. Because of these changes, the U.S. economy was able to weather the first wave of customer ascendancy. Companies that initially crumbled before the onslaught of demanding customers and tough new competitors used these new management methods to claw their way back. Start-up businesses that embodied these principles from the outset outperformed established competitors and experienced meteoric growth as a result.

The management innovations of the past two decades pulled IBM back from the brink and enabled Dell to grow from a college dorm room operation into a world leader. They are at the root of GE Capital's domination of virtually every market in which it operates, and of Progressive Insurance's growth from $100 million in premiums to over $6 billion in an industry that barely grows at all. They are why Wal-Mart overwhelmed Sears and developed a commanding presence in groceries; why Motorola was one of the few electronics manufacturers that kept its Japanese competitors at bay; why Ford became the world's most successful automobile maker; why Intel and Texas Instruments were able to thrive in an industry where so many have failed. The new management techniques enabled these companies to develop better products quicker, and to manufacture them more reliably and at lower cost. They allowed companies to get more out of their plants, operate with less inventory, reduce waste and errors, fill orders more quickly, and respond with alacrity to customers' requests. Increased productivity, lowered costs, better quality, and improved service were the immediate results of adopting these techniques, and they translated into payoffs for every constituency: Customers got better products at lower prices, workers had secure employment, and shareholders earned higher profits.

It was these managerial innovations of the 1980s and early 1990s, rather than the U.S. Federal Reserve or the Internet or the budget surplus, that actually created the boom economy of the late 1990s. Companies did not do well because times were good; rather, times became good because companies did well. The elixirs of economic performance are business productivity and innovation. When companies reduce their costs without reducing value, when they create new products, when they enhance their quality and service, then—and only then—do happy days reign. Customers can get more value for the same money, which means they have more to spend on other things; companies increase sales and profits, which enables increases in wages and capital spending; shareholders see rising equity values; and we are soon riding merrily along on the virtuous cycle of economic growth.

But in the boom times that result, it is easy to forget the hard work that got us there, and to start to think that business is easy and to take success for granted. Too many companies and too many managers did just that in the late 1990s. They committed the unpardonable sin of confusing a bull market with brains, and they took their eye off the operating ball. They let themselves be carried along by the strong economy. They now regret that decision, for recent events have forcefully reminded them that strong economies are temporary phenomena and that we live in extraordinarily unforgiving times. Managers must now pick up where they left off when they got distracted by the excesses of the "New Economy." But more of the same will not be enough. The management innovations of the last twenty years, impressive though they may have been, are just the beginning. In the customer economy, yesterday's innovation is baseline today and obsolete tomorrow. What was once unimaginable quickly becomes routine, and then expectations are raised even higher. It is the nature of customers to constantly demand more—more value for less cost, more innovation, more service, more of everything. Companies that do not keep up with their escalating demands are quickly abandoned. The reinvention of business is not over—far from it.

In retrospect, the management revolution of the 1980s and 1990s was just the first phase of a much longer-term program: adapting every aspect of business to the realities of customer dominance. Operating in the customer economy demands much more than just building tight relationships with customers—so-called "customer intimacy." Indeed, in many cases, that's not even an appropriate step to take. What is required is reflecting the reality of customer power in all the ways in which a company is operated and managed, from how its work is done through how its people are rewarded to how it is organized.

While much progress has been made toward this goal, much still remains to be done. This book's aim is to set forth the next chapter of this program, to outline a further set of business innovations that will define the management agenda for the first decade of the twenty-first century. My purpose is to offer a set of concrete ideas and practical techniques that real managers in actual companies can employ to help their companies dominate their markets in the upcoming decade. I deliberately use the word *dominate* to express the goal, rather than a weaker word like *survive*. In a fiercely competitive environment, the modest goal of "getting by" is unattainable. Only companies that strive to be the best and to outperform all others have a hope of surviving in a world where everyone else is trying to do the same.

The subject matter of *The Agenda* is the ways in which companies are managed, organized, and operated. My aim is neither to prescribe nor to forecast products and services that companies will offer. I do not predict what new gadgets technophiles will carry around, nor if and how insurance and banking will be bundled together. I don't know how cars will look in five years, and I strongly suspect that no one else does either. I concentrate on *how,* not what. My foci are the changes that companies of all kinds and sizes must put in place if they want to operate successfully in the face of the escalating demands of the customer economy.

The management innovations in this book are not the products of my own imagination. I have learned them all by observing the ways in which innovative and well-managed companies are coping with the challenges of the customer economy. The companies that are cited in this book and that offer us a preview of the future represent many different industries. But few are high-tech start-ups or glamorous media firms, the favored darlings of the business press. The companies from which I have learned the most are mature companies in mature industries. They can no longer survive on the legacy of the founder's brilliant invention; they do not float on a rising tide of secular market growth; they are unable to substitute acquisition for execution. These companies succeed not because they are lucky enough to be in a hot market at the right time but because they use new management ideas to outexecute their competitors. My role has been to extract from their experiences a set of fundamental principles and techniques that every company can learn and apply. These principles are relevant to any organization that seeks to do business in the customer-driven world of the twenty-first century: small or large, manufacturer or service provider, high tech or low tech.

I do not maintain that the companies in this book are perfect role models. No one of them has all the keys to unlock the customer economy. Indeed, many have made serious missteps in some areas, despite their success and leadership in others. But putting their experiences together creates a profile of the kind of enterprise that every company needs to become.

In the business agenda for the customer economy, there are nine elements. The first two translate platitudes about customers into concrete action; they specify two specific strategies—whose acronyms are ETDBW and MVA—that distinguish companies from look-alike competitors and create loyal customers. The third and fourth agenda items concern themselves with process, a mild and unassuming word that is turning companies on their sides. In order to achieve the performance levels that customers now demand, businesses must organize and manage themselves around the axis of process; moreover, they must apply the discipline of process even to the most creative and heretofore most chaotic aspects of their operations. Principle number five demands a new approach to measurement, one that locates it not in the domain of accounting but squarely in the center of a systematic approach to improving business performance. The sixth item on the agenda is to redefine the role of managers from autonomous chiefs of narrow domains into team players whose scope is the entire business. The last three harness the power of the Internet to link companies with one another. Distribution must be rethought from the perspective of the final customer, who pays the salaries of everyone in a distribution channel. Companies must knock down the walls that separate them from one another, walls that are the source of enormous overhead and inefficiency, through collaboration and interenterprise process integration. The final agenda item is the most radical. It says that companies need to stop seeing themselves as self-contained wholes and instead position themselves as components of virtually integrated extended enterprises.

The following nine chapters explore these nine agenda items. In each case, I will explain why the issue is critical to contemporary business survival, show how it represents a major departure from the practices of the past, and illustrate how some companies have already exploited the new approach to enormous advantage. The last two chapters of this book offer guidance on how to turn the agenda into practice in your company and on how to keep the agenda fresh in a time of ongoing change.

This book is intended as a guide for businesspeople who are not content to wait for a miracle to save them but are committed to creating their own. As Alan Kay, the father of personal computing, has put it, "The best way to predict the future is to invent it."

When I am asked if this agenda is prescriptive or descriptive, my response is "both." It captures what some companies have already done, and what the rest now must. But slavish imitation will get you nowhere. This is not a cookbook with simple recipes. Business innovation is not a potion that can be bought in a store—it must be brewed at home. It is your responsibility to translate the principles I offer into realities in your organization. While others may have lit the path, no one else can walk it for you. It lies waiting ahead.

2

Run Your Business for Your Customers

Become ETDBW

A few years ago, a consultant brought in a videotape to show the CEO of a medium-size manufacturer of scientific equipment. On the screen appeared the face of the president of the manufacturer's largest customer, who leaned toward the camera and hissed through clenched teeth, "I *hate* you." A similar sentiment was recently expressed by a senior executive of one of their major customers to the leadership team of a large maker of telecommunications equipment: "If you gave us your products for free, we couldn't afford to do business with you."

What was agitating these customers, and countless others in every industry, has nothing to do with products, features, quality, or price. Their suppliers' products were up to date, well made, and reasonably priced. Instead, the customers' enormous dissatisfaction had everything to do with the fact that doing business with these two companies was overwhelmingly complex, problematic, and fatiguing. These companies presented customers with product descriptions so obscure that customers had to struggle to determine which products they wanted to buy; their opaque ordering procedures required customers to spend enormous amounts of time specifying what they wanted; their error-prone delivery processes forced customers to check all shipments and return many of them; their billing systems produced invoices whose deciphering would tax the patience of Job; and the major role of their "customer service" units seemed to be to pass customers from one unhelpful representative to another. These companies were decidedly not ETDBW: not easy to do business with.

Easy to do business with means that from the customer's standpoint, interacting with you is as inexpensive and effortless as possible. It means that you accept orders when and by whatever means it is most convenient for the customer to place them; it means the orders are worded in customer terminology rather than in your obscure nomenclature. It means you make it painless for a customer to check the status of an order; you eliminate that endless series of futile phone calls to uninterested and uninformed functionaries who have been trained only to refer the caller to someone else equally uninformed. It means you send a simple bill that is expressed in comprehensible terms, not your own recondite codes and internal references, and that is designed from the outset to be read and used by the customer; in other words, a bill that someone other than a cryptanalyst can decipher.

The importance of becoming ETDBW is captured by the principle that "product price is only part of customer cost." The payment that your customer sends you isn't the entire cost the customer incurs in doing business with you. The customer must also interact with your sales representative, formulate an order, receive, check, and inventory the goods, receive and interpret your invoice, pay the bill, return the goods that aren't in good shape, and so on. All of these activities cost the customer money, none of which ends up in your pocket. In some cases, the overhead costs of doing business with you rival what the customer actually pays you.

If your ordering procedure is opaque, then your customer has to waste time and money trying to translate it. If you provide no simple way for customers to check on orders, they have to beat their way through exasperating phone calls to canned voices that provide no information. If your delivery system is erratic and unreliable, your customer has to waste time and money developing ways to cope with your malfeasance. If the invoice you provide is hard to interpret, your customer has to spend time arguing about it with your billing people (who will soon run out of time and patience themselves).

If your ways of working are designed for your own convenience rather than for your customers', they will pay the penalty, and in the long run, so will you. The harder it is to do business with you, the greater the burden and the costs you impose on your customer and, of course, the less competitive you become. Lowering your prices by cutting your margins is one way to distinguish yourself from your competitors, but a loathsome one. And for some companies, such as the telecommunications equipment maker mentioned earlier, even giving away their products isn't enough to offset the annoyance of doing business with them. In the customer economy, ETDBW isn't an option. It is a requisite for survival.

Is your business easy to do business with? I doubt it. Your company is much more likely to impose penalties on your customers for the privilege of doing business with you. The experiences of ordering, receiving, using, and paying for your products and services probably lead your customers to put your photograph on their dartboards. To the extent that your customers' experiences are less than bad, that is most likely the result of what one company calls "random acts of kindness toward customers" rather than anything sustainable and repeatable. I'm not saying that you deliberately made your company hard to do business with; it just turned out that way. And you never did anything about it because you never thought it was an important issue.

Being HTDBW (see if you can figure it out) is an almost inevitable consequence of how most managers traditionally thought about the nature of their businesses. The traditional company was inwardly focused. It defined itself in terms of its products and services, and its mission as turning these into profits. Its only allegiance was to its shareholders and managers. Customers were an afterthought, perhaps a necessary evil, who existed solely to buy the company's products. The role of the company was to make and sell its products, and the role of the customer was to acquire and pay for them. Of course, companies masked their disregard for customers behind such politically correct slogans as "The customer is always right," but these were mere platitudes, honored more in the breach than in the observance. Needless to say, it would never cross such a company's mind that something other than its products and services was important or that it should focus on being ETDBW.

When the modern enterprise was a new phenomenon, this self-centered view may have been appropriate. Customers were so desperate for products that they could be safely ignored. Companies found it hard enough to devise, make, sell, and deliver products without worrying about customers too. But that time is long gone. Customers now have the upper hand, and to them, you are the necessary evil. Figure and ground in the canvas of business have been reversed; your customers are now in the forefront and you have been relegated to the background. Today powerful, sophisticated, and demanding customers are willing to accommodate themselves neither to your products nor to how you do business. Customers no longer exist to buy your products; you exist to solve your customers' problems. The company that remains self- rather than customer-centric cannot endure.

Of course, many companies—maybe yours—will assert with a straight face that they are indeed customer-focused. Yet in reality, these claims are empty; most companies only pay lip service to the idea. Too many managers think they have done their duty if they distribute to everyone in the company laminated wallet cards, portentously labeled Our Values, that feature the bold pronouncement "Customers are our first priority." Others issue happy-face buttons to employees and instruct them to smile radiantly at customers. Still others believe that an expanded customer service department with an 800 number and a Web site will solve all problems. Needless to say, none of these rituals accomplishes anything. The concept of "customer focus" cannot be slapped on like a new coat of paint over a product-centric company. It requires rethinking the company, its mission, and its operations in customer terms. It requires that companies experience themselves from their customers' perspective, then redesign how they work accordingly.

Treating a malady first requires recognizing it. If your company is one of the many that is far from easy to do business with, you are most likely hearing these complaints from your customers:

- It is confusing to have to interact with so many different people.
- You are inflexible and force everyone to accommodate to a single way of doing business with you.
- You are reactive and unprepared, acting surprised when customers ask you for something.
- You force customers to maneuver many parts of your company to get anything done.
- You impose overhead burdens on customers by making them interact with you repeatedly and check up on the work you do for them.
- Most important, you don't seem to know or care about what truly matters to customers.

Sound familiar? Fortunately, there are six specific corresponding ways to address and counteract these six common laments and thereby become decidedly ETDBW.

1. Present a Single Face to the Customer.

Managers at 3M are fond of a wry maxim: "The fact that we are a multi-division, multiproduct company isn't the customer's problem." Most companies organize and operate for their own convenience; the customer bears the burden of their internally focused structure. One company, for instance, recently realized with a shock that it listed twenty-three different 800 numbers in the phone book for customers to use to reach them.

Many companies present multiple and fragmented faces to their customers because of historical and impenetrable intracompany divisions. Different groups in a company will have responsibility for different products, and the customer has to call the right group if he or she wants to order a product, ask a question about it, or get it serviced. As a rule, each of these groups knows nothing about the other products or about customers' other relationships with the company. This fragmentation is sometimes the legacy of a history of acquisitions, and sometimes it is the inevitable consequence of the blinders imposed by a product-centered perspective.

No matter what the reason, the result is that customers experience additional costs and inconvenience when doing business with such a company. They have to order from different units, receive different shipments, handle multiple invoices, and address inquiries to multiple locations. I know of one large bank that has entirely separate operations for checking accounts, credit cards, home mortgages, and business loans. It is well known in banking circles that the most profitable customers are those to whom a bank sells multiple products. Yet this bank does nothing to facilitate multiple relationships. From the customer's point of view, dealing with it is no more convenient than dealing with multiple banks. And horror stories abound, like the customer with a million-dollar mortgage who was denied more than a $3,000 line of credit on a credit card, or the customer who was overwhelmed by receiving a dozen different statements from the bank. I also know of a consumer goods company, each of whose product divisions maintains a fierce independence, to the extent that it never occurs to them to combine shipments going to the same retailer. The retailer ends up paying the freight for two half-full trucks rather than one full one, because the right hand of this company has never even heard of the left one.

A company can be fragmented by function as well as by product. If an order bounces from department to department before it is filled, the customer has no single contact for tracking it. In many companies, just determining the price and availability of a product can require calls to more than a dozen different departments: manufacturing to determine production schedules, the warehouse to ascertain space availability, logistics for shipping schedules, marketing to discover promotional discounts, finance for the applicable terms, and so on. When an enterprise does not present a single face, its customers are forced to piece one together. This is a form of reconciliation, and it is very expensive and inconvenient for everyone. Oliver Wendell Holmes once wrote, "Taxes are the price we pay for civilization"; in the business environment, reconciliation is the price we pay for presenting a fragmented face to customers.

A powerful alternative is to create an integrated team that deals with the customer across all products and functions and has the authority to remove any barriers that get in the customer's way. Johnson & Johnson uses this method with its hospital and medical clinic customers. J&J is a highly decentralized corporation comprising numerous independent units that are responsible for different products. In the past, each unit had its own sales force, which meant that customers were often pursued simultaneously by different units. Various J&J companies competed against one another for the customer's attention and incurred redundant costs as they did so. Unsurprisingly, this undercut J&J's performance and profits, and customers complained that salespeople were pulling them in opposing directions.

In the late 1990s J&J reoriented its sales efforts. Sales reps from different J&J companies are now grouped as account teams that handle all of a customer's business with J&J. The teams work together to meet broad objectives, and reps are no longer measured and compensated exclusively on sales for their individual companies. Instead, they are rewarded on the success of J&J's overall relationship with the customer and on the account team's success at helping customers achieve their objectives, such as standardizing product utilization. With one contact—the account team—a customer is not shunted from one sales rep to another and need not worry that his or her concerns will fall between the cracks of J&J's huge organizational chart. The customer, who now brings all problems and questions to the same place, feels valued and supported and, as a result, brings more business to J&J.

Some companies feel they are presenting a single face to the customer if the customer can contact a customer service representative (CSR) with any question. They are deluding themselves, because such a customer service representative is just an overlay on a balkanized organization and has the same outsider status as does the customer. It is only a marginal improvement if the CSR is the one to call an endless series of unresponsive departments to find the answer to a customer's question, since the customer still has to wait forever and the response, when it finally comes, is likely to be incomplete, irrelevant, or simply wrong.

3M Telecom Products, headquartered in Austin, Texas, sells components to manufacturers of telecommunications systems. Its customer service representatives do in fact make life much easier for their customers. They can handle any question relating to orders, order status, expediting, returns, product information, and pricing, and they do so quickly and accurately. They can do this because they are considered full-fledged members of customer account teams. They have access to current information and are integral to operations, not add-ons to it. The CSR presents a single face to the customer from the moment an order is received until the bill is paid. At 3M Telecom, CSRs enable customers to easily get hard answers to tough questions.

2. Segment Operations by Customer Characteristics.

Market segmentation is a familiar tool in product development and marketing. A company will customize its product and its message to address the specific needs of different groups. Once a customer is captured, however, the company typically tosses the newcomer into an undifferentiated customer base and does business with it in the same way it does business with all the rest. In the customer economy, market segmentation should not stop so early. The notion of handling different customers in different ways needs to be extended beyond the sales cycle into the rest of the company's operations.

In the world of auto insurance, when a consumer submits a claim, the insurer typically sends an adjuster to inspect the vehicle. The overt reason is to assess the damage and estimate how much the insurer should pay the claimant; the unspoken reason is to verify that the accident has actually occurred and that the claim is not phony. The most common claim is for a broken windshield, in which case an adjuster doesn't have to assess the damage, since the cost of replacing a windshield can be calculated without ever seeing it. Nonetheless, many insurers inspect the damage. Why? Because the insurer automatically doubts the veracity of its claimants and wants to make sure they never have a chance to cheat the company.

One insurer has recognized that it is unnecessary to presume the collective guilt of all claimants. A customer who has been paying premiums regularly for many years without ever submitting an accident claim is unlikely to decide overnight to embark on a life of crime and to begin with a fraudulent windshield claim. When such a customer reports windshield damage, the company can safely assume that the damage did occur, and the simplest and fastest procedure is to cut a check right away. Customers with more tattered records, however, deserve an adjuster's inspection. Rather than fitting all customers into the same Procrustean bed, the new approach is to take customer variations into account and to treat each claim accordingly.

This principle also works for auto insurance applications. Most companies don't trust applicants to tell the truth about their driving records. No matter what they are told, they double-check with the state motor vehicle department. This same insurer has decided that it is perhaps counterproductive for a service business to make its customers feel like criminal suspects. After analyzing thousands of applications, this company has identified certain demographic characteristics (age or gender, for example) that indicate the likelihood that a customer is accurately describing his or her driving record. If a customer meets these demographic criteria, the story is accepted at face value, and there is no DMV check. This speeds up the application and makes customers happy. At this company, it is only those who fall outside the indicative criteria who require verification.

Many makers of consumer goods also now recognize that different customer groups need to be handled in different ways. For instance, mass merchants, such as Wal-Mart, value delivery at predetermined times to help simplify their complex operations. Smaller customers will often emphasize rapid delivery to help them minimize the inventory they carry. Accordingly, these consumer goods makers convene order fulfillment teams and assign each team to a specific kind of customer and tailor how the team works to match the needs of those customers. Some teams will serve the mass merchants, others regional supermarket chains, and others wholesalers who resell to convenience stores and other small retailers. Building on the same basic fulfillment system, the teams can spin variations that customize order fulfillment to the divergent needs of different customers.

3. Anticipate the Customer's Needs.

A third way that your company can become easier to do business with is to predict what your customer will want, then prepare for it before you receive the request. Anticipation is an edge that every alert company needs to sharpen.

Lucent, the giant manufacturer of telecommunications equipment, has adhered to this principle in several ways. In the past, a Lucent sales engineer would visit a new customer with no preconceived notions regarding what that customer needed. Only after the visit would he or she design a system solution for that customer. Often the engineer's first attempts were wide of the mark because the customers did not express their needs clearly enough at the outset. Needless to say, many iterations ensued, which were costly for Lucent and unpleasant for the customers.

Now Lucent applies the power of anticipation by researching customers before dispatching its sales engineers. Its sales engineers arrive with information about a customer's current setup and so can suggest a preliminary solution immediately, which engages the customer fully from the outset. Everyone has something concrete to examine, and the customer can react to the initial design right away, instead of debating ambiguous abstractions that allow different interpretations. As a result, the customer spends less time and experiences less frustration working with Lucent.

Lucent has also learned to anticipate its customers' repair needs. For example, its managers reacted quickly to news reports that a flood had hit an area where one of its customers, Verizon, had a major switching station. With no delay, Lucent managers accessed their database, called up the wiring diagram of Verizon's switching facility, identified the components and systems most susceptible to damage, and prepared the equipment needed for repair and replacement. By the time Verizon was able to call and ask for help, Lucent had the right stuff ready and waiting for delivery.

A company's customer service operations can also use prediction to become easier to do business with. Consider the difficulties of non-English-speaking customers. They call the standard customer service number and are connected to the next available rep, who, most likely, speaks only English. Confusion ensues until the rep realizes that a bilingual operator is needed. At that point, the customer is put on hold and transferred to an appropriate rep, at which point work can finally begin. This is obviously expensive for the company as well as extremely annoying for the customer.

Several companies are employing techniques to predict which customers are likely to need a bilingual operator. They do this by examining the phone number from which the customer is calling, using Caller

ID. By seeing where the customer is calling from, the company can determine that he or she may prefer to speak in a language other than English. In certain parts of Florida, for instance, the preferred language may be Spanish, while in parts of California, it might be Chinese. The call is then automatically routed to an appropriate bilingual representative, who answers the phone. The customer avoids inconvenience, even humiliation, and feels attended to. And what if the company guesses wrong? No harm has been done because the operator to whom the call was directed is, after all, bilingual.

4. Provide the Customer with a Seamless Experience Across All Interactions with You.

We have all had the experience of interacting with a company for years only to find that today we are being treated as a complete stranger. No one seems to know who we are or what our particular requirements are, and we are put through the same drill as a first-time customer. We check into a hotel where we have stayed for years and are asked what type of accommodations we prefer; we order spare parts from the company where we bought a machine and have to tell the company what kind of machine we have; we pay a bill at one branch office only to discover that another branch claims we didn't. The problem is that the company per se has no institutional knowledge or memory of us. Anything the company knows about us is only in the heads of certain employees. If these employees transfer or leave the company, its knowledge of us goes with them. Unless we happen to be dealing with the right person who has access to the right database, we are lost.

In the early 1990s, customers' relationships with AlliedSignal Aerospace were extraordinarily complex. At the time, AlliedSignal Aerospace was a multibillion-dollar business that sold a wide range of products, including engines, avionics, and landing systems to airlines, owners of private aircraft, and defense and space markets. (AlliedSignal merged with Honeywell in 1999.) A customer had to deal with different divisions in order to buy different products and then with many parts of each of these divisions: one organization to order a product, another to pay for it, a third to have it repaired, and so on.

Things got so bad that Bob Crandall, who was then CEO of American Airlines, told Larry Bossidy, then CEO of AlliedSignal, that if he could buy his parts from another supplier, he would. AlliedSignal recognized it had reached a crisis in customer satisfaction and responded by creating customer account teams. They would be responsible for the overall relationship with the customer. An account team consisted of people from sales, multiple product groups, credit, and customer service, in addition to field service engineers.

These customer account teams have responsibilities beyond sales. Their mandate is to make it easier for the customer to do business with the company, deliver customer satisfaction, and grow the account. Now whenever customers have problems at any stage or in any part of their relationship with AlliedSignal, they contact the same customer account team. Even as individual employees come and go, the customer account team retains its knowledge of the customer; that information has been captured in a shared database available to all members of the team. The results of this effort include a dramatic increase in customer satisfaction and a growth in operating profit from $500 million in 1996 to over $1.9 billion in 1999.

Another company that has achieved spectacular success by adhering to this principle is Charles Schwab, the financial services company. Many brokerage companies viewed the advent of the Internet as a threat to their businesses. Either they tried to avoid it, or they created a separate unit for online investors that was unconnected to the sales reps and service personnel who handled traditional customers. The problem was that this customer segmentation (online versus non-online) was arbitrary, and though it was perhaps convenient for the brokerage, it was very inconvenient for the customer. Most customers didn't see themselves as either users or nonusers of the Internet. The same person might want to deal with a brokerage firm in different ways at different times: by telephone, over the Internet, or by coming into a field office. Dave Pottruck, Schwab's president and co–chief executive officer, recognized this. He told the organization, "Companies don't own the customer anymore. The customer owns the customer. So trying to build walls around them isn't going to work." This led to Schwab implementing its celebrated "clicks and mortar" strategy, which provides a customer with flexible options for doing business with Schwab. Of course, the risk with this approach is that with each encounter a customer could have a different experience. To avoid this risk, the company developed a customer database system that allows every person at Schwab who comes in contact with the customer to know everything about all of his or her other contacts. Whatever mode a customer uses to contact Schwab, the results are the same.

Schwab has also realigned its compensation system so that it encourages its people to focus on the total business that a customer brings to the company, rather than on the narrow slice that a particular representative deals with on a particular day. As Pottruck says, "We don't worry too much about profitability per distribution channel; we worry about profitability per customer." By providing customers with seamless experiences, Schwab roared to the front of the Internet-based securities business.

A number of catalog retailers use the capacity to examine a customer's phone number before answering the phone to create a seamless customer experience. These retailers identify the caller from his or her number and then, if they can, route that call to the same service representative whom the customer spoke to last time. The customers can resume their conversation with the service rep right where they left off, instead of starting over with introductions and background information. This saves time for both the customer and the retailer.

5. Exploit the Power of Customer Self-Service.

Paradoxically, one of the best ways to become easy to do business with is by letting customers do some of your work for you. For instance, IBM allows its customers access via the Internet to systems with which they can select the right product to meet their needs, check its price and availability, enter an order for it, and check on the order's status. IBM's personnel no longer need perform these functions, because customers now can do them for themselves.

This is not terribly unusual; many companies in a wide range of industries are now allowing their customers to enter and manage their own orders. What is remarkable is that customers are eager to operate this way. At first it may seem counterintuitive that customers are not only willing to do your work for you but pleased with the opportunity to do so; it is reminiscent of Tom Sawyer's "allowing" his friends to white-wash the fence for him. Yet on closer consideration, it is not so surprising. For many customers, it is easier to do this work for you than to ask you to do it. After all, even if you handle customers' orders, they still have to explain their needs to you, submit the orders, and ask you for feedback on status. These interactions can easily become a pain for the customer. Your sales rep may not describe your products accurately, may misunderstand the customer's needs, or may incorrectly capture the order. Your order handler may make a transcription error when entering it. Your service personnel may not be available when the customer wants to check on order status or make a change. In other words, even if you are handling the order, the customer still has to handle you, which may be even worse.

Providing customers with access to your computer system so they can enter their own orders may, in fact, be less work for them. A well-designed computer interface makes entering an order painless and can prevent errors. The computer will not misquote a price or misstate product performance data. Your computer system can be made available to your customers whenever they want, so they are not limited to ordering only during business hours, or waiting on hold until a CSR becomes free; they can do things where and when they want. It is easier for customers to do these things for themselves than to have your people do these things for them.

Similarly, many computer and telecommunications systems manufacturers now have customers perform certain repairs themselves. The traditional alternative was for the customer to report a problem and then await the arrival of the next available field technician, who often had no training on the customer's particular model or was not carrying the required part; the outcome was customer frustration and delay. The new approach has the customer make the repair. How, you wonder, can a customer possibly fix an intricate piece of electronic equipment? Ironically, electronic systems have become so complex that practically no one can repair them anymore; all that anyone, including the manufacturer's field technicians, can do is replace parts. The systems are designed in a modular fashion, to facilitate easy servicing in the field.

The new procedure is this: When a customer contacts the manufacturer to report a failed piece of equipment, he or she is connected to a technical adviser, who walks the customer through a script to determine the problem. The adviser tells the customer how to turn off the machine, remove the broken part, and replace it with one stored on site on the customers' premises. Within a few minutes, the equipment is up and running. Customers do not resent being asked to perform the repair; they find it far preferable to enduring the delays involved with dealing with the manufacturer's repair personnel.

In technical terms, the customers in these examples are performing more value-adding work (entering orders, fixing machines), while being freed of a substantially larger amount of non-value-adding work (the overhead of dealing with the supplier). This is a good trade-off for both the customer and the supplier.

6. Use Customer-Centered Measures.

According to an old business adage, "That which is measured improves." If a company wishes to improve how it is viewed by its customers, it would seem natural that it would focus on measuring what matters to customers; but that is rarely the case. Most companies measure what is easy to measure, what they have always measured, and what is important to them—even if it is not meaningful to customers. Then these companies are truly shocked to discover that their customers are upset with them and find them difficult to work with.

Here is a situation that I have encountered frequently. A company has been assiduously measuring and relentlessly improving its order-fulfillment-cycle time (that is, the time that elapses between when an order is received and when it is dispatched to the customer). Through scrupulous streamlining, it has squeezed out unnecessary activity and wasted time. Feeling proud of their achievement, the company's managers now expect to be praised by their customers—only to discover that customers remain very dissatisfied with how long it takes to get their orders filled. The managers are astounded and disheartened; what about all their hard work?

The flaw in the company's efforts was its solipsistic view of order fulfillment. Its managers started the clock when they received the order and stopped it when the goods left their dock. To the customer, however, neither the start nor the end point of the company's measure had any significance. The customers' clocks started ticking when they recognized that they needed the company's product and stopped when the product was received and put to work. To be sure, the supplier's order fulfillment time is a component of this interval, but it is only one.

Other components equally important are the time it takes for the customer to select a product and to place the order with the supplier, for the shipper to deliver the goods, and for the customer to unpack and install them. Reducing the order fulfillment time won't help much if information on the product is hard to get or understand, if ordering procedures are cumbersome or error-prone, or if the shipping method is inefficient. Had the company focused on the right measure from the outset, it would have recognized the broader areas it needed to improve and would have directed its efforts toward reducing this larger time period.

Progressive Insurance, the country's fourth-largest auto insurer, has adopted customer-focused measures and has benefited enormously as a result. Originally Progressive, like other insurers, concentrated on internal measures, such as the productivity of its adjusters. The customer, however, cared about something else: getting through the tremendous hassle of an auto insurance claim. At Progressive and most other insurers, it was often seven to ten days before an adjuster would see the car and prepare a damage estimate, and during that time the customer was getting more and more upset. Pushing for greater adjuster productivity would not solve this dilemma. Then Progressive made the leap and shifted, in its words, "from Progressive time to customer time." It started to measure the time period from accident to adjuster arrival, and to do so in hours, not days; this led to a dramatic reduction in contact time. The result has been an increase in customer satisfaction that has led to a higher rate of customer retention. Larger market share is another benefit, because customers now tell their friends how easy it is to get their claims processed at Progressive. Progressive's current effort is to shorten another measure of primary concern to customers: the total elapsed time from the accident until the claim has been paid.

Many companies deceive themselves into believing they are doing better than they actually are in the area of customer satisfaction by calculating how often they deliver their product by the date they promise customers. This practice is deceptive because the date the company promises is not necessarily the date that the customer asked for. Frequently when customers request delivery on a certain date, they are told that that's impossible and are offered a substitute date. Delivering by that date is commendable, but it means little to customers who have had to rearrange their operations to accommodate the supplier's date. (What is even more outrageous is that most companies don't even meet their own dates more than 40 percent of the time!)

Duke Power, the electric power company, and Solutia, a chemical maker, both have taken the radical step of measuring how often they deliver by the first date that the customer requested. A lower figure here is much more meaningful than a higher figure on the old measure. Remarkably, both these companies have managed to register enormous improvements in this critical measurement; once they focused on the right goal, they found they could actually make progress toward achieving it.

When managers suggest focusing on and improving measurements that really matter to customers, they may be told that those measures are too hard to affect. In some cases, this is just a smokescreen for people who want to avoid taking the difficult steps that improving these measures would require. In others, the objection may have some merit, because the measures are not entirely within the company's control. Still, the objection remains irrelevant. You have to find ways to address the issues that truly matter to your customers.

GE Capital encountered this problem in its business unit that provides financing services to office equipment dealers, by lending money to finance customer purchases. Using its vaunted process improvement techniques, GE Capital managed to reduce the time needed to approve a financing request from two days to a few hours. Then managers discovered that this was barely a blip to the customer; the equipment dealer was concerned with how long it took to turn an order from its customer into payment. This number was hovering at forty-seven days. Reducing or even eliminating GE Capital's two-day segment made little difference. While GE Capital had finished its part and had no obligation to stay involved, it did. Corporate shoulder shrugging doesn't work in the customer economy. GE Capital worked with the dealers to help them redesign their larger forty-seven-day process and have already driven it down to under twenty-five days. Needless to say, the dealers think GE Capital is extraordinarily easy to do business with.

Similarly, GE Aircraft Engines no longer focuses narrowly on how long it takes to repair an engine for an airline customer. The measure that counts is "wing to wing"—how long it takes from the time the engine comes off an airplane's wing until it gets back on—since that is how long the airplane is out of commission. In many cases, the actual repair time turned out to be only about half the wing-to-wing time. So GE has embarked on an effort to help its airline customers reduce the other half of this time period and in so doing is winning their loyalty.

Concentrating on customer-focused measures yields benefits in many ways. Issues surface that otherwise may be overlooked. For instance, measuring order processing time from the customer's perspective can highlight the fact that your ordering procedures are cumbersome and not customer-friendly. It directs your people's energies to where they are most needed by motivating them with new metrics. Customer-focused measures can also be a very useful sales tool; showing customers how doing business with you can improve measures important to them can be a powerful inducement.

THE SIX TECHNIQUES just reviewed are antidotes to the six common symptoms of being HTDBW. Employing them will make your customers look forward to doing business with you rather than cringe at the prospect. You will also reap some other, perhaps surprising, benefits.

In the early days of the quality movement, Phil Crosby wrote an influential book entitled *Quality Is Free*. His argument was that achieving extraordinarily high levels of product quality would not bring added costs in its wake, but would, in fact, reduce costs. A similar observation can be made about ETDBW. Becoming easy to do business with works to your advantage in two ways: It not only saves your customers money, thereby making them more loyal to you, it saves you money as well. Virtually all of the techniques just reviewed drive costs out of your opera-

<u>Agenda Item 1</u>

Make It Easy for Your Customers to Do Business with You

- Present a single face to your customers.
- Work in different ways for different classes of customers.
- Know what your customers will ask for before they do.
- Make your customers' experience a seamless one.
- Let customers do more for themselves.
- Measure the things that customers really care about.

tions. Obviously, you save money when the customer does your work for you. Predicting customer needs prepares you when these needs do appear and helps you manage your resources more effectively; providing customers a single point of contact and a seamless experience frees you of the overhead of reconciliation, coordination, problem resolution, and all the other (expensive) mechanisms used to compensate for problematic ways of interfacing with customers. Virtually all the examples I have cited yielded substantial cost savings as well as major increases in customer satisfaction.

The great jazzman Fats Waller knew all about becoming ETDBW. He said, "Find out what they want and how they want it, and give it to them just that way." He was right. If you do so, you save both your customers and yourself a ton of money, and you will shine in a field of drab and look-alike competitors. If you don't, you become snack food for your ever more powerful customers. But even if you become a joy for your customers to work with, you will have done only half of what it takes to create a truly powerful value proposition for your customers. The other half of that equation is the subject of our next chapter.

3

Give Your Customers What They Really Want

Deliver MVA

I f I were to stop you on the street and ask what business you were in, you would think the question naïve and the answer terribly simple: Your business is defined by your products and services. Deere's business is tractors; Prudential's is insurance; Microsoft's is software. If I were to further ask what customers wanted from your company, you would probably say something like "Innovative and high-quality products [or services], delivered at a fair price." Perhaps after reading Chapter 2, you would hasten to add, "In a way that's easy for customers."

Bad answers.

These answers say a lot about why your company is having so much trouble coping with the customer economy. They reflect a classic introspective, product-centered view of the world. They are relics of an antiquated style of thinking that puts you and your products first and your customers second, assumes your customers actually want what you happen to make and sell, and asserts that all you have to do is make and sell them well.

You couldn't be more wrong. Your customers have no interest in you or your company and only a little more in your products or services. That you and your products occupy center stage in the drama of your own business life does not alter the fact that you and they are merely bit players in your customers' lives. What your customers care about is themselves, and from their point of view, your only excuse for existence is your ability to improve their lives and their businesses. To the extent that achieving that goal involves your products and services, your prized creations on which you lavish love and attention, fine; but cutting-edge, high-quality, low-priced products are only the beginning of the story.

The last chapter examined the imperative of becoming easy to do business with. To be sure, simplifying the customer's life is a necessity, but it is only a start. In the customer economy, you need to do much more than that. You must go beyond merely giving them your products and services; you need to help them solve the problems that motivated them to ask for your products or services in the first place. In short, you have to provide them with more value-added (MVA). ETDBW means that you continue to give the customer what you always have but in a more convenient way; MVA means that you give the customer more, perhaps far more, than you ever have before. It goes beyond simplifying your customers' interactions with you to delivering solutions to your customers' problems, of which your products and services in their native forms are but small pieces.

There is a hoary, apocryphal story about an annual meeting of a major manufacturer of power tools. The chairman stands up to address the assembled shareholders. "I have some bad news for you," he says. "Nobody wants our drills." The audience is shocked. At last report, the company had a 90 percent share of the drill market. The chairman proceeds, "That's right, nobody wants our drills. What they want is holes."

All customers, whether individual consumers or businesses, have problems that require resolution. Your product or service, no matter how good, is inevitably only part of the solution to those problems. For instance, you may be selling automobiles, but that automobile is only part of the solution to the customer's need for transportation. Customers also need gasoline to fuel the car, as well as maintenance services and spare parts to keep it running. They will need financing in order to buy it, insurance to protect it and themselves, and maps to get from one place to another. Similarly, the drill is only part of what the customer needs to get the holes that he is looking for; he also needs a stud finder, the right drill bit, and knowledge of how to use these tools. Individually, each element is a product or a service, but when combined, they comprise a system solution that solves the customers' underlying problem.

When each of these products comes from a different specialized company, the customer has to put all these components together so they work. In certain complex environments, this goes by the official name of "system integration"—and it is often no small undertaking.

When products are well differentiated, customers may be willing to pick and choose from among the best ones and endure the trouble of integrating them. But in a world of commoditized products and powerful customers, the key to success lies in turning your focus away from yourself and your products and toward your customers and the solutions they seek.

You can visualize the principle of MVA as a ladder with your product at the bottom and the solution to your customer's problem at the top. The more help you provide your customers to fill that gap, the more value you add to them, which, of course, differentiates you from your competitors who are still scrambling around at the bottom of the ladder. Also, it is to your advantage to control as much of the ladder as you can—customers will be less likely to abandon you in favor of someone else, lower down the ladder, who offers less value. At the same time, your opportunity for margin and profit increase.

This is not a new idea. In the 1950s, IBM rose to great success with such a strategy. In those days, no one would have accused IBM of having the best computers. While they were workmanlike and more than adequate, its competitors often had superior price performance or more advanced technological features. IBM's genius was to recognize that none of its customers wanted computers per se. What they wanted were solutions to their business problems of the day: payroll processing, accounting, and inventory management. IBM surrounded its basic computers with a host of related products and services that would help the customer solve these problems, such as application software packages, system analysis services, installation, training, and ongoing maintenance. This idea doesn't just apply to computer systems; it can be applied to virtually any product or service. Every business generation seems to forget, and then rediscover, this very basic principle.

In order to deliver more value-added to your customer, you need to ask these questions: What do our customers do with our product or service after they receive it from us? What are the broader business or personal problems that our customers have? What more can we do to help them solve these problems? Thinking in these terms gets you beyond your old product perspective and forces you to think as your customers do.

Consider Trane, the multibillion-dollar manufacturer of cooling and heating equipment that is a division of American Standard. One part of Trane makes components (air handlers, chillers, and more) for cooling systems in large commercial structures, such as hotels and office buildings.

In the past, Trane was content to focus on its products and to compete on their quality. Over time, however, technological parity came to the air-conditioning industry as it has to so many others. Trane found it harder and harder to distinguish itself based on product features alone. In response, the company decided to move from the product business to the system business, from selling equipment to selling solutions.

Trane recognized that its customer, the owner and operator of a commercial building, didn't in fact want to buy air-conditioning components per se. The building owner needed to provide tenants with a comfortable environment. The owner wanted an air-conditioned building, not air-conditioning equipment, or as Trane's managers put it, the customer wanted to buy meals, not groceries. As a result, Trane repositioned itself as a provider of system solutions to building owners.

Instead of exclusively selling components to cooling contractors or other middlemen, Trane now also integrates systems, dealing directly with building owners. Working in this mode, Trane analyzes a building's cooling needs, configures the right system, acquires and assembles the system's components (including components made by other companies), and then installs and maintains the system over time. Trane does not necessarily do all the work itself; the company employs subcontractors to perform specific activities. But it is the prime contractor, with overall responsibility for solving the customer's problem. In short, Trane's managers reexamined the market through their customers' eyes, not their own. They say they have gone from being a manufacturing company with distribution capabilities to a distribution company with manufacturing capabilities—and the latter coincides more closely with the customer's needs. Trane has rapidly grown this part of its business, and it provides very attractive financial returns.

Interestingly, another company has ended up in a position similar to Trane's, after starting from a very different place. That company is Enron Energy Services (EES), a unit of energy giant Enron, which is primarily known for its energy trading and distribution activities. EES was born of Enron's need to differentiate the commodity that it sells (energy). The company's leaders put themselves in the shoes of corporate customers and realized that these customers did not know or care what a kilowatt-hour was and certainly did not want to buy any; they cared about the uses to which they were putting energy, not the energy itself. EES was created to help customers make better use of the energy they were buying. This innovation responded to customers' underlying needs. Today many companies are so focused on the core of their business—creating value for their customers—that they are able to pay only scarce attention to its indirect aspects, such as making sure that energy expenditures are minimized. In essence, EES allows customers to outsource their energy supply chains and guarantees them lower overall energy expenses than they would otherwise have.

For instance, EES began its relationship with a large dairy products company by analyzing the company's annual energy expenses of $50 million. EES calculated how much of that sum was being used by what kind of equipment (from lighting to heating to refrigeration); it inventoried all this equipment by age and efficiency and determined how much labor was involved in purchasing the energy and managing and maintaining the equipment. Then EES entered into a ten-year arrangement with the customer. EES agreed to procure energy and manage the customer's equipment that used it, in return for an annual fee that was about 10 percent less than what the company would have otherwise expected to spend on energy. To make this work, EES applied its own sophisticated energy-buying practices, modified some of the dairy company's equipment, and implemented better operating practices. By selling solutions rather than energy, in just four years EES has grown from a gleam in Enron's eye to over $1.8 billion in sales. Focusing on customer needs rather than on your product line can work wonders.

Note that EES's charges are based on a reduction in the customer's energy costs; EES's own costs are immaterial. The MVA approach allows you to bill your customers on value rather than cost. The traditional approach to pricing is to calculate how much your product or service costs you and then add as much profit as you think the market will bear. With an MVA approach, the focus is less on your costs and more on the value you are creating for your customers. When your solution is positioned in value terms, customers will pay for value received.

British aircraft engine maker Rolls-Royce has adopted a similar strategy. Until recently, airlines that bought Rolls engines assumed responsibility for maintaining them and for stocking spare parts. But for some airlines, these tasks were distractions. Looking through their customers' eyes, Rolls-Royce managers realized that these customers much preferred to focus their resources on promoting their brand and improving customer service. Rolls-Royce promptly created a new offering, called "power by the hour." With this approach, Rolls-Royce retains both the ownership of and the maintenance responsibilities for its engines after they are installed in customers' planes. In effect, the airline rents the engine and pays Rolls-Royce for every hour it is running.

There are other ways to turn your products or services into solutions. Allegiance is one of the largest distributors of medical and surgical supplies in the United States, carrying virtually everything a hospital needs to operate. Years ago, Allegiance operated like any other distributor. It received a hospital's order, packaged and delivered the materials to the hospital's receiving dock, and then forgot about it.

The hospital's real problems, on the other hand, began where Allegiance's ended. All of its Allegiance supplies had to be stored, tracked, then lugged around the (sometimes enormous) premises to their appropriate destinations. In the operating rooms, nurses would gather all of the supplies needed for each procedure, often a very time-consuming task. For instance, a cardiovascular-surgery kit might include hundreds of items, such as different kinds of scalpels, retractors, and sponges.

Allegiance decided to distinguish itself by doing more for the customer. To that end, Allegiance offers to take over most of its client hospitals' inventory chores. In a variation of the practice known as vendor-managed inventory (VMI), Allegiance keeps track of a hospital's inventory, determines when an item needs to be restocked, and then delivers it right where it will be used. As part of this program, Allegiance will make daily deliveries to ensure availability of vital products. Moreover, Allegiance can assemble kits and deliver them ready for immediate use. It can even package all the supplies a patient will need from time of admission until leaving the hospital. These services save significant time, money, and space for Allegiance's hospital customers.

Other distributors have used similar strategies to shed their commodity roles. Grainger is the biggest distributor of MRO (maintenance, repair, and operating) supplies in the United States. It handles everything from air hoses to lightbulbs to small motors. Grainger has recognized that its customers' real problem is managing these high-volume, low-dollar purchases, none of them individually costly but, taken together, quite expensive. Remarkably, the administrative cost associated with procuring these items often exceeds their actual price, because many organizations have allowed their procurement processes to become laden with overhead. Grainger has extended its basic distribution business to include helping its customers reengineer how they perform MRO procurement. Grainger works with customers to develop better ways of finding, ordering, and paying for MRO supplies; this activity reduces the customer's costs and enhances Grainger's value. (EES, too, defines its role as helping its customers reengineer their energy supply chain processes.)

Over the last decade, vendor-managed inventory (VMI) has become widespread in the supermarket industry, where it is often called CRP (continuous replenishment of product) or ECR (efficient consumer response). Given the similarities among brands in the same product category, retailers have acquired new power in their relationships with their vendors. Indeed, the latter can now succeed in only one way—by solving the retailers' business problems in addition to supplying them with goods. Consumer goods manufacturers have come to recognize that supermarkets do not care about their products as such, but they do care about the profits they can derive from those products. Supermarkets see products as merely a troublesome means to a triumphant end.

This perspective translates into opportunity for innovative consumer goods vendors. The smart ones have repositioned themselves as profit enablers rather than product sellers. Their mission is to help retailers boost the profits they realize from selling a manufacturer's products. The first step in this is VMI: A supplier takes over the job of managing its products in the supermarket's inventory. Freeing the retailer's personnel from this task reduces the supermarket's costs.

The next step is category management. Here one vendor is appointed the lead vendor for a given category of goods, such as beverages or frozen vegetables. This designated category manager (also known as the captain of the aisle) is responsible for that entire section of the supermarket, including its competitors' products. The category manager determines how many feet of shelf space should be dedicated to each product in order to maximize the supermarket's overall profits in that category; the category manager then ensures that the supermarket has the right amount of each product in inventory. Numerous benefits accrue to a category manager, from having a close relationship with the customer to knowing exactly how well or how poorly its competitors' products are selling. Category managers are very cautious about abusing their position, because a vigilant customer will replace them with another eager recruit.

Under Jack Welch, GE has been particularly aggressive in spotting the tipping point when a product begins to lose its distinction and threatens to become a commodity that competes on price alone. Well before that point, GE typically repositions the product by adding services that provide customers with complete problem solutions. This has been done across a wide range of the company's business units.

For instance, GE Appliances supports Home Depot's efforts to sell large appliances, like refrigerators, to consumers. GE makes a wide range of products, because consumers want home appliances of just the right size and color for their kitchens. From Home Depot's point of view, this product variation can be a problem, since it would seem to require that the retailer keep a large amount of inventory, which will take up a lot of space (both on the retail floor and in warehouses) and will also be very costly to finance. GE has undertaken to solve this problem by holding large appliance inventory for Home Depot and taking over responsibility for delivering these appliances to Home Depot consumers from GE warehouses. Home Depot keeps only a small range of GE products on the floor for demonstration and maintains in its inventory only the fastest-selling models; the remainder of GE's product line is available via an in-store computer kiosk. When a consumer decides on a specific appliance, the Home Depot salesperson uses the in-store computer kiosk to order the model from GE's inventory and then arranges direct delivery by GE to the consumer's home. In almost all cases, GE delivers within forty-eight hours. Everyone is happy with this arrangement. The consumer is happy to quickly get exactly what he or she wants, regardless of what Home Depot has in inventory; Home Depot is happy because it has freed up floor and inventory space, and it has been absolved of delivery responsibility, all without depriving its customers of any products; and GE is particularly happy, because it does not lose sales if Home Depot runs out of stock and because this value-added service has made it Home Depot's preferred supplier. In effect, GE is relieving Home Depot of some of its most profit-sapping burdens and freeing it to concentrate on selling products—especially GE products.

GE has followed a similar tack in its medical equipment business, which sells MRIs and CAT scanners to hospital radiology departments. GE understands that these customers don't need fancy equipment— they need the ability to serve their own customers, the patients. (Focusing on customers at every level is crucial. Understanding and supporting your customers as they do the same for theirs is a recurring theme in many of these examples.) As a result, GE Medical Systems recognizes that its job is more than selling a CAT scanner. It is to ensure that the hospital that buys a CAT scanner uses it in the most effective way possible. To that end, GE Medical has installed devices in its equipment that allow it to monitor equipment performance. If a machine indicates it is having a problem, GE can dispatch a repair technician before the hospital even knows that something is amiss. GE also provides information on machine utilization that helps the hospital manage its radiology department's equipment more effectively. Similarly, GE Transportation Systems runs some of its railroad customers' locomotive maintenance facilities, helps them schedule their trains, and keeps track of where their locomotives are at any point in time. All of these moves extend the value proposition that GE business units offer in order to help their customers solve their underlying problems.

Though particularly widespread in manufacturing, this approach can also be used in services. GE Capital has teamed with Home Depot to allow shoppers to apply for a home improvement loan at the Home Depot checkout counter and be approved within ten minutes. In the past, American Express Company's IDS unit defined its business as selling individual financial products such as mutual funds, until it realized that its customers' real needs were for long-term financial plans and for suites of products that would help them reach their goals; mutual funds were only one small part of this equation. IDS repositioned itself to accommodate this need, changed its name in 1994 to American Express Financial Advisors and, as such, focuses on its customers' real needs rather than on the products that defined its old identity.

Dell Computer is, of course, renowned for its reinvention of the personal computer industry, creating the build-to-customer-order model that has been so widely emulated. No truly successful company, however, rests on its laurels, because it knows that its competitors will soon be nipping at its heels. To that end, Dell is focusing on a broad set of problems that its corporate customers encounter.

To a corporation, its PCs represent a significant investment. They are treated as assets on the books, and like any asset, they need to be carefully managed. A company needs to know how many PCs it has; where they are; when they were bought; and other similar information. This is easy if you have two or three or even twenty computers. When you have 5,000, 10,000, or 20,000, it becomes a formidable challenge.

Dell provides an Internet-based service that helps its customers manage the computer assets that they buy from Dell. Dell maintains databases on behalf of its corporate customers in which it records every PC it ships. Customers can access the appropriate database themselves to help manage and maintain this important distributed asset.

The trucking industry is an example of an entire industry that has refocused itself on customer problems. Old-style trucking companies defined the customer's need as moving a shipment from here to there. Now truckers understand that the customer's real problem is making sure that they have the right things in the right place at the right time. To help the customer accomplish that, a state-of-the-art trucker (also known as a 3PL, third-party logistics company) will help a manufacturing company customer decide how much inventory to keep in which warehouses, when to move goods from one warehouse to another, and when to schedule the movement of goods from factories to the warehouses. And they will do this in a way that minimizes inventory and shipping costs and maximizes the ability to fill customer orders.

To some, the concept of MVA may sound like heresy against the established orthodoxy of core competences. This doctrine asserts that companies should base their strategies for growth on their basic strengths. It may seem at first as though some of the companies just discussed ventured inappropriately into new territories. Though their laudable goals were to add more value to customers, Trane had no capability in installation, nor Enron in equipment management. What made these companies think they could succeed in these areas? The answer is that core competences are not straitjackets; just as old ones can be exploited, new ones can be developed. Trane and Enron had to acquire some of the key capabilities that their new MVA strategies demanded, but that was not an insurmountable challenge. They were not offering these capabilities in a stand-alone fashion but as extensions to businesses in which they were already very strong. Moreover, when they begin to focus on broad customer needs, many companies discover that they possess competences of which they were previously unaware. Such secondary capabilities (like project management) that are not intrinsic to a company's primary offerings can be highlighted and exploited in the context of a solutions strategy.

Nortel Networks provides one of the more dramatic examples of creating MVA. Until 1999 Nortel defined itself as a designer and manu-

Agenda Item 2

Add More Value for Your Customers

- Think of yourself as a provider of solutions, rather than of products or services.
- Distinguish between what you are selling and what your customer is buying.
- Take a broad view of your customers' underlying problems that go beyond you and your products.
- See what your customers do with what you give them, and either do it for them or help them with it.
- Price in terms of value rather than cost.

facturer of telecommunications equipment. Then its CEO announced that the company was, in fact, not in the manufacturing business, but rather in the business of creating solutions for customers; hence, it outsourced virtually all of its manufacturing. Over time Nortel has gone even further. The company realized that its customers—operators of telephone networks—did not want boxes or even network solutions. They wanted transmission capacity. So Nortel began to offer them capacity, for which customers pay on use. This is analogous to the example of Rolls-Royce; Nortel continues to own the equipment in the customer's network and gets paid as it is used. Indeed, in some cases Nortel has become a partner with its customers in the telephone networks that its equipment is supporting.

At least one major electric utility is working on solving a customer problem that goes beyond the basic service it offers. Every month consumers have to pay a host of bills—for electricity, gas, and water, for local, long distance, and cellular phone service, to cable TV and Internet providers, and more. Paying any one of these bills is not a great problem; paying all of them can be. The utility plans to present its customers with a single bill for all of their recurring monthly services, take payment for all of them, and then remit the amounts due to other providers. This solves a customer problem that transcends the utility's previous offerings but nonetheless represents a real benefit to the customer.

You may think you already know all about selling solutions rather than products, and you may even think that you are doing it. Let me assure you that at best you have barely scratched the surface. The theme of MVA is an extraordinarily powerful one; its implications are profound, and its repercussions echo throughout this book. As Chapters 8, 9, and 10 will show, it is the key to unlocking the power of the Internet. Together with ETDBW, it is the linchpin of the customer-focused company. Yet most companies find themselves sadly unable to do much about either of these essential themes. The reasons for this, as well as what a company must do to enable itself to accomplish these objectives, are revealed in our next chapter.

4

Put Processes First

Make High Performance Possible

At a manufacturer of industrial equipment I know, customers often submit orders with a request that the product being ordered be modified to meet some special need. What happens to such requests could charitably be described as a comedy of errors. The customer service rep (CSR) who receives the request takes it to an engineer, who often rejects it, citing the impossibility of meeting the customer's need. What the engineer really means is that he sees no percentage in spending his time modifying an existing design, since his job description and rewards are focused on developing new designs. Moreover, why should he listen to this CSR? After a great deal of arguing and arm twisting, the CSR is sometimes able to bring the engineer around. But then the scene is repeated with the industrial engineer (who doesn't want to modify his production system), with the scheduler (who doesn't want to disrupt her neat and tidy plan), and with just about everyone else involved in filling the order. Each customer request creates such a crisis; each one is handled in a different way, each has an unpredictable outcome, and each leads to a great deal of energy being expended on internal squabbling. The company has calculated that it takes upward of a month to fill such special orders, but that the actual productive work time involved in doing so is less than three days. The rest of the time is spent arguing.

This company has a process problem. And if this story sounds at all familiar, so do you.

For most of the last decade, I thought I had found a word that summed up the work I did, my outlook on the world, my point of view. The word was *radical*. I used this word not in its political sense but in its dictionary meaning: "fundamental, far reaching, going to the root." The reengineering movement that I started in the late 1980s was all about making fundamental change in how companies conducted business, about rethinking everything from the ground up, about starting with the proverbial clean sheet of paper. I felt, and most other members of the movement would have agreed with me, that *radical* was the key word in the definition of reengineering: radical change in business processes for dramatic improvement in business performance. Reengineering was a take-no-prisoners, burn-it-down-and-start-over approach to making businesses better. Down with tired ideas, irrelevant methods, and obsolete systems. Up with new customer realities, new corporate structures, and new information technologies.

I was wrong.

Don't misunderstand me. I have not cooled off, nor have I recanted my commitment to radical ideas. I am not like a onetime political activist who has settled down into comfortable bourgeois life. I still believe that major changes in the business environment require radical responses. But I no longer view *radical* as the core of my definition, or as the first word of the reengineering lexicon. Now that pride of place belongs to the mild and unassuming word *process*. I no longer see myself as a radical person; instead, I have become a process person.

Process is the Clark Kent of business ideas: seemingly mild and unassuming but actually amazingly powerful. Process is the way in which the abstract goal of putting customers first gets turned into its practical consequences. Without process, companies decay into a spiral of chaos and internal conflict.

Since we are living in a customer-driven world, it would seem natural for companies to orient themselves around what customers care most about. But a moment's reflection reveals that customers aren't at all interested in the activities toward which companies devote most of their managerial energies: the annual budget, the organization chart, the executive succession plan, the compensation program. At most these are only means to an end. Customers care about one thing only: results.

From the customers' point of view, a company exists only to create value for them, to provide them with results. Yet in far too many companies, the actual creation and delivery of customer value is not the responsibility of any particular individual. One searches in vain for people who are focused on and responsible for the end-to-end work of filling customer orders; on seeing new products through from conception to realization; or on resolving customer problems. Instead, the work that creates results for customers is broken into pieces and scattered across numerous departments and units. In these companies, workers, managers, and departments focus on each of the steps that lead to creating results for customers, but no one focuses on all the steps together as a unit. One person takes the customer call, another gathers needed information, a third decides what is to be done, a fourth takes action, and no one oversees the whole thing. These companies, like our manufacturer of industrial equipment, suffer from a crisis of process.

Process is a word now widely used in the business world but often incorrectly. Put most simply, processes are what create the results that a company delivers to its customers. *Process* is a technical term with a precise definition: *an organized group of related activities that together create a result of value to customers.* Each word here is important. A process is a *group* of activities, not just one. For example, filling an order is a process comprised of many activities—receiving and recording the order, checking the customer's credit, allocating inventory, picking and packing goods, planning the shipment, and making the delivery. No single task creates the desired result. Value is created by the entire process in which all these tasks merge in a systematic way for a clear purpose.

Second, the activities in a process aren't random or ad hoc; they are *related* and *organized.* They include no extraneous irrelevant activities, and the included ones cannot be performed in an arbitrary sequence. The process of order fulfillment (as it is often called) is a stream of relevant, interconnected activities that must be performed in sequence to produce the desired outcome. We don't pack before we pick. We don't check credit after we have shipped. We also don't forget to do either one; nor do we decide to check the sports pages for yesterday's scores. We do the right things in the right way every time.

Third, all the activities in a process must work *together* toward a common goal. People performing different steps of a process must all be aligned around a single purpose, instead of focusing on their individual tasks in isolation.

Finally, processes are not ends in themselves. They have a purpose that transcends and shapes all their constituent activities. We don't perform order fulfillment to keep ourselves busy; we do it to create the *result*—goods delivered as requested—that customers care about.

Over the last few years, I have reviewed the concept of process with many thousands of people. After presenting the definition, I usually ask the audience whether their own companies have order fulfillment processes. Typically, only 25 percent raise their hands, at which point I express my surprise. Clearly, all these companies have customers whose orders they somehow manage to fill. I ask them why those methods do not qualify as processes—that is, what's missing? Without fail, the audience cites two words from my definition—*together* and *organized.*

Their companies do perform all the steps that constitute order fulfillment, but the individuals who do these jobs do not work *together.* Each is focused narrowly and exclusively on his or her task; they are disconnected and not aligned toward any common purpose. The credit checker wants to maintain credit standards. The warehouse manager tries to minimize inventory. The shipping department aims to reduce costs. There is no sense that everyone works together toward achieving the goal that serves the collective interest of all—getting product to the customer.

If the participants in this work lack a common purpose, each one will inevitably work at cross-purposes with the others. Everyone has a narrow goal related to his or her department's objectives, which, in fact, have little or nothing to do with the overall needs of the process. While each manager makes sure that his or her department excels at its narrow task, no one ensures the excellence of the whole operation; nor does anyone view fulfillment as a whole through the prism of process.

In addition, the collection of activities that constitute order fulfillment are not *organized*. That is to say, they are undesigned. They lack any coherent structure, any overarching framework that carefully specifies exactly which tasks are to be performed, by whom, when, and where. Rather, work meanders from department to department, sometimes one way, sometimes another. There is no organizing design that integrates all the pieces into a whole process.

A process design prescribes how all the individual units of work must come together to achieve the overall goal. It specifies exactly what work is to be done, in what order, in what location, and by whom. Process design is a prerequisite for repeatability; without it the would-be process is likely to be performed differently each time. No matter how hard individuals work, they cannot overcome a flawed process design, much less the burden of no design at all.

Traditional organizations are not friendly to processes. They are structured around departments, each focused on one task and that task alone. In such organizations, no one knows or cares that others are doing related work. Credit checkers have absolutely no idea of what salespeople or warehouse workers are up to, and vice versa. Each unit speaks its own language and remains aloof from the others. As a result, customers' orders are like travelers passing through a series of rival kingdoms, where border guards give them a hard time before stamping their visas so they can proceed.

With processes broken into disconnected pieces, each hidden in a separate department, no one is in a position to see the end-to-end process, much less make it work smoothly. Departmental managers are narrowly focused on their own turf, while top managers are too far away from the action to comprehend the work being done on the front lines.

In this balkanized environment, bad habits and pointless work flourish. Each department is burdened with assorted checkers, expediters, supervisors, and so on—people whose work is an artifact of the disconnected process and adds not a whit of direct value to the customer, who, presumably, is the target of the effort. Unfortunately, even work that adds no value for customers does add cost.

Errors proliferate in a processless environment. Sharing neither a common vision nor a common terminology, departments miscommunicate, leading to mistakes that require rework or that alienate customers or both. The absence of process also makes companies clumsy and sluggish. Handoffs between departments generate enormous delays. And since no one has authority or perspective on the overall process, no one is in the position to adapt it to special or changing customer needs.

How then have traditional organizations that submerge their processes under functional departmental structures managed to survive for hundreds of years and create the great prosperity of the industrialized world? The short answer: That was then, and this is now. What was once satisfactory no longer is. In a world of pliant customers, genteel competition, and moderate change, companies could generally escape the consequences of high costs, low quality, rigidity, and unresponsiveness to customers. After all, what could customers do? They had nowhere else to go. But in today's customer economy, customers no longer tolerate the poor levels of performance with which they once had no choice but to be satisfied. Low cost, high quality, and rapid response are now taken for granted; they are essential simply for getting the customer's attention, let alone his or her business.

Without rigorous attention to processes, achieving even such minimally acceptable performance—much less anything better—is impossible. In the absence of a process focus, a company cannot consistently deliver the performance levels that customers always wanted and now demand. Instead, it will be overwhelmed with overhead, beset by delays, and plagued by errors; it will operate unpredictably and inconsistently. Specifically, the twin goals of ETDBW and MVA are unachievable without a process focus. A quick scan of the preceding two chapters will reveal that processes were at the core of what companies have done to realize these two goals. Without precise process designs and common integrating goals, employees have little chance of consistently operating in ways that customers find convenient. They will have even less chance of successfully performing and coordinating the broader range of activities needed to deliver higher levels of value-added. As work gets more demanding and more complex, process becomes absolutely essential.

Customers, results, and processes are bound together in an iron triangle. You can't be serious about one without focusing on the other two. The capacity to deliver the results customers expect is largely a matter of how well you design and manage your processes. Processes are the route to results and so to success in the customer economy.

Given its steady, sturdy style—more like the tortoise—the process approach is not much reported by business magazines in search of the sexy hare. Process is the province of quiet companies that speak softly but generate big profits. Glamorous start-up companies seldom focus on process because they don't yet need to. In their entrepreneurial stage, they can live off booming demand for their unique products.

For established companies in mature industries, however, process is vital. IBM, Ford, Duke Power, 3M, Cadbury Schweppes, GE Capital, Mead Paper, Progressive Insurance, Air Products and Chemicals,

Detroit Edison, UPS, Motorola, and John Deere are just a few of the dozens and dozens that are now intensively focused on their processes. Virtually all companies in some industries, such as chemicals and electric power, are becoming process oriented. In these and other highly competitive industries, secular market growth isn't sufficient to carry a company to success. Only superior execution can, and that depends on having superior processes.

The revival and continuing strength of many companies on this list is, in fact, a direct consequence of their process orientation. IBM, for instance, is one of the most celebrated business turnarounds of the last thirty years. The popular press has correctly attributed much of this to Lou Gerstner's extraordinary leadership. But what specifically did he do to transform IBM? His starting point was a strategy of integrating IBM's lines of business in order to make the company customer-centric. This led to a relentless focus on managing and standardizing processes across IBM, as a result of which cycle times on product development and order fulfillment were reduced, procurement costs were lowered by hundreds of millions of dollars, and a company that was on the brink of failure was brought back into the ranks of the solidly successful.

Another company to benefit from adopting a process focus is Progressive Insurance, which now has annual premium revenues of more than $6 billion. In the early 1980s, that number was roughly $100 million. That is sixty-fold growth in two decades. While that growth rate might be unexceptional in biotechnology or PC software, it is practically unimaginable in the auto insurance industry, which grows at only 3 to 4 percent a year. Progressive's intense focus on its processes led to dramatic improvements in their performance, which, in turn, sparked the company's extraordinary growth.

Even today's high technology wunderkinds will have to join the process camp at some point; no company can be buoyed by market growth forever. Eventually, products standardize, competition intensifies, demand slides, customers become more exigent, and success becomes the province of those who can execute better than their adversaries. In a phrase, the long-term winners will be those that master process.

The payoffs of process mastery can be breathtaking. Costs melt away, quality goes through the roof, and time spans shrink to a fraction of what they were. In 1999 my firm surveyed dozens of companies that had adopted the process approach to work and business. In order fulfillment, cycle times had typically decreased by 60 to 90 percent, and "perfect orders" (those delivered on time, with no mistakes) had increased by 25 percent. The cost of performing procurement transactions had been slashed by more than 80 percent, while procurement times had shrunk 90 percent. In product development, the percentage of successful launches rose by 30 to 50 percent. The time required to bring a new product to market was shortened by 50 to 75 percent. These improvements in process performance paid off in the critical enterprise currencies of customer satisfaction, customer retention, and corporate profits.

The good news is that these remarkable improvements are not atypical. In fact, they are the norm. The bad news is that achieving them requires a wholehearted commitment to process and an abandonment of the thinking and practices inherent in functional organizations. Making that commitment begins with focusing on the two words my seminar attendees find missing in their companies—*organized* and *together.*

Being *organized* means having concrete, specific designs for processes so that their performance isn't determined by improvisation or luck. Being *together* means creating an environment in which all process workers are aligned around common goals and see themselves as collaborators rather than adversaries. Both of these were missing at the equipment manufacturer with which this chapter began.

These twin principles—disciplined design and common alignment—are easy to describe but nearly impossible to implement in a traditional, functional organization. Hence it is necessary to make the company fit the principles by making myriad fundamental changes. Neither principle can perform the job alone. Each needs the other.

People who are aligned around a common goal but lack the discipline of a well-designed process will go nowhere, albeit together. Likewise, the best-designed process has no chance of survival when people aren't aligned around the process and its goals.

A major electronics firm learned this fact the hard way. In the early 1990s, the company was plagued by long cycle times in bringing new products to market. Management spotted the cause: flaws in the product development process. The existing process was plagued by handoffs, misunderstandings, and a poor comprehension of customer needs, among other problems. They promptly redesigned this process from scratch; their new design incorporated the latest methods for developing new products quickly and cheaply.

The new process called for teams from engineering, marketing, and other departments to work together in the same location. Each team would have full responsibility for a product from conception through launch, including such diverse activities as producing documentation, creating advertising, and even developing customer training materials. Because each team would have control over every aspect of the process, all activities would be performed in a coherent, streamlined fashion, free of the old bottlenecks and delays.

This was the theory, but it didn't work. The first pilot teams not only failed to speed up product development, they barely managed to operate at all. They were, in effect, sabotaged by the existing organization, which saw them as interlopers. Functional departments were unwilling to cede people, space, or responsibility to the teams. The corporate training unit refused to relinquish control over the training materials. The advertising department refused to let the teams create product advertising because, it asserted, that was its prerogative.

Instead of achieving the harmony in product development that the designers intended, the team plan worsened the discord it was supposed to cure. What was wrong with the new process? Actually, nothing. The problem was that each old functional department retained power over its turf, which prevented those areas from becoming aligned around the process and its goals. As one top manager put it, "We finally realized that we could not overlay a high performance process design on our functional organization." The company recognized it would have to make deep, fundamental changes in order to reinforce the process approach. In so doing, it transformed itself into what can be called a *process enterprise.*

A process enterprise is one that encourages, enables, and allows its people to perform process work. Process work is work that is focused on the customer, work that takes into account the larger context in which it is performed, work that is directed toward achieving results rather than being an end in itself, work that follows a disciplined and repeatable design. Process work is work that delivers the high levels of performance that customers now demand.

In innumerable ways, traditional organizations interfere with the ability of their people to perform process work. A process enterprise, in contrast, supports and encourages it. As a result, all its processes deliver sustained high performance. Note the key words: *all* and *sustained.* It is no great trick for a company to floor the pedal and get superior performance—for a short time. By harsh downsizing or pushing people harder, you can squeeze out instant acceleration, at least until the workforce runs out of gas. But overworked people burn out, lose their drive, and eventually leave. A process focus accomplishes the opposite—it encourages people who are aligned around a common purpose to continue performing reliably at a high level.

Everyone in a process enterprise knows the enterprise's processes and where he or she fits in, what results customers need, and who is responsible for delivering them. Everyone focuses on outcomes and knows that the real enemy is not other departments within the company but competitors outside the gates. Everyone looks outward at the customer, not upward at the management hierarchy.

How can you recognize a process enterprise? GE Capital, where process is the lingua franca, uses the following characterization.

- There is as much allegiance to processes as to functions.
- Employees internalize process goals.
- Employees understand how the process is performing.
- Everyone knows customer requirements and strives to meet them.
- Employees help manage each other instead of escalating conflict.
- Processes are measured objectively—and frequently.

Some executives, when confronted with the power and imperative of creating a process enterprise, attempt to go about it in their customary ways: by reorganizing, changing managerial responsibilities, or building new computer systems. While many of these steps are important, they are not of the essence. Pierre Leroy, president of John Deere's Construction Equipment Division (CED) and Deere Power Systems Group, has put it succinctly: "Process is a revolution in thought that leads to changes in business." First and foremost, processes represent a new way of thinking about the work of an enterprise. The first step in creating a process enterprise is to make this new way of thinking the norm in the enterprise; everything else will then fall into place.

Four distinctive features characterize the new way of thinking to which Pierre Leroy refers.

First, processes are *teleological* (from the Greek word *telos*, meaning "goal" or "mission"). That is, they focus on the outcome of work rather than on work as an end in itself. In an organization that pays attention to its processes, everyone in the company understands the *why* as well as the *what* of their work. How people are trained and how performance is measured must reinforce the outcome orientation of processes.

Second, processes are *customer-focused*. Thinking in terms of processes compels a business to see itself and its work from the perspective of the customer, rather than from its own. Deere CED no longer thinks in terms of marketing and selling products and services; now it views this work through the lens of forming partnerships with customers to solve their business problems. Deere used to focus on optimizing its own production schedules; now it concentrates on delivering solutions to customers on time. These new perspectives inevitably lead to new ways of working.

Third, processes are *holistic*. Process thinking transcends individual activities. It concentrates instead on how activities fit together to produce the best outcome—the results that must be delivered to customers. The key goal—superior value for the customer—is achieved when an assortment of warring departments is replaced with a seamless web of collaborators working together for a unified purpose.

Finally, process thinking is based on the belief that business success flows from *well-designed* ways of working. It explicitly rejects what might be called (with an acknowledgment to Thomas Carlyle) the great man (or woman) school of business, which attributes a company's success to a visionary chief executive, a marketing genius, or a brilliant product developer. If such an inspired individual develops the great strategy, the brilliant ad campaign, or the killer product, then the company will succeed; otherwise, it will not. The process approach rejects this idea on the grounds that it relies on luck and is therefore unsustainable. One cannot control whether lightning will strike, or depend on it to strike regularly. Process companies seek to institutionalize success by designing high-performance ways of working. They do not denigrate the talents of remarkable individuals, but they recognize that all human talent can and should be leveraged by an overall process. They believe that a company achieves its highest potential by designing processes that mobilize everyone's abilities rather than depending too much on any single individual, however gifted she or he may be.

Process thinking is needed for all work and all people. It is not a concept relevant only to the upper reaches of the organization or to those performing ethereal "knowledge work." It is equally needed on the factory floor and in the sales office. Traditional janitors, for instance, see their job as pushing a broom. Without brooms, they cannot work; unable to move something stubbornly stuck to the floor, they sweep around it. Process janitors, in contrast, see their job as achieving an outcome: a clean facility. They understand this goal and the part it plays in the ultimate goal of satisfying paying customers. Consequently, if they are not given a broom, they will go find one. Unable to clean something with it, they will find a better tool.

Process thinking must be inculcated in the organization as part of a broad and universal educational effort. In conventional, nonprocess companies, people know little outside the narrow confines of their individual jobs. Company managers find it pointless to educate people in anything beyond the specific skills they require to perform specific tasks. Adding to this isolation is the fact that companies tightly control the release of information and share it only if necessary, as if the organization were a spy agency rather than a business. But for a process to realize its potential, everyone involved in performing it must understand the whole process and how their individual efforts contribute to it. They need enough information about customers, competitors, and the company's finances to make the decisions that are part of process jobs. Duke Power gives all its linesmen a class that provides basic information about the electric power industry, such as deregulation, utility cost structures, and customer requirements. It gives them an appreciation of the business process concept, a detailed understanding of their own process, and grounding in the interpersonal skills needed to work collaboratively.

Everyone in a process enterprise should be able to answer these questions: What process are you part of? Can you describe it in twenty-five words or less? What is its purpose? How does your process create value for customers? How do you personally contribute to this value? How do others working with you also contribute value? What do the people immediately before and after you in the flow of the process do? By what measure does the company judge the performance of your process? What is the current level of that measure? How do you know when you personally are doing well? What other processes interface with yours? What do these processes need from yours, and what does yours need from them? What efforts to improve your process are now under way? People who can answer these questions have successfully internalized process thinking.

Indeed, while it may be hard to spot from the outside, one of the most distinctive features of a process enterprise is that everyone in it is thinking. Even in a process enterprise, people still spend the bulk of their time performing individual tasks. But they no longer heed the old motto "Do your work and don't think." Now it is "Do your work but think about your process." Everyone, bar none, has to understand the larger purpose (the teleology) of their work. They must see where their tasks fit in the grand design, know when and how to cooperate with others, and never forget the target of all this—a hugely satisfied customer.

Overcoming traditional thinking is necessary but not sufficient if a company is to have sustained high-performing processes. Another obstacle that must be overcome is the absence of anyone with overall responsibility for a process. In a functional company, existing managers are responsible only for narrow segments of a process. No one is empowered to create or impose a new process design, to knock down barriers, and to make the process work as it should.

Consequently, every process in a process enterprise requires a *process owner*—a manager responsible for ensuring that the entire process keeps flourishing on an end-to-end basis, from start to finish, over and over. A word of clarification: Everyone involved in performing a process, from salespeople to truck drivers, should "own" the process in the sense of sharing the commitment to make it thrive. The process owner, however, is the manager in charge of designing the process, building its supporting tools, installing it in the organization, and ensuring its ongoing high performance.

At Duke Power, a unit of Duke Energy, Rob Manning is the process owner of a process called "deliver products and services," which essentially means installing new electrical service for customers, many of whom are building contractors putting up new subdivisions. Before Manning assumed this role in 1996, this process was in very poor shape. Though it was performed in each of the company's geographic regions, nowhere was it anyone's specific responsibility. The process was performed in part by customer service reps who took an order and promised that the work would be done on a certain date; in part by schedulers who assigned people to the project; and in part by linesmen who actually did the work. But none of them thought much about one another or the whole process. Each was located in a different department that concentrated on enhancing its own performance. No one coordinated all the work of the various departments to strengthen overall performance. There was no *organized* and no *together*. As a result, the process was invisible, ad hoc, and performed differently and inconsistently across the company's various geographic regions. One obvious manifestation of these problems was Duke's frequent failure to hook up electrical service on the promised date; in some of its service territories, the company met its promise date only 30 percent of the time. Needless to say, contractors were angry about paying their electricians to wait around for Duke to connect the power.

When Rob Manning assumed the process owner role, his first job was to evaluate the existing process and create a better design. He investigated why the company so often failed to meet the installation dates it promised customers. One reason, he discovered, was that the person committing the dates lacked accurate information about exactly who would be available to do work on a given date. This individual might know the total number of people available for an assignment but not their specific skills, and so he or she might promise the customer a date when the people actually needed for the job were unavailable. Moreover, crews often didn't complete all the work they were assigned for a day because they left the depot later in the morning than they should have.

Manning and his team redesigned the process to address these problems. For example, it used to take about seventy minutes every morning for installation crews to load their trucks and get on the road. Now the company's warehouses have been reorganized so that parts and tools required by the crews are laid out the night before. As a result, the crews load up and head off in ten minutes, giving them an extra sixty minutes a day to speed installations and slash customer waiting time. The company also deployed a new scheduling system that provides detailed information about available field personnel, thereby enabling more specific and accurate assignments. The new process also included people whose role was to negotiate commitment dates with customers and keep them apprised of any changes.

Central to the work of process design is the selection of performance measures. As Manning puts it, "Measures are my best friend." A process owner must designate which aspects of the process ought to be measured, determine the levels of performance that customers require, and calculate the indicators that best measure progress toward the desired goals. A process owner is responsible for deploying the measurement systems, evaluating how well the process is performing, publicizing the performance levels to everyone involved, and taking whatever steps are necessary to improve them.

By concentrating on the design and measurement of his process, Rob Manning achieved dramatic improvement in its performance. Commitments to customers are now consistently met more than 98 percent of the time, across all of Duke's regions. But Manning's job did not end once he had straightened out the process. Since every process must keep pace with changing times, advances in technologies, and the growing needs of customers, measuring and improving his process is Manning's—and every process owner's—never-ending responsibility.

The process owner, however, does more than design and measure the process. He or she also supports and enables the people who actually perform it by educating everyone involved and serving as a resource for them. For a process that involves many people, especially people who are geographically dispersed, the process owner is likely to need local representatives. Rob Manning has process coordinators spread across Duke Power, each of whom supports about thirty people in the field. The process coordinators collect performance data, answer questions, and help solve problems. A process coordinator is definitely not a traditional supervisor keeping tabs on thirty people all day. Field teams make their own decisions that are consistent with process goals and measures. A process coordinator is there as a resource to whom they can turn should they need to.

A process owner serves as an advocate for the process, both to the people who perform it and to those in the rest of the company. Rob Manning describes himself as a process evangelist. He spends a significant amount of his time persuading process team members that meeting customer needs is their most important goal and that his process design is the best tool available for reaching it. He also represents his process in the corridors of power, obtaining the resources it needs to get its mission accomplished.

At IBM, the process advocacy role is entrusted to the company's most senior managers. Each process has a full-time owner, called a business process executive, who is responsible for creating and implementing the design. In addition, each process has an advocate on the worldwide management council (WMC), the fifty or so senior executives who run IBM's lines of business. At each WMC meeting, process advocates report on the performance of his or her process and the progress it is making. Interestingly, the advocate must do this personally, not by calling in a staff member.

At some companies, process owners are line managers, and the people who perform the process report to them. This does not mean, however, that they or their local designates are traditional supervisors or managers. The people who perform a process do not need, indeed cannot abide, an overseer. Aware of the customer's needs and the overall process design, they are measured on and held accountable for the process's performance and do not need someone looking over their shoulders. Process work requires independence, autonomy, and decision making.

On the other hand, at a company like Duke Power, the process owner does not directly manage the people who perform the process.

Regional managers provide the people, and the process owner develops the design they will follow. The differences between these two forms of process ownership are not terribly significant. I have asked several senior people at Duke Power whether a person performing a process in a region reports to the regional manager or to the process owner. Each time I have received the identical reply: "It doesn't matter." Since everyone involved—process team members, process owners, regional managers—is measured and held accountable for the same process outcomes, all managers share the same agenda, and so the question of reporting relationships becomes one of administration rather than strategic direction. (This issue will be central to Chapter 7.)

Whatever variation on the theme a particular company chooses, process owners must be among the most senior managers in an organization. A common error for companies that are intrigued by the promise of process but reluctant to rock the boat is to give some of their existing middle managers the title of process owner. But of course, having a title doesn't guarantee that one can do the job. The process owner must be senior enough in the company to have end-to-end authority over the process. He or she needs enough clout to advocate for it to other senior managers. There is no such thing as a successful junior process owner.

Each process owner is, in fact, the steward of a key business asset: one of the organization's business processes that determines how the company works and creates all of its value. It is well known by now that intellectual assets are the real measure of a company's value, not the conventional components of the balance sheet. A process design is a particularly valuable form of intellectual asset. It is concrete and directly usable, not diffuse and abstract. Flawlessly designed and executed processes are what create superior products, exceptional marketing programs, flawless fulfillment, successful sales efforts, and enviable customer satisfaction. Today a company's processes, even more than its short-lived products, define its identity and shape its opportunities for growth and diversification. Such invaluable assets need someone to look after them.

Installing process owners may be the most visible evidence of a company's commitment to process, but if it stops there, little will be accomplished. Even with process owners in place, traditionally organized companies will defeat the best-designed processes. Executives must be prepared to jettison many of the familiar aspects of their companies in order to align everything around the new process focus.

To begin with, the basic structural unit in a process enterprise is not the functional department but the process team—the people (usually an interdisciplinary group) who collectively perform a process from beginning to end. Process teams are not short-term assignments or ad hoc overlays on a functional organization. Rather, the process team is an employee's primary workplace. A person's primary allegiance must be to the team and its members, not to a functional department that consists of others with the same specialized skill.

A process enterprise will need a revamped facility that enables these teams to operate. At American Standard the order fulfillment process is performed by diverse specialists, from accountants to shipping personnel. While these employees used to work in separate departments, they are now all located in the same quarters. Sharing the same work space offers them a better view of the entire process, and co-locating different talents effectively broadens everyone's horizons. Team members can exchange ideas easily, and the daily interactions lift their sights to the process as a whole. When work is perceived as process work, space must be process space.

It makes sense that if front-line personnel and managers focus on processes, then their compensation should be based—at least in part—on how well their processes perform. All process teams at Allmerica Financial, a *Fortune* 500 insurance company, receive bonuses based on reaching specific performance goals set by the process owners. These goals include targets for the amount of time required to handle applications from beginning to end and the percentage of contracts issued without error. (Chapter 6 will explain how the process owners set these targets.) The process owners can award additional bonuses to members who make outstanding contributions to a team's results. At an increasing number of companies, compensation is based on three factors: process performance, personal contribution, and corporate performance. One benefit of these new reward systems is that they remind everyone that creating customer value, not keeping busy, is the real point of everyone's work. They remind everyone that in a process enterprise, there are no winners on a losing team.

Teamwork can't be limited just to the front lines. Process owners and the rest of the management team must also learn to cooperate in order to pursue the larger goals that the whole enterprise seeks. Otherwise, creating a process enterprise will merely turn functional silos into process sewers, and the enterprise will suffer from a new kind of fragmentation. Customers are served by competition between processes no better than by warfare between functions. The individual processes of an enterprise must integrate, and the people working in and responsible for these processes must cooperate with each other if the enterprise as a whole is to work successfully. (This idea, too, will recur in Chapter 7.)

To help ensure this kind of integration and cooperation, some companies are appointing senior executives to be chief process officers, CPOs (albeit sometimes with different titles). The CPO is responsible for establishing an overall process model that identifies all the company's processes and how they interface and interact with one another, and for promulgating policies for managing them. In effect, the CPO specifies the job of the process owner. The chief process officer also convenes and chairs a process council consisting of all the process owners and other key executives. The council is the locus for resolving cross-process issues of politics, priorities, and resource allocation.

At these council meetings, the business leader plays a key role. He or she must ensure that the attendees work as a team and not merely represent parochial interests. Accordingly, he or she strives to reinforce the company's overall vision while making sure that the needs of particular processes don't overwhelm the needs of the company as a whole.

Managers sometimes have mixed emotions about process enterprises. On the one hand, they see the logic and the power of this way of doing business. On the other, they feel anxious about the impacts that converting to a process enterprise will have on them personally. First of all, their own numbers will be reduced. A good rule of thumb is that a process enterprise needs only about half as many managers as does a traditional organization. Front-line personnel who understand the design and logic of their process, work together in teams, and are held accountable for results do not need much managerial oversight. Instead of the classical worker-to-manager ratio of 10 or so to 1, in a process enterprise the ratio is in the range of 20 or 30 to 1. Second, the managerial jobs that remain are very different from their predecessors, centering on design and measurement of process and on development of people rather than on supervision of work. And managerial teamwork is something completely unfamiliar to most traditional managers. No wonder that the managerial ranks are often less than completely enthusiastic about undertaking the transition to process.

On the other hand, most front-line personnel embrace it. A process enterprise treats its employees as responsible adults who prefer to push themselves rather than be pushed, who know what needs to be done, and who will accept responsibility for doing it. It is no place for passive workers who do what they're told, but it is made to order for engaged, autonomous, and motivated businesspeople who work not for their bosses but for their customers.

Powerful customers have killed the paternalistic organization. In the old days, companies could afford to shower people with regular raises, hefty benefits, and career-long security in return for unquestioning loyalty and obedience. Any resulting costs could be safely passed along to the hapless customer. In the customer economy, however, a company can no longer guarantee anything to its employees. Paternalism must give way to partnership. The company and its employees are in the same boat. To say that this is a major shift from traditional labor relations is an understatement, yet I have found most workers in process enterprises to be comfortable with it. Listen to what a few people who actually work in process enterprises say about it.

- Jerry P. is a team leader in a manufacturing plant. "In the past, nobody cared about the next person," he says. "If something went wrong, it was somebody else's problem. Now it's team-work, and we work together as a group to fix problems. People who do the work know it best, and now the company takes feed-back from them. People now enjoy their jobs. It's not a drag coming to work each day. People have more pride in what they're doing."

- Ed B. is a member of an accounts receivable team in a manu-facturing company: "The best part of how we work now is that you can see where you fit in, how all the parts of the company fit together."

- John D. is a thirty-three-year veteran of an electric power com-pany and a former president of the union local. "In the old days there were strict trade craft rules," he recalls. "A repairman didn't do an electrician's job or vice versa. Now the lines are blurred and people can do more to work to their capabilities. There are fewer foremen, and the front lines have the power to decide their own work. People have more impact on the busi-ness, and you can see the difference in their attitudes. They feel more ownership of the business. Morale is excellent."

Lest you find the magnitude of the switch to process overwhelming, let me tell you that you may well be on the road to becoming a process enterprise without even knowing it. Not all companies align themselves around processes self-consciously, or as part of an explicit commitment to customers. In many cases, they begin with other things in mind and discover the transcendent power of process only after the fact.

One of the major business phenomena of the 1990s was the advent of so-called ERP (enterprise resource planning) systems. These inelegantly named software products offered customers an integrated set of application modules (for finance, production, logistics, and so on) that shared a common database and seamlessly interfaced with one another. Many companies in the 1990s implemented ERP systems for narrow technical purposes: to avoid the Y2K problem, to replace antiquated systems that were hard to maintain, to lower the cost of the hardware platform needed to run their software, and the like.

Companies that undertook ERP with these goals in mind were almost universally disappointed in the results. In some cases, they experienced catastrophic failures and never even managed to install the system. In others, after many headaches, the systems eventually worked but delivered only modest payoffs. The reason was that these companies did not appreciate the real nature of ERP. Because its modules are so tightly integrated, an ERP system is, in effect, a tool for supporting end-to-end business processes, a great rarity in the world of packaged software. Listen to the following comments from two companies that have successfully implemented ERP systems.

The traditional flow was for the account rep to set up the order. The credit department then checked it. Next, the order was sent to plants where traffic and inventory people got involved to plan the shipments and bills of lading. Sourcing then ordered materials from various locations. The order was then invoiced, entered into receivables, and the sale was booked. Now, instead of flowing from one department to the next, a team of people handles the order from beginning to end.

We have learned how bad we really are. We've been a run and gun organization. Anyone could do anything, and the rest of the company would adapt. If it was raining on Tuesday, we'd do things one way. If it was Wednesday and sunny, we'd do something else. Because of the ERP system, we are formalizing how we work and implementing it across the organization.

The first quotation expresses the fact that an ERP system leads to cross-functionality and teamwork: the *together* theme of process. The second one captures the fact that an ERP system introduces discipline into an organization: the *organized* dimension of process. An ERP system is a Trojan horse that carries in its belly our two old friends, discipline and teamwork, *organized* and *together*. It introduces processes into an enterprise whether or not it wants them or is ready for them. When companies prepare effectively for this by orienting themselves around processes, they succeed with ERP. When they do not, they fail.

Scratching the surface of most other contemporary business issues will reveal that they, too, are fundamentally about processes. For instance, the only way to achieve six sigma quality is through careful process redesign. GE, the master of six sigma, says that "processes are the basic vocabulary of six sigma." As Chapter 9 will show, what is most important about the Internet is that it can be used to integrate intercorporate processes, processes that transcend corporate boundaries as well as functional ones. Similarly, supply chain integration, an issue high on many agendas, is addressed best as an exercise in intercorporate process improvement. A focus on processes is also crucial in successful mergers and acquisitions. Simply joining two companies under a common holding company umbrella is neither a merger nor an acquisition; it is merely propinquity. If the purpose of uniting two companies is to yield significant cost reductions or take advantage of marketplace synergies, then their processes must be standardized and integrated.

When initiatives like these are understood and managed through a process lens, their success rate skyrockets. In other words, many companies come to a process approach indirectly, as a result of discovering that processes are the most effective way to implement some other major initiative on which they are already embarked. Once a company realizes this, processes become the underpinning not only of the initial project but of most others that follow. There are many on-ramps to the process highway.

The business world is notorious for its fads—simplistic solutions to complex problems that have a moment in the spotlight before shriveling in the harsh glare of reality. Creating a process enterprise is something else—a deep change in the way we think about and organize productive work. It is an abiding change, of the kind that comes along not every couple of years but rather every couple of centuries. It delivers breathtaking improvements in operating performance, but these come at a price: the wholesale rethinking of the structure and management of the enterprise. Job descriptions, skills and training, measurement and reward systems, managerial roles, facilities, and a host of other systems upon which a company relies daily all need to be realigned. Companies that have reaped the benefits of process have done so by making a steadfast commitment to that approach.

A halfhearted engagement in processes is as bad as no engagement at all. At one large chemical company, the CEO began a major program of process-focused performance improvement. The company's managers identified their processes, assigned them owners, and embarked on redesign efforts. Before long, they achieved massive cost reductions, huge decreases in inventory, and major improvements in both revenue and customer retention. But shortly thereafter, the CEO retired. The new CEO came from outside the company and, in a paraphrase of the Bible's description of Pharaoh, knew not process. He saw the apparatus of process as unnecessary overhead and retreated from his predecessor's initiatives.

Unsurprisingly, business performance began to decline. The new CEO's conventional responses—downsizing and layoffs—caused it to decline even more. After he snatched at a further series of contemporary business fads, from global consolidation to portfolio divestitures, business sagged even more. In fact, as of this writing, the performance of the company is far worse than it was before the focus on processes first began. The underlying cause of this discouraging backslide is that the first CEO was not aggressive enough in implementing processes. He managed to install the new designs but did not realign all aspects of the business around them. His successor encountered not a deeply process-oriented enterprise, but a traditional one with a process overlay. Had it been otherwise, he would have been unable to roll back his predecessor's advances so easily.

Fortunately, more and more CEOs now understand what it takes to harness the power of their processes. The tide is clearly running in the process direction. Most manufacturing industries are already in the process tent. Financial and other service companies are lining up at the entrance. By the end of the decade, companies that are not becoming process enterprises will be the exception rather than the rule. In the marketplace of business ideas, process has soared in value because it works better than anything else. Once an experimental notion, adopted only by the visionary, the brave, or the desperate, the process-based way of running a business is fast becoming the norm.

This does not mean that you are guaranteed success or nirvana if you publicly embrace the process approach. Execution matters enormously. Companies that adopt the forms without changing their thinking, that use the terminology without changing their cultures, will not succeed. Simply retitling old jobs, renaming functions as processes, or focusing exclusively on the management ranks is a guaranteed route to failure.

Even achieving success with processes brings its own challenges. For one thing, process enterprises need measurement and reward systems that are more sharply tuned than those employed by traditional organizations. That people throughout the company need to learn and adopt process thinking means that training and education budgets will jump dramatically. Moreover, not everyone will happily board the process bandwagon. Some workers may resist the responsibility that a process enterprise imposes, and more than a few managers may resist giving up their traditional power and perks. The cultural shifts associated with processes—from individual to team, from boss to customer, from improvisation to discipline, from conflict to sharing, from buck passing to personal accountability and collective responsibility—are difficult changes for people to accept.

Yet the most common refrain I have heard from people who have lived through the experience is this: "The transition was awful, but I'd never go back." Whatever hardships the transition inflicts, creating a process enterprise offers huge benefits to shareholders, managers, and employees. It delivers sustained high performance across the board. It is flexible in its use of resources. It gives everyone a common focus and alignment. It enables managers to truly manage by giving them the tools they need to influence outcomes. It offers front-line performers more satisfying jobs and the self-respect that comes from being treated like adults, free from the paternalism and patronization that characterized yesterday's hierarchies.

The process enterprise is here, and it is here to stay.

Agenda Item 3

Create a Process Enterprise

- Obsess about the end-to-end processes that create all value for your customers.
- Ensure that every person understands processes and his or her role in them.
- Appoint senior process owners to measure, manage, and improve the processes.
- Create a process-friendly company by aligning facilities, compensation, and structure around processes.
- Develop a culture of teamwork and shared responsibility.
- Set up a process council so that you don't replace functional silos with process sewers.
- Manage in process terms everything you do to make your company better.
- Make process into a way of life.

5

Create Order Where Chaos Reigns

Systematize Creativity

I n contemporary myth, a successful company is a taut ship—a showcase of efficiency where work is precisely defined, expertly performed, and tightly managed. Only people who have never been inside a real company believe this myth. The fact is that many parts of many companies are completely out of control. Individuals may work hard and be constantly busy, but the place as a whole is in chaos. Endless effort is expended for naught, people work at cross-purposes, and the fact that anything gets done is almost a miracle. Every situation is handled differently, with people improvising and making up their work as they go. This chaos can turn up anywhere, but it is endemic in the parts of a company that deal in new situations: not in manufacturing or logistics or finance, but in product development and sales and marketing.

At one electronics company I know, sales of large systems happened largely by accident. Sales reps pursued prospects based on their personal intuitive preferences; engineering might or might not modify a product to meet the needs of a prospective customer; prices were quoted to customers before finance had the opportunity to evaluate them; customers received different answers when they asked the same question of sales, engineering, or finance; and so on.

At one chemical company, products seemed to get developed despite the best efforts of the organization. If marketing came up with a product concept, engineering would often reject it as not feasible—code for "too much trouble" or "not very interesting." Marketing people would routinely reject new technologies suggested by research as impractical—meaning they did not understand them. Occasionally—but only occasionally—a "product champion" got so impassioned about a new concept that he or she managed to ram it past all these gatekeepers through sheer force of personality. But no sooner did the new product start to emerge than the waters closed back over it. Development suddenly argued that building a new plant to make the product would take forever. Finance said the proposed price would lose money. Sales claimed that no one would buy the damn thing anyway. In this chemical company, new products got to market only by accident. Each department worked hard but in isolation; each wheel was spinning, but the transmission connecting them was never engaged.

The Keystone Kops could have run these operations better. Unfortunately, scenarios like these are all too familiar. In many organizations, much work is best compared to Brownian motion, where particles bounce around completely at random.

It may be unbelievable to outsiders that apparently well-managed, successful companies actually operate this chaotically. The reason that they do is fairly simple: They still operate the same way they did when they were much smaller—that is, with great informality. A very small company can get by without sharply defined ways of working, because the people who work there know each other and communicate well enough to improvise successfully. In the halcyon environment of small-business life, everyone knows everyone else. Engineering is just down the hall from sales; the finance chief joins you for lunch in the cafeteria. The company's key projects are common knowledge. Even the CEO answers to his or her first name, and formality is parked outside the plant gate. Good people, working together, can rise to the occasion and make almost anything happen.

With growth, however, come problems. The company's old ways of working do not "scale up." As it hires more people, fewer of them know each other, or the customers, or the company as a whole. It becomes harder for anyone to know what is going on, and like modern academics, the company's employees soon find they know more and more about less and less. Yet no one ever gets around to designing systematic modes of operating, and the old improvisational ways of working remain deeply embedded in the company's genetic code. When many people are trying to handle many situations with no clearly defined way of doing things, the results are unsurprisingly disastrous.

Besides scale, there are other reasons why the informal ways that used to suffice for an organization no longer do. For one, work has become much more complex than it used to be. Selling, in the old days, was largely an act of personal heroism. The key to successful selling was knowing the products and the customers. The effective sales rep would present his or her product or service in the best possible light, forge a bond with the buyer, and triumph over the competition.

This approach may still work in the real estate boiler rooms depicted in *Glengarry Glen Ross,* but it has little to do with the way sales are made in the real world. As I hope you remember from Chapter 3, today's customers don't want products; they demand solutions, and solutions don't come in a box. They must be designed, fashioned to meet the customer's specific needs. Making such sales takes a lot more than personal charisma. Today's selling is system selling, solution selling, consultative selling; it entails analyzing customer needs, designing alternative solutions, scrutinizing costs, developing and implementing systems, and more. This is not the work of a heroic individual sales rep; gone are the days of Willy Loman lugging his sample cases on the lonely road. Modern selling is a team sport, and a complex one at that. Winning at it takes discipline and structure. Making it up as you go along is a recipe for disaster.

The same applies to product development. The American myth is that products are developed by lone geniuses working in their labs, who turn sudden inspiration into practical innovations. That wasn't quite true even in Thomas Edison's day, and it certainly isn't true today. Reality is far more complex. Talent and inspiration are necessary but not sufficient. To create and launch nearly any new product today requires many people with many different skills. Engineers must envision and design the product, using customer input provided via sales reps; then marketing experts must assess the product's potential and help shape its specific features. Financial types must analyze the cost of making it and determine a competitive price. Manufacturing specialists must decide how to make the product in volume. Lawyers must assess how it can be protected from imitators.

The keys to success here are coordination and discipline. Activities must not only get done, they must fit together and be done in the right order if the new product is to see the light of day. Getting customer input too late is tantamount to not getting it at all. Yet most companies lack any reliable mechanism for ensuring such coordination. They simply have no guiding intelligence, no standard way of operating that integrates all the pieces, no repeatable design. Instead, each department goes off on its own, with little or no grasp of the larger picture.

Today's fast-changing business world is an inhospitable environment for ad hoc and informal ways of creating and selling products. Ross Johnson, former CEO of RJR Nabisco, is reputed to have said about his company's mainstay product, "Some genius invented the Oreo. We're just living off the inheritance." Time was when the business of many companies depended on Oreos: products with seemingly endless lifetimes. In those days, developing new products was a matter of no great urgency; whenever new products appeared would be good enough. That's no longer the case. Today's products have lifespans of months rather than decades. No matter how splendid your products are, you had better have a pipeline of equally splendid ones under development. If you don't, your success will have the shelf life of celery. Developing new products is now too critical to leave to chance. So is selling. Customers no longer display loyalty; they must be resold on an ongoing basis. Ways of working that might have been adequate for engaging the occasional new customer fall apart when they must be applied to rewinning the existing customer base every day.

In short, to succeed in today's world, the critical work of selling and developing products must be built on discipline and structure; it must move from the ad hoc to the methodical. To employ the language of Chapter 4, these reflexive activities must become full-fledged, systematic processes.

To many people, the appeal and the power of process has principally come from its cross-functionality, its *together* aspect. By focusing on end-to-end sequences of work, processes knock down the walls of functional silos, eliminating handoffs and the errors, delays, and costs that inevitably flow from these discontinuities. By focusing on the customer and on a common outcome, process thinking aligns everyone in an organization and avoids the bizarre consequences of incongruent functional goals and misaligned measurement systems. But the other key word in Chapter 4's definition of process was *organized*. The structure, discipline, and design of a process are as much an antidote to chaos as alignment is a cure for fragmentation.

By specifying a precise sequence of steps and pinpointing responsibility for performing them, we introduce composition and order into areas where chaos would otherwise rule. The payoffs include repeatability, predictability, and manageability. No longer do people have to put their energies into figuring out how to work; they can concentrate on doing the work itself. Performance soars as a result: When you don't waste time on futile efforts, you can get things done much faster and less expensively.

Discipline does not eliminate the need for individuality or creativity. On the contrary, it actually encourages them by providing a framework for individual work that allows each person to leverage his or her own activities. Structure ensures that the parts come together as a whole.

Consider the disorder that once gripped a major manufacturer of private two-way radio systems, of the sort used by police forces, security departments, government agencies, and electric utilities. These are large-ticket items, customized to meet each buyer's particular needs. They include such components as a transmitting tower, a base station, the receivers themselves, multiple accessories, and training for the users.

"Selling" these systems involves far more than a sales rep buying lunch for the purchasing agent. The customer's needs must be determined and assessed. A system that meets these needs must be designed, and its costs must be evaluated, as well as its feasibility, profitability, and consistency with the manufacturer's business strategy. After that comes the creation of a detailed bid, the search for the right people to work on the implementation effort, negotiations with the customer, and more.

All this work can't be done by any one individual, however talented or heroic. It requires disciplined coordination of work performed by many different parts of the company. Until recently, however, this manufacturer's selling efforts were as organized as a food fight.

As other departments saw it, the sales force "never saw a deal they didn't like." No matter how unclear the outcome—or uncertain the profit—they would chase every lead to the bitter end. Eager to head off competitors, sales reps would often quote a price to a customer long before anyone had any real idea what the system would cost. (The lament at this company was that what was said in the first five minutes of the first sales call committed the company for the next three years.)

As information about the customer's needs seeped from department to department, it became garbled and subject to personal interpretation. The people who had to design the actual system were so far removed from the customer, and the information they had to work with had become so distorted by the time it reached them, that they had to invent interpretations of the customer's requirements. The advantages and disadvantages that competitors brought to the table were not considered early enough in the game to make a difference in the company's proposal. Product managers promoted the use of the products they were responsible for, even if these didn't fit the customer's needs very well. People bounced from project to project; a team working on one customer assignment would wake up to discover that half its members had been reassigned overnight. No one was in charge of project "team" meetings; whoever had the loudest voice prevailed. The customer did not know whom to call and, in any event, heard a different story from every person he or she spoke with.

However absurd and self-destructive this behavior seems, this story is much closer to the norm than to the exception for today's corporations. That such companies ever do get sales is due largely to a few extraordinary people who rise above the chaos that surrounds them. Some enterprising sales rep goes flat-out. ("We are not going to lose this one.") He or she becomes a crusader, working long hours to collect information, jawbone peers, circumvent the bureaucracy, whip up hope and enthusiasm, and generally do whatever it takes.

A similar figure in the product development area has become enshrined in corporate mythology: the product champion. The product champion, through force of great will, manages to drive a product to completion, despite the best efforts of the organization to kill it. Indeed, corporate folklore has it that a product will succeed only if it has a strong champion.

Both the heroic sales rep and the product champion try to compensate for organizational disorder by personally harnessing uncoordinated activities into a purposeful whole. They are substitutes for discipline and process, but in the long run, they can't succeed. For one thing, heroes have a lamentable tendency to quit or burn out. For another, any company should be alarmed when it succeeds in spite of its normal ways of operating. The fact that sales need heroes and products need champions is a terrifying indictment. Coming up with a new product or a major sale should not be an unusual event that depends on extraordinary individual acts; it ought to be the natural result of well-designed and smoothly operating processes.

What our manufacturer was missing in its sales efforts, and what most companies lack in sales, product development, and other such arenas, is discipline and process. Many companies still labor under the false impression that these notions apply only to back-office activities, such as purchasing, order fulfillment, or answering customer inquiries. Somehow they feel that imposing discipline and structure on creative work—developing products, creating marketing campaigns, selling products and services to customers—would inhibit people and force them into a narrow box from which they could not escape. These companies somehow associate the concepts of discipline and process with bureaucracy and inflexibility. Nothing could be further from the truth. Teamwork and discipline are at least as valuable in creative front-office work as they are in back-office activities. The radio systems manufacturer's old way of selling suffered from a deficiency of both. The many individuals involved had differing agendas, and there was no over-arching way of selling that brought them all together.

In time, discipline and process did come to these sales efforts. The company's managers diagnosed their haphazard way of doing business and identified its fundamental flaws, which ranged from diffuse decision making to blurry communication with customers. They then designed a precise twenty-five-step formula to be applied to every sales opportunity. The formula is worth examining for an insight into how process structure tames the beast of chaos.

The process begins when a sales rep identifies a sales opportunity. Rather than having each step of the process performed by a different person, a team is convened at the outset to explore and investigate the opportunity. This team includes the sales rep responsible for the account, but he or she is joined by people from the product groups, from engineering, from systems integration, from contracts, and from other key parts of the organization. They collaborate on the first five steps of the process:

1. Work with the customer to spell out the opportunity, developing an overview of the nature of the customer and his needs—information that will be used at every succeeding step.

2. Assess this opportunity in the context of our plans and capabilities. Does this opportunity fit our technical and business strategies? Will we be able to deliver what the customer requires? Can we get this done in the time frame the customer demands?

3. Analyze the competition: How would other suppliers approach this opportunity? Are we likely to win this one? How should our approach reflect the competition's strengths and weaknesses?

4. Develop a preliminary business case. This is a rough but complete estimate of the cost of this deal, the revenue it will deliver, and the contribution to corporate profit it will make.

5. In light of all these factors, decide what priority should be given to this opportunity. If we have a real shot at winning this one, do we want to? Is it a good use of our energy? At this point, low-priority cases are abandoned to conserve resources for the best opportunities.

Steps six through eleven dig deep into the customer's requirements and develop a project strategy.

6. Assemble a multiskilled project team with relevant specialties (engineering, sales, marketing, finance, and the like). The team's assignment: Handle this opportunity all the way to its successful conclusion. Allocate resources to make sure that people won't be pulled off the project.

7. Refine customer requirements, through in-depth discussions with the customer.

8. Identify the risks associated with pursuing this opportunity, from technological uncertainties to competitor response.

9. Finalize the business case, based on all information gathered thus far.

10. Have management review the team's strategy. Disapproval scraps the project.

11. Double-check with the customer that we have an accurate understanding of the customer's needs. Correct all inaccuracies.

In the next six steps, the company invests significant resources in developing the solution to the customer's needs.

12. Allocate any additional resources needed for solution development.

13. Develop and evaluate alternative designs for a solution. Select the approach that will be proposed.

14. Develop an analysis of likely competitor approaches to this opportunity and how they will be priced.

15. Update the risk management plan, clarifying the situations that might cause this project to go awry.

16. Work out revised profit-and-loss scenarios.

17. Create the formal quote that will be submitted to the customer, and have it reviewed and approved by all concerned parties.

The next five steps finalize the project strategy and present the proposal:

18. Review the customer's formal Request for Proposal (RFP). Note that instead of being caught flat-footed by the sudden appearance of the RFP, the company has been developing its approach all along and is ready to respond with alacrity when the RFP at last appears. If necessary, the project strategy is tuned to match the RFP. If the RFP is very different from what was expected, the project is abandoned.

19. Review the proposed technical design and the related support services, to ensure that they are consistent with the RFP.

20. Finalize the bid that is to be submitted.

21. Spell out the bid in a formal proposal.

22. After final review and approval by all concerned parties, present the proposal to the customer.

The final three steps of the process come after the customer chooses us:

23. Negotiate details of the contract. This is to ensure that our responsibilities are clearly spelled out, thus avoiding demands for costly services "for free" later on.

24. Conduct a post-mortem on the project to assess what did and did not work well.

25. Brief the rest of the organization on any competitive intelligence that came out of the project.

This is a close-up of a carefully designed process. Our purpose is not to analyze its details but simply to show how discipline can be applied even to seemingly unstructured and "creative" areas such as sales.

Some experienced sales professionals might argue that there is nothing remarkable or innovative about this process. They might maintain that it is just basic sales operations. But that is precisely the point. Any process is better than no process. Before the company formalized these twenty-five steps, each sales opportunity was handled in a different way. Important steps were often neglected, and things were frequently done out of order. Management reviews, for example, were regularly skipped or done late, long after the company had carelessly invested major funds in a no-win project. Quotes were submitted too early. Projects not in the company's long-term interests were arbitrarily pursued. Installing the process ensured that each of the required steps was performed every time, without exception. What had previously been in the domain of luck and personal inclination has become the province of structure and formality.

This approach has dramatically improved sales performance. The company wins more of the projects on which it bids—a share more than 15 percent higher than it had before the process was created. Moreover, time and money are no longer squandered on hopeless or inappropriate projects. This business is now a much more effective organization—and more profitable as well. According to my estimate, the unit's profits have jumped roughly 500 percent as a result of better pricing, rising market share, and smarter resource allocation.

Some might question the broader applicability of these experiences. After all, not everyone sells products as complex as private two-way radio systems. That is true, but such systems selling is becoming the norm in many industries. For instance, selling consumer goods to a supermarket is no longer merely an exercise in order taking. It requires developing a cooperative promotional and advertising plan, crafting a custom price that rewards increased consumer purchases, installing a vendor-managed inventory program, and addressing a host of other issues. As products are surrounded by value-added services (a theme explored in Chapter 3), selling anything becomes much more complex and much more in need of discipline.

Many other companies are also applying discipline and structure to sales and reaping enormous rewards as a result. BellSouth, for instance, has adopted a process approach to selling advertising space in its Yellow Pages. The process design enforces such disciplines as a longer-term perspective on customer relationships, assignment of a sales opportunity to the sales rep best qualified to handle it, and capturing and using customer data for strategic purposes. The process has also turned a series of interdepartmental handoffs into an integrated group of activities performed by a cross-functional team. Cycle times have been slashed by two-thirds, rework dramatically reduced, and last-minute fire drills all but eliminated, which has resulted in both greater customer satisfaction and reduced costs. In the early 1990s, Electronic Data Systems (EDS) implemented a disciplined sales process called SVS (Strategic Value Selling), which was one of the key contributors to the company's 93 percent sales increase between 1996 and 1997.

It is worth stressing again that structure doesn't turn people into automata. On the contrary, it is liberating: Discipline provides a framework that ensures that creative and talent-intensive activities are done by the right people, at the right time, with the right information. However, it does require change and adaptation. Sales reps can no longer operate as lone wolves. They have to learn to follow a process, to work in teams, and to restrain their improvisational impulses. This is not always an easy adjustment, and senior managers need to make sure that the process is actually followed. At EDS, the vice-chairman somewhat ominously advised the sales force, "It may be okay to win a deal without SVS, but you'd better not lose a deal without SVS." (Perhaps the most chilling part of this warning is the use of the word *may*.) Unsurprisingly, the sales force quickly learned to appreciate the power and beauty of SVS.

What these companies have done with sales, others have done in product development. One good example is Caterpillar, the manufacturer of heavy construction equipment. Caterpillar has redesigned the way it conducts what it calls NPI (New Product Introduction). The process now has four major phases:

1. Strategy.

A cross-functional team of business analysts, engineers, and others takes charge of launching a new product. The team meets with customers and dealers to identify needs, develop requirements for the product, and set its business objectives.

2. Concept.

The team converts customer requirements into technical specifications, determines the new development that will be required, and assembles a business plan that covers the proposed product's marketing, manufacturing, pricing, and future technical support. These are all developed at the outset, so that the company does not later find that it has developed a product that cannot be sold or supported. Reality check: Caterpillar's executives review the plan for plausibility and consistency with the company's criteria for new products.

3. Development.

This is where significant dollars are spent. Turning the concept into an actual design requires enormous effort and constant review to ensure adequacy and completeness. The reviews are rigorous. At Caterpillar, it is quite acceptable to kill a project that doesn't meet target criteria.

In less coherent companies, an embryo product quickly takes on a life of its own. Once a team takes responsibility for it, its members have a vested interest in nursing the project through to the bitter end. Even if it seems destined to fail, they bull ahead, hoping for divine intervention. They have every incentive to avoid cancellation. In most company cultures, anybody associated with a scrubbed project is tainted with an aura of failure and is by no means assured of getting back onto the fast track or indeed any track. Better to stick with a losing project than to have none at all.

Needless to say, this mentality leads to zombielike product development projects—neither living nor dead—that are not in the company's best interest.

Caterpillar's systematic reviews (called "stage gates") are antidotes to the industrial hazard of perpetuating lousy ideas. Most important, the company's realism is reinforced with a cultural precept, which effectively says, "Killing a project that will ultimately fail is a success, not a failure." It is a success because it avoids the folly of betting good money on dead horses. To reinforce this attitude, teams that can prove a project is hopeless and have the courage to follow up on that know they will be reassigned to new projects. In short, Caterpillar makes it pay to be honest.

The development phase also involves a great deal of analysis and simulation that culminates in the building of a prototype for a new product—a version of the machine that can be tested in the lab. After testing, the design is revised and refined to ensure that performance and cost targets will still be met. Caterpillar then assesses its overall readiness for the new product. Is the marketing organization up to speed? Is finance ready to support it? Is the distribution system ready? At the end of this phase, the project is again reviewed, in the light of these evaluations and the new plans. If major problems loom, the project can still be terminated.

Caterpillar builds a limited number of actual units of the product and puts them into the field for testing. Real customers use them for real jobs so that Caterpillar can make sure that they meet customer needs and the product has the needed quality and reliability.

4. Production and Support.

Finally, the product is unveiled to the customer base. Production is ramped up, and everything is prepared to build and distribute the new model in large quantities.

NONE OF THIS is especially profound or surprising, but Caterpillar's determination to coordinate its product start-ups has led to enormous benefits. It used to take seven or eight years for the company to create a new product; now it takes three years or less to go from concept to customer. A new 360-ton off-highway truck, for instance, was developed in eighteen months. This allows the company to pull the trigger more quickly and respond sooner to market changes. (Interestingly, there are more than a few similarities between the radio systems maker's sales process and Caterpillar's product development process. At some level of abstraction, development is the same, whether it is products or sales that are being developed.)

Why, exactly, does discipline lead to this kind of speedup?

First, the right steps are done at the right time. There is no need to stop the process to go back and do something that was overlooked because no process was being followed. There are no disconnects or problematic handoffs that result in errors, rework, and pointless delays. Second, the repeated evaluation of all projects means that time and money are being spent as efficiently as possible. If more projects are terminated early, fewer go on to fail at the more expensive stages. Accordingly, the most promising projects get all the time, money, and attention they need.

In addition, getting customer input at an early stage guarantees that the design meets the end-user's needs, not the company's internal speculative fantasies. And if managers get people from marketing and pricing involved all the way through development, they can be confident that the final product will be positioned to sell well at a good profit. In the final result, products that do reach the market are much more likely to be successful for both customers and the manufacturer.

Many companies have begun to apply the discipline of process to product development. Eli Lilly, for instance, has reduced by more than 50 percent the time it takes to turn a scientific discovery into an actual drug. IBM has cut the time needed to bring new hardware products to market by 75 percent.

If there is any field of business that might be thought impervious to discipline, it is computer software development. The way most software is brought to market makes even the loosest product development in other industries look positively rigid.

Software developers are universally regarded (particularly by themselves) as cowboys and free spirits. They may have enormous talent but show little if any interest in discipline or rules. They have traditionally seen their work as creative, artistic expression rather than as something akin to engineering.

Chaos is too kind a word to describe the way Hewlett-Packard's Software Engineering Division used to produce new software. Large numbers of engineers worked in splendid isolation, following their own private muses. Often they began writing a new program before its specifications were actually nailed down. Features were added or removed helter-skelter. Critical steps such as customer needs analysis might be done, or then again they might not, depending on someone's mood; and if they were done, that might happen after the software was largely completed. Testing was inevitably performed in a last-minute crisis mode, as programmers frantically tried to get their creations out the door. Rarely have so many smart people added up to such a dumb group.

Not surprisingly, Hewlett-Packard's new software was invariably late, over budget, and full of errors. In the mid-1990s, the company's then chief executive, Lewis Platt, ruefully estimated that 70 percent of the serious problems reaching his desk were software problems.

Managers found that trying to address these problems was like trying to herd cats. For a while, the division's managers simply accepted this kind of mess as inherent in the nature of software. But then, several years ago, they rebelled. They decided chaotic software development need not be inevitable. So they developed a disciplined process and introduced it to their software writers. The process meshed all facets of software creation, from design to testing and standardization. It insisted that customer needs be identified early, that schedules be based on analysis rather than guesswork, that needed tests and checks be performed when they ought to be, that progress be rigorously tracked, and that defects be discovered and treated early rather than late. The new process was governed by a rigorous measurement system, and it guaranteed predictability and repeatability.

To prove their commitment to discipline, HP's leaders committed software heresy. In the software world, a product's features had always come first—they defined the product. In turn, schedules had always yielded to accommodate features. As for process, there wasn't any. No longer. At HP, process now ruled. The managers told their people that process would come before schedule, and schedule would come before features, which would flow out of the process itself. Following the new process was not optional. As the leader of the software unit told his people, "Adherence to the process is part of the salary continuation plan."

As expected, some of the software unit's freer spirits saw this as a throwback to the Ford assembly line, or maybe the dark Satanic mills of the Industrial Revolution. They maintained that the new system would turn them into drudges, little better than bobbin boys of the 1820s. The leaders of the change told them differently—that the goal was not to crimp their creativity but to strengthen it. By following a structured process, they could be creative in more effective and more important ways. Their mission was to be creative about the product, not about the process.

In their concerns, the free spirits voiced a common misconception. The opportunity to improvise and develop unique ways of working may seem like a freedom, but it is really a burden. It dooms people to constant turmoil over who is supposed to do what and when. Lack of process actually subverts creative work. By contrast, discipline and structure channel and leverage creative energy. They free people to focus on the work they do best rather than fretting about how it should be organized.

HP's managers have a nice way of judging how much process is needed in a company. They say that you don't have enough process if it takes exceptional people to do ordinary things—if it requires great heroics to perform work that should be routine. On the other hand, you have too much process if your exceptional people can't sometimes do exceptional things—if the process becomes a straitjacket that confines and limits people. The truth is that far more companies suffer from not enough process than from too much. Most enterprises operate in conditions much closer to chaos than rigidity.

HP reaped great rewards for its willingness to tame the beast of software development. The average time it took to get a software product out the door plummeted by more than 50 percent. The amount of software produced, measured in lines of code, fell by more than 10 percent, since useless features were no longer being included; this made the software cheaper to produce and easier to maintain. Software is now produced within budget and on schedule, terms never heard before. And quality improved dramatically as well; the number of serious bugs in HP software went to zero. And all of this was accomplished without reducing the power and innovativeness of HP's software lineup.

Beyond the direct performance improvements, more subtle benefits accrue from introducing discipline and structure into previously chaotic environments. One is that the work becomes more reproducible, more predictable, and less dependent on luck, heroics, and extraordinary talent. You no longer need people who can get things done in spite of the system. Discipline allows ordinary people to create extraordinary results by leveraging their talents and abilities. This makes the company less dependent on (and hostage to) a small group of talented people, who often know all too well that they are close to indispensable. Talented and capable people are still important. But they no longer spell the difference between abject failure and great success.

A company dependent on heroes can find itself in desperate straits if they suddenly depart. A disciplined process, however, belongs to the company—and if some people go, others can be plugged into the system in their place.

Discipline also allows an enterprise to be managed, in many cases for the first time. Chaos can't really be managed; at best, it can be observed. Go into a company that has not taken a disciplined approach to product development or sales and ask some basic questions: Where do you stand with a particular effort? What is its likelihood of success? How many deals will close in the next sixty days? How many products will be ready for customer shipment in the next six months?

Without discipline, these questions are not only unanswerable— they are essentially meaningless. Without the well-defined series of stages that structured development imposes, you have no way to discuss what stage you're at. With discipline, however, business is no longer a roll of the dice. It is something that can be measured, managed, controlled, and improved.

But all these benefits don't come free. They are purchased at the price of great cultural change in an organization. Achieving a disciplined approach requires gaining a new perspective, a new set of attitudes on the part of everyone in the organization—managers as well as people on the front line.

Perhaps most difficult for many people is accepting the importance of discipline. Many highly talented people whose careers have developed in creative (read "chaotic") environments have learned that it is their personal drive and talent that makes for success. It is a strain for them to accept that improvisation and freelancing are the marks, not of a good performer, but of a bad one. The salesperson who believes that walking through walls and twisting arms are the keys to success may find it distressing to be told that there are rules that must be followed, and that personal talent has to fit within a context. People must also learn to accept the new primacy of teams. No longer is it the lone wolf, the inspired genius, the solo contributor who is the hero of the story. Rather it is the group, all the people who work together to create the result.

These are extraordinarily difficult adjustments for many people to make. American culture has long idealized the cowboy, the explorer, the inventor toiling in his isolated workshop. Sometimes more imaginary than historical, these valiant characters remain deeply ingrained in our consciousness.

In many corporate cultures, all this makes process a hard sell, however beneficial it promises to be. Some people will sincerely believe that introducing discipline and process will destroy creativity and drive out all that has made the organization successful. Others will feel threatened, fearing that they will be unable to perform in the new system. Or they may simply feel devalued by it. Some of these concerns are valid. Not everyone is able to make the transition to a disciplined environment. Some people may lack the style and the skills that a new process requires. Even some who could succeed may choose not to and vote with their feet.

At Hewlett-Packard, turnover in the software unit tripled for a time after the great change. Those who left were the incorrigibles who either could not or would not adapt to the new way. But the ones who stuck around were pleased, and perhaps surprised, by the results. Hewlett-Packard conducts an annual survey of employee morale. In one taken after the introduction of discipline (and after the exodus of the resisters), the software division registered the highest *esprit* of any unit in the company. People said they were able to work more effectively and that they enjoyed their jobs far more than they had before the change. The notion that discipline channels rather than limits creativity is not just rhetoric but reality.

How do you make all this happen? The critical ingredient is unswerving executive leadership and constant reinforcement. An occasional memo will not do. The new way of thinking and behaving must be endlessly repeated and stressed by the company's leaders, who must make it plain to all that there is no going back.

The cultural shift must also be reinforced by readjusting the compensation system. Compensation can encourage changes in behavior and send a signal of what is important. Even when people get the right results, they must not be rewarded if they succeed the wrong way. It won't take long for them to realize where their real interest lies. They will recognize that while it might be fun and personally fulfilling to be a free spirit, it won't get results anymore.

Innovation need not be synonymous with chaos, nor must sales be a hostage to heroics. In a world where products become obsolete overnight and customers have to be rewon every day, we cannot afford to let such work depend on luck, since luck has a nasty habit of giving out when you need it most. Mark Twain said, "The greatest of all inventors is accident." We can use process to make a liar of him. Process isn't bureaucracy; it is clarity. The absence of process isn't freedom; it is anarchy. It's not a hard choice to make.

Agenda Item 4

Tame the Beast of Chaos with the Power of Process

- Recognize champions and heroics for what they are: signs of dysfunction.
- Leverage your people's creativity with the power of process.
- Make innovation repeatable through detailed process design.
- Don't let people tell you that creativity conflicts with process.
- Be resolutely committed to discipline and teamwork.
- Accept the fact that not everyone will get it.

6

Measure Like You Mean It

Make Measuring Part of Managing, Not Accounting

In the world of business theory, measurement is an important management tool. Measures are supposed to provide managers with valuable current information about the performance of their company, which they can use to make effective decisions that will improve that performance. In the real world, however, a company's measurement systems typically deliver a blizzard of nearly meaningless data that quantifies practically everything in sight, no matter how unimportant; that is devoid of any particular rhyme or reason; that is so voluminous as to be unusable; that is delivered so late as to be virtually useless; and that then languishes in printouts and briefing books without being put to any significant purpose. Other than that, our measurement systems are just fine.

In short, measurement is a mess.

I have collected a number of observations by managers that characterize the state of measurement in today's organizations:

- "We use two percent of what we measure. The rest is CYA." Companies spend extravagant amounts of time and money collecting measurements, most of which they have no idea what to do with. One telecommunications company collects more than ten thousand measures of activity throughout the company, the great majority of which are never even looked at, much less used.

- "We are masters of the micro. We measure paper clip acquisition times." Many companies have no idea what they should be measuring, so they substitute the appearance of precision for its substance. They measure what is easy for them to measure, whether or not it matters.

- "If you want to know my inventory levels on March 2, I'll tell you in mid-April." The data provided by contemporary measurement systems are lagging and out of date by the time they are presented to the managers who are supposed to make use of them.

- "We measure far too much and get far too little for what we measure because we never articulated what we need to get better at, and our measures aren't tied together to support higher-level decision making." There is little thoughtful design behind most measurement systems. Companies collect measurement data without having any clear purpose for it in mind and without having any real idea of what the measurement information actually represents or communicates.

- "Business leaders don't concentrate on measurement because they were turned off by accounting in business school." Despite the lip service many managers give to the power of measurement, they actually see measurement as an appendage to the business rather than as part of it. To them, business is about creating and making products, relating to customers, making sales and deliveries, and collecting cash, while measurement is the domain of the accountants, the bean counters. They see it as a tool for coroners rather than for physicians, for those who conduct autopsies in the aftermath of business activity but not for those who are concerned with a living, breathing business.

- "It's hard to do measurement right because our executives don't believe it's important." A certain kind of machismo prevails among many managers, to the effect that "Real executives don't need measurements." These executives seem to believe that they can know what's going on in the business without relying on sheets of printed data, that it is in fact an admission of weakness for them to pay too much attention to metrics. They believe that bold vision and firsthand experience are the key requirements for effective leadership, and that measurement is needed only by those poor souls who, unable to connect to the heart of the business, take refuge in the dim shadows that a business casts on an accounting spreadsheet. These executives may go through the ritual of measuring their businesses, but it is a hollow sham.

The perilous condition of most measurement systems should in fact not surprise us; it is almost inevitable, given the genesis and evolution of these systems. Their first shortcoming is that they are overwhelmingly financial in nature. Measurement systems were initially developed to enable a company to report its financial results to shareholders and tax authorities; these systems were then inappropriately pressed into service to support management decision making, where for the most part they are useless. When a manager knows revenue, cost, and profit, he or she understands what has happened but not how to achieve better results in the future. When you see that costs are high, sales are low, and profit is falling, you know action is required, but you do not know what kind.

Financial measures—profitability, return on investment, discounted cash flow, or any other of the technically complex measures used by financial engineers—tell you little if anything of what you need to know about your business. To cite an oft-used cliché, "Using financial measures to manage your company is like driving while looking in the rearview mirror." Or like trying to manage a baseball game today by using last year's win-loss record to tell you whether to call a hit or a bunt, whether to keep in your starting pitcher or bring in a reliever.

The second problem with traditional measurement systems is that their nonfinancial elements are fragmented and piecemeal, devoid of any underlying logic. They developed as departmental managers were called upon by their superiors to improve the performance of their various domains. Toward this end, managers invented measures to track how their people were doing; they measured cost, accuracy, speed, and productivity, often using dozens of variables. Rarely if ever certain what purpose this served, they substituted quantity for utility, multiplying the number of things they measured in the hope that at least some of them would be significant. Managers were compiling these statistics with the unarticulated belief that if their employees performed well according to them, then the company as a whole would achieve its overall objectives. This was a vain and idle hope because no explicit connection was ever made between the individual items being measured and the overall desired results for the company.

Given these realities, it is unsurprising that most managers have disdained paying much attention to their measurement systems. They can be forgiven this attitude because, for a long time, it had few negative consequences. Before the advent of the customer economy, managers in fact had little need or use for sophisticated measurement systems. First, in a world of placid customers and genteel competition, performance improvement was a relatively low priority. Higher costs could be passed along, dissatisfied customers could be safely ignored, and innovation was optional. Furthermore, when improvements were necessary, they could be made without using sophisticated measurement systems. In many ways, businesses then were less complex than they are today: Customer demands were more narrowly focused; product lines were thinner; distribution channels were fewer; the technologies of manufacturing were less intricate. The size and the scale of most operations was a fraction of what they are today.

Then, managers could in fact run their businesses through intuition and relatively simple interventions. If sales were down, they could exhort their regional sales managers to push their sales reps harder; they could cut or raise prices; or they could fire all the sales managers; but they could not do much else. When the options for treatment are so limited, there is little need for intricate diagnosis. The analytics associated with sophisticated measurement were overkill.

In contrast, today there is relentless pressure from customers and shareholders to improve performance and to do so immediately. Moreover, in today's enormously complex businesses, it is not obvious what steps are required to get the demanded improvements. A company's measurement systems must be able to reveal the sources of performance inadequacies. Yet measurement systems have not caught up with the realities that companies now face. They still provide managers with little more than lagging financial data and a laundry list of miscellaneous performance figures.

The chaotic state of contemporary measurement was impressed upon me when I attended a senior executive meeting of a major electronics company, at which the company's leaders were reviewing their dozen or so key performance measures. These measures included customer satisfaction, sales closure ratio (that is, the percentage of proposals turned into accepted bids), market share, order fulfillment time, employee satisfaction, working capital, service cost per customer, customer retention, new product break-even time, revenue per employee, and return on equity.

To use the peculiarly British phrase, this list of measurements was a dog's breakfast—a little of this and a little of that. It included some overall company objectives (such as return on equity and market share), some operational metrics (service cost per customer and order fulfillment time), and some miscellaneous items (employee satisfaction, customer retention). But the critical shortcoming with this list was that the managers who reviewed these items so carefully in fact had no idea as to what they could do to improve any of them. If the numbers were good, they would smile; if the numbers were bad, they would cluck their tongues and express concern and make a careful note that something would definitely have to be done to improve that number by the next executive meeting; and then they would move on to the next number. This company's measurement system did not connect the numbers to each other in any meaningful way or provide executives with any real guidance as to how to improve them.

Overall company objectives—market share is an example—obey what has been called the principle of obliquity: Major overarching goals cannot be pursued directly. Managers have no direct control over market share. Rather, it is the outcome of other factors over which they do have control. The question is, however, precisely which factors? If market share is down, what levers must we pull to increase it? Among our options are lowering prices, introducing more products, improving manufacturing quality, and simplifying our invoices. Indeed, managers can choose from hundreds of possible remedies to boost a company's performance. How do they know which are the right ones? Without an explicit connection between desired outcomes and controllable phenomena, the electronics company could use its measurement system as an observational tool but not as a remedial one, and so its executives were condemned to watch helplessly as numbers went up and down, seemingly at random.

It was not always thus. In simpler times, the dynamics of business were easier to comprehend, and when a measurement indicated trouble, managers intuitively knew what to do. But now the age of intuition is over. Businesses are so complex and so rapidly changing that a "gut feel" for what is important is extraordinarily difficult to develop and impossible to maintain. Managers no longer really understand their businesses, and so they can't know how to intervene to make them perform better. They are consequently reduced to either playing a passive role or to instigating initiatives more or less at random in the hope that something will make a difference. In modern and complex businesses, leaders' intuition about how to make things better is sadly deficient—and their measurement systems are of little or no help.

In fact, traditional measurements are not only usually useless, they can even be dangerous and can actually impede a company's efforts to better its performance.

A major telephone company, confronting unprecedented competition in the aftermath of deregulation, was trying desperately to improve customer satisfaction—yet its measures of customer satisfaction seemed stuck in concrete. Its managers' intuition was good enough to point them to the caliber of the service the company delivered as a key determinant of how satisfied customers were and how likely they would be to jump ship to a competitor. Yet their efforts to improve service were sandbagged by their measurement system.

When a customer called to report a problem, a customer service representative (CSR) took the information. The CSR was measured on personal productivity, meaning how many calls he or she handled each day (or its equivalent, average duration of a customer call). Next in line was the dispatcher to whom the CSR passed the complaint and who was responsible for sending a field technician to solve the problem. The dispatcher was measured on field crew utilization—that is, how much of the crew's working hours were spent at customer sites rather than on traveling between assignments. Finally, each field tech was measured on productivity—the number of job tickets punched each day.

These measurements were not abstract statistics; they shaped people's behavior. The CSR, dispatcher, and field technician all did their best to perform well in terms of these measurement systems, both out of personal pride and to get better job ratings and thereby bonuses and promotions. Unfortunately, all this measurement and diligence actually worked against the company's goal of satisfying customers, who weren't even mildly interested in average call duration or field technician productivity. They were interested in immediate restoration of their phone service—but the measurement systems ensured that no one else was. The CSR's criteria pressured him to get through each call as quickly as possible and move on to the next customer, even if that meant not getting all the needed information. The dispatcher's measure encouraged her to schedule groups of repairs in nearby locations, so that travel was minimized, regardless of how long that kept customers waiting. The field technician was focused on getting in and out of a customer's premises as quickly as possible; the quality of the repair was secondary. If the equipment broke down again, that would be another call and somebody else's problem. The possibility of a technician conducting preventive maintenance that would keep equipment from breaking down in the first place was completely eviscerated by the imperative of punching the job ticket and moving on.

In effect, people throughout the company were asked to meet goals that were unrelated to what the customer wanted: reliable phone service, meaning service that never failed or was fixed both quickly and well when it did. In theory, the connection was that the faster everyone worked, the more quickly the customer's service would be restored. In practice, the connection did not connect.

This example is not atypical—quite the contrary, it is commonplace for a company to find that its efforts to improve performance are stymied by its measurement systems. At one large manufacturing company, a sales rep brought in a small order from a new customer who promised that quick delivery would ensure big orders to follow. As one would expect, the sales rep flagged the order as a priority and expedited its flow through the organization. Eventually it came to the logistics people who were responsible for shipping. They realized that this order represented a dreaded less than truckload shipment, which, if sent before being batched with similar small shipments to make a full truckload, would increase shipping costs. Guess how the logistics department was being measured?

The shipping department was unconcerned about antagonizing the customer and losing future orders, since such considerations figured nowhere in its measurements. Instead, behaving entirely rationally according to the reigning measurement system, it held the urgent order until it could be delivered more cheaply. Perhaps the employees were unaware of the consequences, or perhaps their vision was circumscribed by what they were held accountable for—shipping costs and nothing else.

I know a semiconductor manufacturer where factory managers would often shut down their plants for the last week of the month, even if they had a spurt of urgent orders from impatient customers. The reason was that the plant managers were being measured on variance from plan, and once they had made what the monthly plan called for, it was against their interests to make more, whatever the customers might want. It is also very common for salespeople to be measured and compensated based on the amount of business they write—that is, the total amount of their sales. This of course encourages them to close sales at almost any price, or to finalize them by promising all sorts of "free" additional services (free to the customer but not to the company). The result is a lot of business—unprofitable business.

In other words, the old saw that says, "Be careful what you wish for, you may get it," has a business version: "Be careful what you measure, you may get it—and it may kill you."

Companies need a new approach to measurement, one that is tuned to the demands of the customer economy. This approach begins with the recognition that measurement is in fact an essential part of managing, not of accounting. A Talmudic dictum teaches, "Study is not the essence, but action." Similarly, measurement is not the essence, but improvement. The purpose of measuring is not to know how a business is performing but to enable it to perform better. Measurement must be neither an end nor an activity in itself but part of an integrated system for enhancing business performance. Therefore a contemporary measurement system should provide no data without a rationale and a purpose; people must know why things are being measured and, more important, what they are supposed to do about them. A contemporary approach to measurement also recognizes that modern businesses are complex systems, for which intuition no longer suffices. Today any action that a manager takes can have myriad and unpredictable consequences throughout the organization. Therefore measurement must be based on a carefully thought-through analysis of the business, one that links the objectives of the business to the things over which managers and front-line personnel have control. Only then can the recognition of a problematic measure lead to the right actions that will correct it and to improved performance of the business as a whole.

In other words, a contemporary measurement system stands on two legs. The first is a formal, structured, and quantified model of the enterprise—the kind that scientists and engineers have long used to describe physical systems—that enables managers to mobilize a company's resources to ensure that it achieves its paramount goals. Such a model connects a company's overarching objectives with its controllable dimensions. It is analogous to a wiring diagram that shows precisely how pulling on this lever here opens that door over there. It shows managers both what they ought to measure and what they ought to do with the measures. The second leg is a deliberate process for using measurement data to improve enterprise performance, a structured and focused program that uses measurement information to identify the causes of inadequate performance and then does something about them. These two elements are linked and related. Let's begin with the notion of a business model.

A few years ago, a major credit-card company was trying to improve two critical business measures. First, it wanted to increase customer retention: raise the percentage of its customers who renewed their cards when they expired. A customer cannot use a card that he or she does not have. Second, it wanted to increase card utilization, to get customers to use the card much more often, in order to boost the company's revenue from the commissions it received from merchants.

The company had no shortage of ideas about how to achieve these goals: lowering the annual fee to encourage customers to hold on to the card; adding services and premiums, such as frequent-flyer miles or points for every dollar spent, to boost card usage; increasing advertising to enhance the company's image and make customers want to continue identifying with it; and the like.

None of these was an intrinsically bad idea; in fact, the opposite was true. An argument could be made for each of them—and was. The hard part was deciding which were good enough to fund out of a limited budget. The debate took place at the outer margin of certainty, where important debates often occur. Eventually, the company's leaders chose a course of action, but their supporting evidence was so skimpy that advocates of other positions refused to accept it. As one wag put it at the time, "The decision has been made—now let the debates begin."

The debate went around in circles because the participants did not actually understand the dynamics of their business. Which product features were most important to customers and how those features could be enhanced to boost customer retention and spending were matters of opinion rather than fact. To get the facts, the company's managers decided to build a model of the business.

The first draft was qualitative. It started with the idea that customers' behavior was driven by a combination of their satisfaction with the company's card and what they thought of the competition. While the latter was largely out of the company's control, the former was not. The model specified that satisfaction with the card was shaped by its value (in turn, a function of its cost and the value-added services it included); customers' experiences using it; their experiences interacting with the company (say, over billing); and the company's overall corporate image. The second draft was quantitative. The company used its extensive databases, which included actual customer behavior (renewals and product usage rates), as well as surveys of customers' views on the model's various components, to calculate numbers that specified the relative importance of each factor: how much impact, for instance, various value-added services would have on a customer's propensity to renew or use the card.

Some of what the model revealed was quite unexpected. One service enhancement that the managers had believed very important and deserving of investment turned out to have but little impact on either customer usage or retention. Here intuition would have led them seriously astray. Another enhancement was found to have a major impact on usage, though not on retention. Corporate image, on the other hand, had a surprisingly high effect on retention, albeit very little on usage.

As a result, the company readjusted its priorities and allocated its resources differently. Pulling back from some other initiatives, it placed a high premium on developing a coherent corporate image. Advertising was aimed in that direction, too, instead of toward individual product features. At the same time, the company made a major investment in the product feature that customers indicated was heavily correlated with their usage. As all these steps were taken, the customers responded just as the model had predicted. Usage and retention—and in turn, profitability and growth—all went up.

Using the model, this credit-card company showed how its products and services affected desired customer behavior. Still, even with its very important benefits, the model was far from sufficient. It needed to be coupled with a model of the company's operations and how they, too, affected the customer. Reconfiguring product and service offerings is not the only way that companies can improve their performance: increasing the speed at which products are picked from the warehouse shelf, improving the accuracy with which customer inquiries are dealt, and lowering the cost of conducting a test for a product still under development are some other ways. While these may all sound like fine efforts in the abstract, they are actually of no specific value unless they can be correlated with specific desired enterprise outcomes. Connecting these individual activities to company results is the great challenge in the arena of performance measurement and improvement.

Measuring a company's outcomes, like market share, return on equity, and customer satisfaction, is important because these are the only things that really count. But as I have said, enterprise outcomes can be pursued only obliquely; you have little direct control over them. On the other hand, the most controllable actions are those performed by individuals. If we measure, say, how much time it takes someone to pick ordered items from the shelf, or to calculate an invoice, we can hold these individuals accountable for their performance and expect them to improve it. The difficulty here is that while readily controllable, these activities and the measures of their performance are of relatively small intrinsic significance. The impact on the business as a whole, of the rate at which one warehouse worker picks items, or of the accuracy of one accounts receivable specialist's calculations, will be infinitesimal. What is needed is a model of the business that connects and balances these two extremes: the critical and the controllable. Such a multilevel model starts at the highest corporate level and continues all the way down to individual activities.

Allmerica Financial has created and utilized such a model with great success. Allmerica, based in Worcester, Massachusetts, is a 160-year-old financial services company that today has about $2.5 billion in capital. It divides its business between helping customers manage assets (through variable annuities and life insurance) and helping them manage risk (via property and casualty insurance).

In the mid-1990s, the company was lumbering along in the middle of the pack in all its markets. Its performance was adequate but not spectacular. Since it had always been a mutual company owned by its policyholders, top financial performance had never ranked among its top priorities. But when Allmerica went public in the mid-1990s, it suddenly became answerable to public shareholders who were extremely interested in financial performance and growth. Consequently, the company undertook a serious effort to understand exactly how to improve performance.

Its managers identified three essential goals for achieving its financial ambitions. These became the company's overall objectives and were placed at the top of its business model. The first was customer retention. It is by now a commonplace that holding on to your existing customers is a prerequisite for success. Losing customers and being forced to replace them is very costly, especially in industries like insurance, where much of the early income pays agent commissions. Replacement also takes time and energy that could be better spent acquiring new customers.

Its second overarching goal was employee retention. As a service-intensive business, Allmerica needs capable, skillful employees who can serve customers well and perform the often-complex technical tasks associated with insurance. High turnover rates would decimate both the technical expertise needed for underwriting and the high morale needed to provide outstanding customer service.

The company's third overarching goal was to add more products and acquire more partners to distribute them, both of which would help increase revenue. New products can be sold to existing as well as to new customers, and new distribution partners would give Allmerica access to new markets.

Though identifying the three requisite outcomes was an accomplishment, it was not the same as achieving them. The next step was to examine the factors over which the company had control and determine how they could lead to the desired objectives. For example, it was obvious that customer retention depends on customer satisfaction. People don't switch to a new company randomly but (in part) because they are dissatisfied with the old one. If Allmerica could not control customers' behavior directly, it could influence their satisfaction.

The insurance industry has a measure of customer satisfaction called the Dalbar rankings. The J.D. Powers of the insurance industry, Dalbar anonymously purchases products from insurance companies and then tests their service capabilities across a host of customer service demands. At the time it undertook this initiative, Allmerica ranked thirty-seventh out of fifty companies on the Dalbar list. Though not an embarrassing number, it was hardly inspiring. The company set out to pinpoint exactly what it could do to satisfy customers better and thereby keep them longer. Customer interviews and data analysis revealed the factors key to shaping customer satisfaction. One, for instance, was the timely and accurate delivery of an insurance contract (in essence, a policy). If the company took too long to process the customer's application and send the actual contract, the customer was likely to go elsewhere the next time he needed insurance. He was also likely to feel angry if, when it finally came, the contract was full of errors that needed to be corrected. Thus, timely and accurate delivery of a contract was identified as a primary goal of the company's performance improvement efforts. If, in retrospect, this seems obvious, it was not at the time. As I have said, in a complex environment, managerial intuition about what is important is often wrong. Formal analysis must trump gut feel.

Allmerica was able to determine what customers wanted in terms of both the delivery time and the accuracy of its policies; then it translated these figures into performance requirements for the employees involved in contract delivery. Underwriters were given a goal of a specific turn-around time for producing and delivering contracts. This figure was not selected arbitrarily or pulled out of the blue, as was the performance goal of punching job tickets for the phone company field repairman. Rather, it was selected because of its impact on contract delivery time, which would shape customer satisfaction, which in turn would impact customer retention, which in turn would impact financial performance. The company then implemented systems to track these measures and put in place programs to improve them.

Before moving on, I want to make a number of points about this model. First, Allmerica's actual model is far more complex than the abbreviated version I've just described. In its asset management business, the company identified and now measures more than sixty aspects of performance that influence customer satisfaction. Nonetheless, a good model must be simple enough for everyone to understand, enabling people throughout the organization to position their daily work in the context of the company's overall objectives. Too much detail and complexity are confusing and, ultimately, useless. In simplicity there is profundity.

Second, any real model must be multidimensional. My explanation of Allmerica's model focused on just one dimension of one goal: time, as a driver of customer satisfaction. Needless to say, it is foolhardy to optimize one dimension at the expense of all others. If you invest too many resources into expediting the application process, for example, your costs might leap, forcing you to charge more, or your quality might suffer; these would in turn alienate customers (albeit in new ways). The trick is to set and achieve targeted performance levels in many dimensions simultaneously, not in just one.

Third, any model that a company creates of its business has to be regarded as a working hypothesis. The relationships it expresses between specific controllable actions and desired outcomes is only provisional until it is tested and validated through experience. Moreover, the model needs to be kept updated over time; changing circumstances and customers' expectations may perturb the quantitative and even the qualitative aspects of the model. Certain things may start to count more or less than they used to, while new connections may need to be established.

By translating its overall goals into a manageable number of key measures, Allmerica targeted the things that really mattered. Resisting the temptation to experiment with endless possibilities, it instead concentrated on the most highly leveraged opportunities for improvement. Within two years, Allmerica rose to number four in the fifty-company Dalbar ratings, a leap of thirty-three rungs up the industry's prestige ladder. At the same time, it cut expenses by tens of millions of dollars. What is remarkable is that Allmerica simultaneously achieved seemingly incompatible goals—lower costs and higher customer satisfaction—by understanding exactly what underlay each. Improving these factors yielded increased customer retention and growth, just as the company had desired—and as its model had predicted.

Allmerica's methodology was the opposite of the haphazard and disorganized approach that many companies take toward measurement and performance improvement—try this, try that, try something else, and then go back and start all over again. It created a precise model of how its operations—that is, the things over which it had direct control—ultimately affected the behavior of its customers, then used the measurement data highlighted by this model to improve what it could control in a disciplined way.

In line with a growing trend, Allmerica also linked people's compensation to their new measurements. Individuals there are rewarded if they achieve goals for the measures over which they have control and if the company as a whole reaches its goals. By selecting the right measures, publicizing them, focusing people's attention on them, and giving people a personal stake in their outcomes, Allmerica made its achievements not a matter of luck but a matter of management.

Duke Power is another company that has successfully developed and implemented a model of its business as part of an effort to improve its performance. To reach its goal of top-quartile returns for shareholders, the company created a multitier model resembling Allmerica's. Its internal name, the Gameplan, indicates that the model, in addition to being a measurement tool, embodies Duke's overall approach to winning in the newly competitive world of electric power.

Duke's two principal mechanisms for delivering required returns to shareholders were, unsurprisingly, increasing revenue and lowering costs. The model put these goals at the top and identified the ways of achieving them. Increasing revenue required retaining existing customers, adding new ones, and selling more electricity to all of them. Cost cutting entailed spending less for both capital and line operations. Then Duke linked these overall objectives to activities performed by individuals throughout the company.

To reach the objective of customer retention, for instance, Duke identified and focused on what customers wanted: "hassle-free," inexpensive, and reliable electrical service. "Hassle-free," according to customers, meant that the company had to be easy to reach, quick to schedule work at the customer's convenience, and dependable in keeping appointments. The company's managers then proceeded to ensure that every aspect of the company's operations would become hassle-free by this definition.

To that end, Duke started measuring the percentage of installations that it completed by the date it had promised the customer. This measure was not selected arbitrarily; it followed ineluctably from the chain of logic that began with the company's overall goals. A high percentage of on-time installations was needed to make installation "hassle-free," which in turn would contribute to customer retention, which in turn would lead to the company's central objectives. (Recall from Chapter 4 that a focus on this metric helped ignite the company's efforts to redesign its installation process.)

Duke Power now has about two hundred measures, a far cry from the ten thousand used by the telecommunications company cited earlier. Duke's two hundred have been selected carefully. Each one measures an important aspect of the company's progress toward its twin prerequisites for financial success and shareholder confidence—boosting revenue and cutting costs.

Every month all two hundred measures are collected and distributed to all of Duke's managers. Each is expressed on a single page that shows the current value of the measure for the company as a whole, its trend over recent months, and its value in each of the company's locations. Together they offer the company's leaders an invaluable real-time guide that gives them a finger on the pulse of the company where it counts. Managers are now able to track progress on a manageable number of key indicators that really make a difference.

Each team leader sees a subset of these two hundred measures. The "scorecard" that each team leader gets lists a half dozen or so significant measures that are associated with the team's work and that they can influence. These are the primary areas where a team can have the greatest impact on achieving the company's objectives.

For a leader of a team of linesmen in the field, for instance, these numbers might include the percentage of customer service orders that the team completed on time; the percentage of repeat customer service work required of that team (obviously the first number should be high, and the second number low); the costs the team incurs in restoring routine outages; and the costs it incurs in installing new service. The team is accountable for achieving targeted levels of performance on each of these measures: a certain percentage of on-time installations, so much cost per service restoration, and so on. When the team leader receives the monthly scorecard, he or she will see the team's current performance versus the targeted performance for each measure. These numbers attract everyone's attention. When team leaders see a measure that is not doing well, they focus on it. To curb the temptation to over-compensate and thereby let other measures slide, the teams are held accountable for a minimal performance level across the board in all measures. As at Allmerica, performance reviews and compensation depend on their scorecards. And as at Allmerica, Duke's creation and disciplined use of its Gameplan model has transformed the company's business performance.

The business models that Allmerica and Duke created, while insightful, are of no use unless they are linked with a formal way of using the measurement information they generate. This is the necessary second leg of a contemporary system for measurement and improvement. Duke, Allmerica, and a host of other companies have deployed such a structured process. It begins by establishing target performance levels for each of the measures that the business model identifies as being important. These include overarching goals (such as customer satisfaction) as well as controllable operational activities (such as the speed and accuracy with which a contract is delivered, or the amount of time an individual underwriter spends processing applications). Mechanisms are then put in place to calculate the actual value of each of these measures on a regular basis. Each of these measures is then compared with the target that has been established. If all measures are achieving their targets, then all is well. If they are not, then we are in the domain not of measurement but of management and improvement. Managers must now intervene to address the root causes of the inadequate performance so that overall business goals continue to be met.

Intervention at the personal level is called for when an individual is not meeting his or her performance target—when an underwriter fails to turn around applications as quickly as the model demands, for example. The question that managers must answer is why the underwriter is not meeting the goal. Perhaps he or she lacks the necessary skills or training, or the tools provided are inadequate, or this individual is just the wrong person for this job. Once the problem is identified, the appropriate remedy can be applied.

Suppose the underwriters are, in fact, turning around applications quickly enough, but the company as a whole is not. Then the fault lies not with the people but with the larger process of which their work is but a part. No matter how hard people strive, they cannot overcome a problematic or limited process design. If the gap between required and actual process performance is small, then managers need only tinker with the existing process design in order to address its inadequacies. But if the gap is substantial, then managers will need to discard the current process design and create a new one. (The first of these options is usually known as continuous improvement, the latter as reengineering.) Both Allmerica and Duke needed to resort to major process redesign to achieve the performance improvements I cited.

Perhaps, however, the company is turning around applications as quickly as it should, and is achieving all the other operating performance goals stipulated by the model, but it is still failing to realize its desired overall results. That is, everything seems to be working fine, but measured customer satisfaction is lower than it is supposed to be, or measured customer satisfaction is satisfactory but customers are nonetheless leaving the company. How can this be? The problem in this case lies not with how people are executing the processes, nor in their designs, since those targets are being met. Rather, the problem lies in the model itself and how it connects the company's goals to its work. Perhaps the targets have been set too low, so that even attaining them does not bring about the desired outcomes. Or perhaps those who built the model did not understand their customers and markets well enough, and so the company's imperatives have been erroneously defined. It may not be rapid turnaround of contracts that leads to customer satisfaction, for instance, but something else. When operating performance is satisfactory but enterprise outcomes are not, then the model needs to be rethought. It might have been faulty from the outset, or it might have become obsolete as a result of changes in customers' needs or competitors' actions. In either case, the model needs to be updated, and the whole cycle can then begin again.

You may see in this approach echoes of other work. It builds on the pioneering efforts of Shewhart and Deming, in its resolute commitment to disciplined measurement and ongoing improvement. It also has points in common with such measurement techniques as the balanced scorecard, EVA, and the service-profit chain. Our approach yokes the strategic frameworks of the latter to the improvement focus of the former in order to create an integrated system of measurement and management. At companies like Allmerica Financial and Duke Power, measurement is not an afterthought, a sideshow to the main tent of the business. Rather, it is intrinsic to the companies' operations and management.

I need to add two postscripts to this discussion of measurement and improvement. The first relates to the design of the metrics that you use to measure what the business model indicates needs to be measured. In some cases, this choice is straightforward; how to determine the percentage of installations completed by a promised date is clear. Even in these cases, however, unexpected subtleties have to be considered. For one, people often "game" measures, meaning they live up to the letter of a measure but not its spirit. A linesman might interpret his goal of completing a work order as simply getting to the site on time, whether or not the work actually gets done. If, when he shows up, he realizes he doesn't have the appropriate equipment to do the job, he might mark the first work order as "complete" and create a new one that he can perform when he gets the equipment. Managers have to be very careful that everyone is interpreting the measures as they are intended.

In other cases, just deciding how to measure what needs to be measured is complex, because some phenomena can be measured in many ways. What's the best way to measure customer satisfaction? You can use surveys to ask current customers how satisfied they are, but that's expensive and often inaccurate. A more accurate way may be to observe a customer's purchase behavior over time, but that data may come too late to be useful; by the time the customer has stopped buying, his dissatisfaction may be terminal. Some companies measure customer satisfaction by the inverse of their complaint volume, but not all dissatisfied customers complain; also, salespeople may label complaints as inquiries, or fail to register them promptly. A measurement system's designers need to be alert to the problems associated with the mechanisms they employ, and be prepared to address their shortcomings.

A good measure must be accurate, actually capturing the condition it is supposed to describe. It must be objective, not subject to debate and dispute. It must be comprehensible, easily communicated and understood. It must be inexpensive and convenient to compute. It must be timely—that is, not requiring a long delay between the occurrence of the condition and the availability of the data. Constructing measures that meet these criteria is not as easy as listing them; it remains more art than science.

Our second postscript is that the most accurate measurement system in the world will fail if it is implemented in an inhospitable environment. Creating business models and using measures to drive performance improvement are more than technique; they are a way of life. They represent a fundamental shift in how managers view themselves and their business. This approach demands an objective view of the business, and a recognition that measurement is not an accounting afterthought but an essential and integrated dimension of running a business. It must be supported by a culture that values objectivity over opinion, commitment to improvement over excuses for why it can't happen, honesty rather than irresponsibility, openness rather than defensiveness, and problem solving over problem avoidance. It requires that people respect data and facts more than intuition and wishful thinking, and that everyone collaborate first to understand what performance needs to be achieved and why it is not, and then to close the gap.

If these conditions do not obtain, then even the best-designed measurement system will be met by lip service, passivity, excuses, and vicious compliance. Endless arguments about the validity of the measurements will replace serious attempts to improve them.

Ironically, the approach to measurement and improvement that the customer economy demands can be best described with a phrase that is a hundred years old. At the turn of the twentieth century, in a simpler and more optimistic age, Frederick Winslow Taylor coined the term *scientific management*. Taylor was the pioneering industrial engineer who believed—and clicked his stopwatch thousands of time to prove—that there was "one best way" for any worker to perform any task. Scientific management was aimed at making coal miners or steelworkers perform exactly as Taylor prescribed, to ensure their own maximum efficiency and their companies' maximum profit. Over the past hundred years, Taylor's term fell out of fashion; indeed, it became an oxymoron. For most of the twentieth century, management was anything but scientific. Managers largely worked in the dark, with barely the faintest clue as to what was really going on in their companies. Their decisions were based far more on opinions, anecdotes, and raw exercises of power than on the deep insights that follow from scientific analysis. Real management was based more on guesswork than on information.

Perhaps it is now time to revive Taylor's term. The process of constructing a model of a business, gathering data to test it, and then using that data to drive efforts to improve results certainly employs scientific staples, notably careful measurement and the formulation and testing of hypotheses. It may or may not be "science" in the strictest sense of the word, but it is certainly superior to the undisciplined and haphazard style of management that too many companies still practice. As Admiral

Grace Hopper, one of the pioneers of computing, said, "One accurate measurement is worth a thousand opinions." It is high time for managers to get used to this idea.

Adopting this new way of measuring and managing, and reaping the benefits that it brings, can be accomplished only if senior leaders show the way by action as well as by word. When a company's top leaders demonstrate a commitment to open inquiry—to what Jack Welch calls facing reality as it is, rather than as we wish it to be—when they willingly sacrifice vanity and sometimes money to create better results, then Frederick Taylor's vision of scientific management, albeit in a different form from what he intended, can at last become a reality.

Agenda Item 5

Base Managing on Measuring

- Take measurement out of accounting and make it part of every manager's job.
- Abandon the measures you have inherited from the past.
- Develop a model of your business that links your overall goals to specific things you control.
- Put in place measures and targets for the key items in this model.
- Design measures that are objective, timely, easy to calculate, and easy to understand.
- Make ongoing performance improvement inevitable by incorporating it into a disciplined measurement-based process.
- Let facts and measurement triumph over intuition and opinion.

7

Manage Without Structure

Profit from the Power of Ambiguity

As the father of four grown children, I am often asked for counsel by young parents regarding the care and development of their offspring. Since I am involved in the business world, they sometimes ask how they can tell if their youngsters harbor executive capabilities. I advise them that if their eight-year-old pride and joy brings home a report card with an Unsatisfactory grade in "Plays Well with Others," then they have a future divisional president on their hands.

Corporate managers definitely do not play well with others. They are as territorial as lions or wolves, and the more senior they are, the more territorial. This behavior is not genetic; it is induced by the ways in which companies are organized. Executives have traditionally coped with the scale and complexity of their companies by dividing them into pieces and assigning each piece to a different manager. One is responsible for manufacturing, another for sales; I am in charge of the unit that makes and sells lawn mowers, while you run the construction equipment part of the company. While this scheme does offer clarity and focus, it also tends to narrow that focus too far.

As a manager, my part of the company, large or small, is my sovereign domain. I am accountable for its performance, I have control over the resources needed to achieve that performance, and I am measured and rewarded exclusively on it. Consequently, I ignore anything outside my domain and leap to the barricades to defend it from any intruders. My decision making is guided only by what is best for me and my part, and the rest of the company can go hang. I will (grudgingly) take directives from, and report performance to, my superior, but I engage with no one else. Toward my peers, I am likely to exhibit intense animosity. After all, I am, in effect, competing with every other manager for resources, executive attention, and promotion to the hallowed circle of corporate leadership.

Georges Clemenceau, French prime minister at the end of the First World War, observed, "There is no passion like the passion of the functionary for his function." His words were nowhere more truly realized than in the modern corporation.

Every company has its own horror stories of how fragmenting a company into independent parts leads to bizarre and even destructive behavior. The following stories are merely representative.

- A major provider of computer services has long been organized into a number of divisions, each of which offers a different type of service (outsourcing, contract software development, e-business development, and so on). Unfortunately, the company has traditionally missed out on many of the largest megadeals, in which a large customer wanted to contract with a single provider for the full range of services. The reason is that no one was pursuing these opportunities. Every division was focused exclusively on its own service, ignoring opportunities to cross-sell. A divisional sales rep had no incentive to see if a customer might want other services, since he would receive no reward for doing so. Divisional heads zealously shielded their customers from their sibling divisions, since they feared that any money spent with another division would mean less for them. Even if that were not the case, no division head wanted to invest effort to develop an account when a significant share of the benefit would be reaped by other divisions. After all, each divisional head saw himself or herself as being in competition with the others.

- A major electronics company was organized into a large number of autonomous business units, each of which procured components on its own. As a result, the company's purchasing was spread out among a great number of vendors, and none of the units ordered in enough volume to have any significant leverage with its suppliers. The company calculated that it was spending hundreds of millions of dollars more per year than it would have had it had the ability to aggregate its purchasing across the company. But the fierce independence of the units precluded that possibility. Each asserted that it was "different," that it had unique requirements, and that it would suffocate if forced to purchase from the same suppliers as the other divisions.

- A major chemical company was suffering from numerous problems with its legacy software systems, and the corporate CIO proposed acquiring an Enterprise Resource Planning (ERP) system for use across the company. His proposal unleashed a tidal wave of protest. Functional managers wanted no part of any system that, because of its process orientation, would breach their barricades and force them to cooperate with one another. Plant managers were terrified of using a standard system that would facilitate interplant comparisons, which might make them look bad. Divisional heads instinctively rejected any corporate initiative as an affront to their autonomy. Needless to say, none of these objections were expressed in these terms. Rather, alarms were raised about such weighty issues as accounting policies and corporate data standards. Naturally, these issues were remanded to a committee for careful consideration, where at last report the initiative still languishes.

- An oil company had three major units: one to purchase petroleum, one to refine it, and one to market it to service stations. Each unit was run on a self-contained, stand-alone basis, working at arm's length from the others. Information was not shared among them. As a result, the refining unit typically produced more or less than the marketing unit required; the traders who bought oil missed opportunities to get it cheap because they found out too late that the other units needed it; and the company as a whole was awash in inventory and cost.

- A giant food corporation was created through a series of acquisitions, but each of the acquired units has continued to operate independently under the new umbrella. As a result, customers cannot order from one price list, obtain volume discounts based on their total purchases from the corporation, or receive a single delivery of a mixed set of products. For its part, the corporation has to manage a large number of independent supply chains, with the excess costs that entails; it also often has to send out two half-full trucks that carry products from different units, because there is no way to combine them in one full truck.

- The corporate strategic planning group at a high-technology company identified a new theme in computing that represented an important opportunity for the corporation. However, the planners found no takers when they shopped the idea to the heads of the company's divisions. The problem was that the new theme was in fact new, and it did not match the charter of any of the existing business units. Divisional heads were intently focused on their assigned businesses and had no time for anything outside their formal purview. By the time the company went through the arduous process of creating a new unit to exploit the new theme, precious time had been lost and a more nimble competitor had gotten there first.

- At a large manufacturer, one division found itself with excess manufacturing capacity, while another was short of capacity. It would have been logical for the first to make its excess available to the other, so that both would win. But the head of the first division preferred not to do so, even though they would both lose as a result, since he calculated that the other would lose more. In competition among division heads to become CEO, it is often not necessary to be good, just better than the others. Most division presidents would much rather score a 5 while their peers are scoring 4, than score an 8 while others are scoring 9.

Then there is the division of a medical products company so protective of its independence that it refuses to print the name of its parent corporation on its stationery; and the insurance firm where I was told, "Our division presidents never talk to each other, and when they do, they lie." I could continue with variations on this theme indefinitely, and I imagine you could match me tale for tale.

Such grotesque behavior is not limited to the mahogany-paneled confines of the executive floor. It cascades down into the organization, as each manager gives marching orders to his or her subordinates, ever more narrowly confining people's responsibilities and vision. The divide-and-conquer approach to organization has become divide-and-be-conquered; in the modern corporation, the whole often turns out to be much less than the sum of its parts.

Though not new, these problems have reached new heights (or depths) in the last thirty years, as the idea of the strategic business unit (SBU) has become standard in the business world.

Until the middle of the twentieth century, companies were, for the most part, organized into functional units. That is, corporations were divided into large, separate departments, one for manufacturing, another for finance, and others for logistics, sales, marketing, and so on, with each focusing exclusively on its particular function. As enterprises grew, however, this approach became less effective; the departments grew too large to be manageable. Moreover, companies were attracting a wider diversity of customers and expanding their product lines to accommodate them. As a result, departments were forced to broaden the focus of their specific activities. Manufacturing might be expected to make both calculators and cruise missiles, for example, while marketing could be called on to reach, simultaneously, consumers and industrial buyers. In response, the idea of the strategic business unit (SBU) emerged.

An SBU is a self-contained business that provides certain products for certain customers and is run on a stand-alone basis by its own general manager. It develops, makes, sells, and services its own products with its own people. The parent corporation provides each unit with capital and expects a specified financial performance in return; other than that, the SBU is usually on its own and operates independently of all the rest. (In some companies, SBUs get access to advanced technology developed by a corporate research center.) Each SBU is a "tub on its own bottom," a business that, under the direction of an entrepreneurial president or general manager, has free rein to pursue its own interests. Most business historians credit GE with introducing the concept in the early 1970s. Today GE has SBUs that produce jet engines, manufacture and sell plastics, and deliver a variety of financial services, while the SBU concept has propagated across American industry, becoming the de facto norm.

This neatly segmented approach to enterprise structure has advantages, notably clarity and simplicity. In the SBU model, every unit is driven to optimize its performance and is given the resources and the autonomy to do so. The head of each unit does whatever he or she decides is best for the business. Any conflicts between unit heads are pushed up to the parent company's senior executives for resolution.

The logic is that by splitting the whole into separate parts, each of which has a leader with the autonomy to achieve its goals, the needs of the whole will, inevitably, be met. In theory, an SBU structure enables a company to avoid the complexity, inflexibility, and even ossification that result when a single leadership team attempts to direct the activities of a large and diverse enterprise. But as with everything in business (and perhaps in life), there are drawbacks as well as advantages to this approach.

Almost as soon as it came into being, some began to question the SBU notion. If every SBU operates independently, what is the purpose, rationale, or contribution of the corporation as a whole? For the SBU, is there any advantage in being owned by a parent company that happens to own other units? At first, the responses to this question were expressed in strategic terms. According to the dogma of the 1960s and 1970s, the essence of corporate strategy was to assemble a portfolio of SBUs that included a mix of fast-growing, stable, and cash-generating businesses, and to use the cash generated by some to fund the growth opportunities of others. That the SBUs might not benefit individually from their common ownership would be compensated by their collective growth and that of the parent corporation. The apotheosis of this thinking was found in conglomerates like ITT and Litton, congeries of businesses with little in common except a consolidated balance sheet.

In the last two decades, this portfolio theory of the corporation has become outdated. Now it is broadly agreed upon that corporations need to be more than holding companies, that some glue needs to unite their business units. One widely accepted perspective is that each unit of a company needs to express the company's core competences. Various units may make different products for different customers, but they should all build on a common foundation of expertise. Another theory is that the parent corporation adds value to its constituent units through a standard set of management disciplines. Thus, while GE's units are in businesses as dissimilar as broadcasting and medical systems, they are bound together through a set of management practices that were developed under the aegis of Jack Welch and that are disseminated via the company's famed Crotonville learning center. Workout and six sigma quality are just two of the best-known management techniques that GE has implemented across its SBUs.

Today, despite the popularity of the SBU concept (particularly among executives charged with leading them), it has reached the end of its useful life. The disadvantages inherent in the SBU approach, the kinds of problems described in my litany of horror stories, can no longer be abided in the customer economy. Companies can no longer afford the internal redundancies and inefficiencies, the customer inconvenience, and the organizational inflexibility that come from being divided into a mass of independent units. SBUs do provide a way for dividing a large company into manageable units, but in doing so they destroy the power of the company as an integrated whole.

The demise of the SBU has not been a sudden one. Over the last decade, a series of chinks have appeared in the walls that surround, protect, and define SBUs. They were not ideological cracks; that is, they did not represent a deliberate challenge to conventional thinking about corporate structure. Rather, they were tactical responses to specific business situations. But their net effect has been to call into question the validity of the SBU-based corporation and to offer, in its stead, something with a very different character.

The first notable fissure was created by the concept of "shared services." In the early 1990s many corporations were desperately searching for ways to cut costs and reduce overhead. They had already tried downsizing, with decidedly mixed results, and were looking for other easy-to-implement techniques. Eventually, many realized that there was a lot of duplication in their SBUs. Executives discovered that many people scattered across their companies were performing the same routine administrative tasks, such as sending out or paying bills, managing accounts receivable and accounts payable, ordering office supplies, updating personnel records, and answering employee questions about benefits, among others. Many who were performing these tasks did not have the volume of activity needed to be truly efficient; in other words, they were unable to exploit any economies of scale. Furthermore, there was a lot of variation in how the work was done, which inevitably led to variation in its quality. Some units followed better ways of working than others. Some people were well trained and did good work, but others were not. Finally, these administrative activities were distractions from the real work of the business units and drew attention away from what should have been their primary foci.

The "shared services center" (SSC) was the response to this problem of redundancy: a centralized group chartered to perform transactional activities for the whole enterprise. Instead of paying your own bills, the SSC would do it, and charge you for its work. Employees with questions about the company's pension plan would call the SSC for answers. Dedicated to such tasks, the SSC could exploit economies of scale. Its managers could focus on improving quality and lowering costs of this work; it could justify investments in productivity-enhancing technology. The combination of these factors often led to spectacular cost savings.

One example is Ahold USA, which is part of the Dutch supermarket titan Ahold; its units include Stop & Shop, Giant Food Stores, BiLo Supermarkets, and other major grocery chains. In the past, each had operated autonomously according to the SBU model, but ceaseless pressures on margins in the supermarket industry eventually forced Ahold to explore shared services. In 1999 it implemented an SSC for financial transactions. As a result, 400 people now do the work previously performed by 560. Through centralization and standardization, Ahold also drastically reduced the cost of acquiring and maintaining the software systems it uses to perform these transactions.

Sometimes overlooked in the enthusiasm surrounding the success of the shared services concept is the fact that it challenges the autonomy of SBUs. No longer is the leader of an SBU entirely the captain of his or her own ship. Some of the work needed to keep the business going is now being done by people over whom the SBU chief has no direct control. An SBU does not manage or control the SSC that provides it with transactional services; rather, it plays the role of the SSC's customer. In some companies, SBU heads resisted this breach of their independence, arguing that it was unfair to hold them accountable for the SBU's financial performance if they were incurring an expense (the SSC's bills for services rendered) over which they had no control. These objections carried little weight. The prospect of reducing costs trumped the risk of violating SBU autonomy. But the outraged SBU heads had a point. The pristine isolation of the SBU was indeed starting to fade.

The second insult to the SBUs occurred in response to customers' escalating demands for simplicity. If an SBU structure made internal management easier, it also complicated the customer's life. For instance, let's say a retailer buys products from a diversified consumer packaged goods (CPG) company, which has SBUs specializing in different product categories. The retailer has to negotiate individually with each SBU. That means separate orders, deliveries, and bills—in short, a massive increase in work. In an era when retailers were relatively powerless, they had to put up with this. But in the customer economy, retailers can insist that a CPG company present it with a single face.

Toward this end, some corporations considered organizing their business units around customers or markets instead of around products. Instead of one focusing on snack foods, another on cheese, and another on meat products, one unit would serve mass merchandisers, a second wholesalers, a third retail grocers, and so on. But this is not realistic. For each unit to operate as a genuine self-contained SBU, it would have to develop and manufacture all of its own products. This would mean enormous redundancies and no economies of scale in areas such as research, manufacturing, and procurement.

A more practicable approach was discussed in Chapter 2: Create customer-focused account teams that represent multiple SBUs. A team might be comprised entirely of salespeople or it might include customer service reps, logistics specialists, and others involved in interacting with customers. These teams would represent a single interface to all of the company's SBUs for the customer. But while this approach goes a long way toward solving the customer's problem, it also has the unintended consequence of softening the SBU's sharp edges. The SBU head can no longer command his or her sales reps to focus exclusively on the SBU's products and goals. The reps are now members of a team that must balance each SBU's objectives with those of the company as a whole. Sometimes an account team may have to sacrifice one SBU (by offering its products at a deep discount, for instance) in order to win more of the customer's overall spending for the corporation. This is a major departure from the traditional SBU.

The third crack in the SBU's defenses has to do with process standardization. Let's take another look at Duke Power's efforts to install electrical service on schedule (Chapter 4). Duke Power is organized into geographic regions that divide up its service territory in North and South Carolina. Formerly, every region was in effect an SBU. Each regional vice president was responsible for reaching specified financial goals and was equipped with the staff and resources to do so. Within that mandate, regional vice presidents were essentially autonomous. Cooperation among them was rare. Dealing mainly with their own region's customers, they had very little reason to communicate with one another.

When Duke Power's top executives decided to improve the performance of the installation process, they had to decide whether to standardize the method across the company or to allow each region to implement its own version. Had the regions and their customers been very different from one another, multiple installation processes might have been necessary. But since that was not the case—you install electrical service in North Carolina the same way you do in South Carolina—the company decided it needed only one process.

To accomplish this, the company appointed a single process owner, whose job it was to create a standardized process for the whole company. This process owner and all the owners of the company's other processes were positioned as peers with the regional vice presidents, all of whom reported to the head of the business. Consequently, controlling the work has been separated from controlling the people who perform the work. The process owners design the process, and the regional vice presidents are responsible for seeing that it is carried out. What had been complete regional self-contained authority has now been divided, with some responsibility going to the process owners and some staying with the regional vice presidents.

The issue linking these three phenomena—shared services centers; a single face to the customer; and process standardization—is that they demonstrate the futility of trying to segment companies into independent SBUs. The world is not unidimensional, and companies aren't diamonds that cleave neatly along a facet into self-contained components. It is impossible to neatly divide an enterprise into SBUs that can operate independently of one another. In today's world, any two "independent" business units will inevitably overlap, sharing customers, product lines, backroom activities, or front-office processes. In a multidimensional world, the autonomous SBU is a fiction. We ignore this at the risk of higher costs and customer dissatisfaction—neither of which is acceptable any longer.

The solution to the structural problem of the SBU is, however, not to be found in more structure; it is to be found in antistructure. The passing of the SBU is also the passing of the primacy of organizational structure. Nothing less than the existence of well-defined organizational boundaries is being called into question, and with it both the notion of managerial autonomy and the significance of the organizational chart.

This notion will come as something of a shock to many executives, who suffer from the widespread malady of "structuritis." This syndrome's principal symptom is the propensity to issue a new organizational chart as the first solution to any business problem. Some companies find the exercise of reshuffling the management deck and assigning everyone to a new box so cathartic they stage it regularly, even annually (or worse). Many embrace periodic makeovers with the intensity associated with pilgrimages to fonts of religious faith. In companies suffering from structuritis, the organizational chart is a topic of endless fascination and an object of great veneration.

Needless to say, these periodic reorganizations generally accomplish little, since they fail to address the root causes of most real business problems. All too often, reorganization is a substitute for deep strategic thinking, disciplined performance improvement, and substantive change.

The time has come for managers to worry less about organizational structures and organizational charts and more about marshaling their resources for the benefit of the customer. That an enterprise, as a whole, can be decomposed into independent units is an outmoded idea. Emerging in its stead is a structure far more subtle and complex, in which no manager has complete independence; rather, those at the top collaborate for the collective benefit of the entire company.

To see how this works, let's again look at Duke Power, where neither a process owner nor a regional head has complete autonomy. The former controls the process design, the latter the people who carry it out. Making this division of responsibility work requires extraordinary cooperation between process owners and regional heads. In designing a process, the process owner must take into account the regional staff's capabilities, while the regional head, when selecting his or her people, must consider the requirements of the process. Neither one can say to the other, "Do things my way." If either tries to assert total control or usurp the other's responsibility, the entire enterprise fails. Duke does not have a hierarchy with clear lines of authority; instead, its executives float in a soup of shared accountability. If the process owner and the regional head work well together, both succeed; if they don't, both fail.

Those still addicted to the clarity of traditional structures might ask, To whom does someone performing a process in a particular region report: to the process owner or to the regional head? As I said in Chapter 4, I have posed this question to a number of senior leaders at Duke Power, who, remarkably, offer the exact same answer each time: "It doesn't matter." That's because the process owner and the regional head have identical goals. Each is measured and rewarded by the key metrics that the company identified in the Gameplan discussed in Chapter 6. Both are evaluated by how well the regional staffs perform the processes and how well the company performs financially.

Duke Power is notable for having minimized conflicts created by divisive or incongruent goals. Instead of the process owner promoting process measures while the regional head focuses on profitability, both of them care about both measures and are motivated to work together to boost these shared measures. Therefore it doesn't matter to whom a person performing a process reports; he or she will get the same guidance and imperatives from either source.

To some, Duke Power's organization may be reminiscent of the much-maligned matrix organization. The matrix idea emerged in the 1970s as an early attempt to enable a company to focus on many things at the same time. In matrix organizations, a person could have two or three managers. An engineer based in California might report to the manager of engineering, the manager of California operations, and the manager of the product line on which he or she was working. The matrix's fatal flaw was that these managers typically had divergent goals. They had sharply distinguished responsibilities and were evaluated by different measures, and so they inevitably focused narrowly just on their particular areas—just on engineering productivity, or the costs of the California operations, or the success of one product line. Each relentlessly pursued a narrow agenda, typically at the expense of other concerns, and with little or no regard for the whole company's performance. In this system, anyone reporting to two or three managers was caught in an endless tug-of-war and wasted precious time and energy trying to determine whose needs took priority. The inevitable politicking was intolerable. The Duke Power structure obviates this flaw by aligning everyone around common goals.

Cooperation at Duke Power isn't needed only between process owners and regional heads. The process owners also collaborate closely with one another, because processes aren't islands unto themselves. They, too, overlap, since the same workers are often involved in several processes at the same time. For example, the same field personnel perform the processes of installing lines and maintaining them. At first, this overlap created conflict. The two process owners each tried to persuade the regional heads to assign more people to their process.

Before too long, however, the two process owners realized that this conflict was wasteful for both of them, and they worked out a new arrangement. The two realized that there is seasonality in demand for their work. Accordingly, certain field personnel were assigned to work exclusively on each process, so that high-priority work could always be performed right away; the rest formed a floating pool available to work on either one. The maintenance process owner agreed to schedule routine jobs in the spring and fall, whenever possible, thus creating greater installation capacity during the summer when demand for that was highest. Duke's shared goals encouraged these two process owners to breach the walls surrounding their independent areas of responsibility. The power of mutual benefit made their collaboration not only practical but inevitable.

At Duke Power, the era of well-defined fiefdoms run by autonomous managers has passed. But that doesn't mean that adjusting to this new regime was easy. For Duke's managers, long accustomed to proud independence, collaborating marked a profound shift. Cooperation in pursuit of shared objectives is not a trait that our traditional organizations develop or encourage in their managers. At first, the process owners and the regional heads instinctively acted more as rivals than as partners. The problem wasn't resolved until all the managers sat down together to develop a sort of constitution for collaborative decision making. Known as a *decision rights matrix,* this document specified the roles different managers would play when various major decisions had to be made, such as changing a process design, hiring people, or setting a budget. It detailed which managers would actually make the decision, which had to be consulted beforehand, and which had to be informed afterward.

In effect, the decision rights matrix became the organization's road map for managerial collaboration. Ironically, once the matrix was developed, Duke's managers found that they rarely had to consult it. The process of developing it led them to internalize it. The document's clarity gave the managers a concrete sense of how the new organization would work. The very process of creating it gave them an appreciation for a new style of management.

This style of management collaboration mirrors the teamwork that is now commonplace among front-line workers. Indeed, nothing less should be required of executives. It would be hypocritical of leaders to make demands of their employees that they are unwilling to make of themselves. But ending managerial autonomy means much more than just having managers work together on ad hoc project teams. At Duke Power, collaboration is the very essence of management work, not an occasional departure from it.

Looking back, the rise of shared services centers, of single faces to the customer, and of process standardization signaled the beginning of the end of the traditional view of enterprises as sharply structured organizations with highly autonomous managers. But this shift is not yet over. These three phenomena are starting to leverage one another, leading to even looser structures in many organizations. Some companies, in order to present one face to the customer, are, in effect, combining process standardization with shared services. That is, once a company decides that a process should be conducted in the same way across all of its units, under the aegis of one process owner, it is only a short step to take the people who perform this process out of those units and turn them into what amounts to a shared services center for nonadministrative work.

This is what has happened at a major manufacturer of building supplies. In the past, this company was organized into conventional independent business units, each with its own product line, such as insulation or roofing. Each unit had its own general manager whose mandate was to optimize the profits in her or his specific domain, regardless of how well or poorly the other units were performing. But this system began to erode with the arrival of enormous customers like Home Depot and other national home improvement chains, behemoths who saw no reason to endure the repercussions of the manufacturer's fragmentation. In response, the manufacturer removed the performance of the order fulfillment process (taking orders, shipping goods, receiving payment, and so on) from the product-based SBUs, which then focused entirely on product development and manufacturing.

Order fulfillment became the responsibility of three new units, one for each of the company's major types of customers: large, big-box retailers like Home Depot; large construction contractors; and intermediaries, distributors who resold products to smaller retailers. Each of these units could take orders for any product, would coordinate delivery, and would present the customer with a single bill and invoice.

Today you will find few remnants of the conventional model of independent business units at this manufacturer. The product units don't have all the capabilities of a completely self-contained business. While they develop and manufacture products, they don't deal with customers. Likewise, the customer-facing units provide the interface to customers but don't actually make the products. Nor has the company returned to a functional organization, in which all manufacturing is performed by one department and all marketing by another. Rather, this company is like an epoxy glue that works only when its ingredients are mixed together. Adding a customer unit to a product unit equals creating a complete business—but only when you combine them.

One striking point about this complete business is that it doesn't appear anywhere on the company's organizational chart. No single manager is responsible for it. But when the heads of a product unit and a customer unit work together, they forge an alloy, the equivalent of a traditional general manager who is responsible for his or her domain. Needless to say, only through extraordinary collaboration can product and customer chiefs smoothly integrate their diverse capabilities and, in effect, operate a complete business.

Is this manufacturer organized according to products or markets? The answer—both and neither—reflects the multidimensional reality of today's business world. Products, customer segments, geographies, and markets are all significant facets of a company, and no single one of them can be allowed to dominate the others. Any cleavage of a company along a single dimension will inevitably lead to inconsistencies and redundancies. Although the dimensions of product and market are equally vital to the building products company, neither can work nor succeed without the success of the other. I want to repeat that theirs is not a traditional matrix structure that allows different managers with diverging priorities to pull workers in conflicting directions. Here different managers have different primary foci, but they are also given every incentive to align their interests, thus providing the key that drives the overall company's success.

Within this configuration, who is paramount is irrelevant and, in fact, only a matter of subjective perspective. A product chief might think the company is organized by products and that the market units are merely distribution channels shared by the product units; the market unit leaders might think the opposite. Who is the sharer? Who is the sharee? Who cares?

With the reconsideration of unit boundaries comes a reconsideration of profit-and-loss responsibilities, which in the past were the realm of the SBU heads. Now they must be allocated more broadly. Each market unit is accountable for the profitability of its market segment. Each product unit is responsible for the profitability of its product class. The costs of the product units are allocated across the market units for their profit-and-loss computation and vice versa.

In an important sense, the fixed SBU structure was an artifact of the limitations of mid-twentieth-century accounting technology. Until recently, companies could pick only one dimension for profit-and-loss responsibility because physical records and the early computer systems that simulated them didn't allow for more. There was just one way to organize the chart of accounts, and you were stuck with it. Accordingly, SBU heads were the only people accountable for a bottom line.

With contemporary information technology, however, one can slice and dice what is sometimes called an information cube in arbitrary ways. The same record of a transaction in which a product was sold to a customer can be analyzed in customer, product, geographic, or any other relevant terms. Not only is there no primary dimension for structuring the organization, there is no limit to the number of possible dimensions. This is as it should be. In order to manage products effectively, one must know which are profitable and which are not; the same is true for the efficient management of markets and customer segments. Having to choose one way or another to organize a business is a losing proposition.

Carly Fiorina has recently reorganized Hewlett-Packard consistent with this approach. Previously, HP was a compilation of 83 separately run units, each focused on a single product line. Fiorina has reorganized these divisions into three product-generation units, each responsible for creating products in broad categories, such as computers or printing systems, and into two customer-facing organizations, one for business customers and one for consumers. (There is also a services unit that has characteristics of both a front-end and back-end organization.) What had formerly been full P&L responsibility is now shared. The customer-facing and product-generation organizations have shared goals and metrics to assure they're equally driven to deliver results.

As is the case at Duke Power, this kind of organization must operate collaboratively and by consensus rather than by hardwired fiat and dicta. Various market units present their product needs to the product units, which navigate through potential conflicts and create goods to satisfy the broadest possible customer requirements. Conversely, different product units plead their cases to the market units, which devise customer-facing processes to accommodate diverse products. In this environment, reporting lines become both unclear and largely irrelevant. An order filler, asked whether he or she works for a product line or a customer segment, would probably answer with a shrug of the shoulders. Why should it matter?

In place of the conventional all-powerful SBU manager, the unit manager in this kind of company becomes an advocate for the unit's needs. A market unit manager lobbies for his market segment, a product manager for her products. The various advocates negotiate and design plans for front-line people to follow.

Interestingly, there is precedent for this cooperative way of working in the conventional role of the product manager, who in a manufacturing company brings together, without exerting control over any of them, all the resources needed to ensure the success of a product. Still, in the past the product manager would have been operating under a traditional head of a self-contained SBU. Now even business unit managers have the same loose charter as traditional product managers.

This new kind of nonstructure needs a different kind of manager with a new set of skills. Comparing his positions before and after the changes were made, one executive at Duke Power observes that they are as dissimilar as night and day. Another has said that the three critical requirements for his new job are "influence, influence, and influence." In the absence of strict hierarchies and absolute authority, managers can accomplish things only by working with others, not by issuing orders.

The traditional managerial role bestowed authority and power on whomever happened to be filling it at the time. No longer. Now management roles are only what their incumbents make of them. If they are forceful representatives for their constituencies as well as effective team players, then both they and the company will succeed. If they are not, they will be relegated to the sidelines of business life. Managers will no longer have the crutch of authority that their positions represent; they must walk and manage on their own.

This new kind of organization is virtually structured and essentially unstructured. It is extraordinarily flexible and responsive to evolving needs, and it requires very little managerial overhead to make it work effectively. But its strength is also its weakness. The absence of sharply delineated domains and clear lines of exclusive control, however, fosters an environment that lacks clarity and is awash in ambiguity. In an amorphous, fluid organization, where different managers represent distinct concerns but nobody has absolute control, it is very easy to slide into conflict and endless argumentation. For example, what happens when two different markets pose conflicting requirements for a product unit? Or when two process owners both need increased resources to get their jobs done? Such issues, quickly resolved by the old authoritarians, might paralyze the new egalitarians. The danger of a structureless environment is that everybody can lobby for his or her issue to the point that nothing ever gets done.

It should be clear that shared measures and objectives are prerequisites for the collaborative style needed to avoid this danger. If people have different missions, nothing will persuade them to sacrifice their objectives in favor of anyone else's. Only when people unite to pursue overarching goals that transcend their narrow domains will the separate dimensions of an organization coalesce into a whole. But shared measures and objectives are not enough.

Without a doubt, the most important prerequisite for making this structureless organization work is a dynamic and strong leader. Structureless does not mean leaderless. To the contrary: A true leader, rather than a bureaucrat or a dictator, is an absolute requirement if an enterprise is to harness the power of structural ambiguity. A strong leader supplies, through force of personality and vision, the cohesion that would otherwise be provided by formal structure. Such a leader projects a compelling vision of the enterprise, which focuses every member of the management team on the enterprise's larger objectives. It is this leader who fashions a team out of a disparate collection of managers with different orientations.

This kind of business leadership is a new requirement. In supplier-dominated economies, companies could afford to coast, and their top executives could afford to see themselves as stewards. No longer. In the customer economy, a rigid organization "led" by a traditional manager will break apart at the seams. Only an organization without seams can withstand the heavy buffeting that it now endures. Today's leader must hold the enterprise together, because nothing else will do it for him. The decline of the SBU must be matched by the rise of the inspirational and charismatic enterprise leader.

Despite what I tell young parents, managerial behavior is learned, not inherited. It's not too late for existing managerial cadres to learn this new style of managing. They may even find that its personal rewards—the camaraderie and *esprit* that come from a shared sense of purpose—more than compensate for the effort in making the adjustment. Let's hope so. Otherwise we will need to have some long talks with the nation's third-grade teachers.

Agenda Item 6

End the Tyranny of the Organizational Chart

- Get over the idea of sharply defined business units with autonomous managers.
- Redefine managers as representing markets, products, or processes, rather than as having total control over them.
- Make managerial teamwork and cooperation the rule rather than the exception.
- Teach managers to put the needs of the enterprise as a whole first.
- Employ rewards that emphasize the group over the individual.
- Substitute inspirational leadership for formal structure.

8

Focus on the Final Customer

Turn Distribution Chains into Distribution Communities

Do you know who your customers are?

It would seem axiomatic that in a customer economy, every company must know, understand, and have strong relationships with its customers. But in a great many industries, companies don't do this because they simply have no idea who their customers are. The reason is that they are shielded from their real customers—the people and companies who make use of their products and services—by their distribution chains (also known as channels): wholesalers, distributors, retailers, dealers, and a whole set of other intermediaries.

Some companies do deal directly with their customers. Boeing sells directly to airlines, steelmakers sell to the auto companies, consumer banks sell to homeowners. But the great majority of products and services reach their final destination only after passing through the hands of one or more intermediaries who buy and resell, buy and resell. From consumer goods to industrial motors, distribution channels bridge the gap between the maker of a product and its ultimate purchaser. At the same time, they separate the two.

Distribution channels form an opaque screen that lets little information through. On one side sit the product makers, who know everything about their products and precious little about their customers; on the other are the intermediaries, who know exactly the opposite. When information can't pass through the channel, everyone suffers.

Chapter 3 explored how Trane, the major maker of air-conditioning equipment, is transforming itself from an equipment maker into a provider of comfortable buildings. That story focused on the part of Trane that makes components of large systems for large buildings. Another part of Trane sells smaller units to owners of small buildings, like homes and small businesses. Customers buy both new Trane equipment as well as replacement parts for equipment they already have. But Trane itself has only a small share of the market for replacement parts for its own equipment. Why? Because Trane has little idea who owns its equipment or when they are buying parts. It reaches its customers only through a network of distributors and contractors. Owners of Trane equipment are mostly buying generic versions of Trane parts from distributors, and Trane has no way to urge them to do otherwise. This problem is not unique to Trane. It is endemic to a host of industries from automobiles to electronics.

On the other hand, Trane's distributors and contractors can face challenges because they experience delays in getting up-to-date information about Trane's products. The shrink-wrapped notebook updates and CD-ROMs that companies today use to get information into their distribution channels are cumbersome and prone to delay. A Trane contractor, therefore, is likely not to know enough about the latest Trane offering to promote it with confidence immediately; in preparing a sales proposal, the contractor will have to pore through volumes of notebooks and CD-ROMs to find the right product data and pricing information, running up costs and increasing the possibility of error.

Traditional distribution systems are also inefficient and rife with unnecessary costs. After all, the same product is being sold multiple times as it wends its way through the distribution channel, and though each of these transactions adds cost, it adds no value. An air conditioner is no better because it has been sold by the manufacturer to the distributor or by the distributor to the contractor. Distribution systems are also awash with inventory. Intermediaries are never sure what customers will order or how long it will take the manufacturer to respond to a request for product, so they pile up inventory—lots and lots of it.

Consider the part of the food industry called dry groceries—basically, the packaged items in the central aisles in the supermarket. On the average, more than one hundred days pass from the time one of these products comes off the manufacturer's production line until the consumer picks it up off the supermarket shelf. That's over three months. The problem is not slow trucks. The problem is that these products are going through a lot of hands: More than 40 percent of all food items stop at least twice between the manufacturer and the retail shelf. Each time the product must be unloaded and stored and picked and reloaded. The total amount of inventory sloshing around this distribution system exceeds $100 billion.

These problems are not new—they are in fact inherent in multitier distribution channels. What is new is that they are no longer tolerable. In the days when customers were weak and powerless, this system could be endured. Customers had to put up with the excess costs, the delays, and the poor performance. They will do so no longer. A company that tries to reach today's powerful customers through traditional distribution channels is like a surgeon who tries to operate while wearing thick gloves.

Companies have come to realize that they need to be closer to their final customers in order to hold them, to up-sell and cross-sell them, and to garner high-margin follow-on sales. They need to be closer to their final customers in order to be able to serve them quickly and accurately. They need to be closer to their final customers in order to drive out the huge costs and inefficiencies, the redundant work and piles of inventory, that clutter existing channels. This much companies realize. What they don't know is how to do it.

Unfortunately, in the last years of the twentieth century, many companies were led astray by a siren call that ultimately dashed them on the rocks: disintermediation. Stripped to its core, disintermediation simply means getting rid of intermediaries, the middlemen who intervene between company and customer, so that these two can do business directly with each other. Through disintermediation, went the theory, costs are reduced, service is improved, inventories are reduced, and all are made happy—except the now-superfluous intermediaries. The miraculous tool that was to enable disintermediation and banish intermediaries to the nether regions was, of course, the Internet.

The term *disintermediation* first entered the business lexicon during the revolution in financial services that was precipitated by the extraordinarily high interest rates of the 1970s. Prior to that, consumers were depositing their funds into bank savings accounts, which the banks used to invest in loans and money-market instruments. As classic intermediaries, the banks paid minuscule interest for the right to parlay the depositors' money. Facing inflation and higher interest rates, however, consumers discovered the advantages of money-market funds, which allowed them to invest directly in the same instruments as the banks. Likewise, at the corporate level large borrowers started to bypass banks and go straight to the commercial paper market for financing. Analysts of the time wrote jeremiads forecasting the imminent collapse of the U.S. banking system if these trends didn't end. Needless to say, the reports of the banks' death were, in Mark Twain's words, "greatly exaggerated." They have survived as financial intermediaries by shifting to other forms of value-added service.

To its proponents, the Internet was to be the ultimate disintermediator, allowing customers to order directly from the producer, bypassing traditional distribution channels. The explosive success of Amazon.com, despite the fact that it actually operates as an intermediary between publishers and book buyers, stirred the imaginations of people in virtually every industry about the possibilities of reshaping distribution.

Amazon is the most prominent name in the B2C (business to consumer) part of e-commerce. Founded as an online bookstore, it now offers a wide range of products from electronics to music. Although, as I write, it is yet to be profitable and there is no guarantee that it ever will be, Amazon has achieved metaphoric status far beyond its own industry. Its success has produced a brisk neologism—the verb *to Amazon,* meaning to see one's business seized by an Internet-savvy competitor that deals directly with customers, eliminating the costs of a distribution channel. For some months in 1999 and 2000, consultants and journalists were terrifying executives in virtually every industry with the prospect of being "Amazoned." Anxious not only to survive but also to appear cool and au courant, many executives sought to co-opt the new Amazoners by embracing disintermediation.

Amazon has a lot to answer for. Although the company has been extremely successful in popularizing electronic commerce, it is also indirectly responsible for widespread confusion, mass hysteria, and more than a few disasters brought about by established companies reacting to their fear of "being Amazoned." Like claret, Amazon's singular business model does not travel well or far. Indeed, the company's success may derive mainly from its perspicacious choice of books as its primary merchandise. Unlike most other consumer items, books are, in many ways, the perfect product for electronic commerce.

The great majority of people decide whether to buy a book based on a modest amount of information: author, title, subject matter, reviews, and the recommendations of others. All of this information can be conveyed electronically to a prospective book buyer. Indeed, Amazon conveys this information more effectively than do many bookstores.

For most other products, however, the consumer wants to experience directly what he or she is about to buy. The Internet cannot reproduce the sensory tastings and testings that go into buying a sofa, a sailboat, or a suit. Most people will not buy a chair without sitting on it, feeling how it conforms to their specific anatomy, and deciding how the fabric feels and how the color looks in their living room or den. These things are not easily learned from a computer screen, even one perfectly tuned for color accuracy.

Not only is a book easy for a buyer to select, it is easy for Amazon to ship. Books are small and light and can be transported easily in a delivery truck. On the other hand, the costs of directly delivering a sofa from a manufacturer to a consumer are prohibitive, which is why they, and most other products, are shipped on a truck packed with other merchandise to a location near the consumer, where the whole shipment is broken down and items individually delivered to their purchasers just over the last few miles. We have a name for such transfer points: stores.

Amazon is also fortunate in that it does not have to send out with every book it ships a representative to teach the customer how to read, to place it on the customer's bookshelf, to explain complex passages, or to mend a torn page. In other words, books require no training, installation, support, or maintenance. Most products do.

The truth is that for most products, Internet-based disintermediation was an extraordinarily naïve and unrealistic fantasy. For most products, distribution intermediaries do not just add cost; they also add value. They are more than just a series of stopping points for goods en route from manufacturers to final customers. Intermediaries add value that the final customer needs and that the manufacturer is not well positioned to provide. Intermediaries help customers select and acquire products, provide support and maintenance services, and more. The problems with conventional distribution channels—high cost, excess inventory, poor information flow—are very real, but the solution is not to eliminate them altogether in favor of a disintermediated model. That would be merely replacing one bad idea with another.

Instead, manufacturers and their intermediaries must collaborate to leverage each other's capabilities in the interests of creating a distribution system that maximizes value for the final customer while simultaneously minimizing its own costs. We have to start thinking about distribution from the outside in—that is, from the standpoint of the final customer—rather than from the inside out, the perspective of the manufacturer and provider of products and services. We need to change our lexicon. Instead of distributing *to* the customer, we must see ourselves as distributing *for* the customer. The question is no longer what's the easiest way for us to get rid of our product, but rather what's the best way to deliver the greatest value to the customer at the end of the road, who pays all our salaries.

Suppose, for instance, that you are the owner of a small business who needs to air-condition your building. You will have to decide how much equipment is needed to adequately cool the building and which air-conditioning products will best meet that need. You will have to determine what related products, such as grills and ductwork, are necessary. Then you will have to acquire and install it all. Over time the system will require service and spare parts. All of this needs to be done, but you are incapable of doing it yourself. The manufacturer is too far away to do you any good and in any event is not set up for dealing with lots of small customers like you. It has chosen to focus on designing and making products, not on solving the myriad problems you have.

So you turn to an air-conditioning contractor, part of the manufacturer's distribution channel. But the contractor may also have difficulty solving your problems. He or she may lack the most up-to-date product information or the engineering sophistication to do precise BTU calculations. Hence you may not receive the best possible recommendation for equipment. Since the distributor from whom the contractor gets equipment holds inventory in anticipation of your order, his (and therefore your) costs will go up; and the distributor may not have the equipment you need on hand, and so you will have to wait.

Trane has recognized in this situation an opportunity to work with its contractors and distributors in a way that benefits everyone. It has deployed an Internet-based system that leverages, not disenfranchises, its distribution channel. Trane's Web site, named Trane ComfortSite, provides a wide range of services: Some of them are informational, designed to help contractors and distributors serve the final customer, and some of them are transactional, designed to cut the costs of commerce.

First, Trane ComfortSite offers its contractors up-to-date product information, which enables a contractor to configure a Trane system that delivers the required air conditioning with a minimum of fuss and a maximum of accuracy. The site's proposal generator, which allows the contractor to put together quickly a proposal for a potential customer, eliminates a lot of clerical work, avoids potential errors, and saves everyone a lot of time and hassle. The site offers training modules on installing Trane equipment as well as tools to help contractor technicians diagnose and fix specific equipment problems. (A "comfort calculator," which a contractor can use to determine a customer's precise energy requirements, is also planned.)

On the transactional side, the site accepts contractor orders for Trane products, including spare parts. It also enters and forwards orders for complementary products like screens and curbs that are made by other companies. Contractors can enter their warranty claims for reimbursement by Trane, thereby reducing their costs and improving their cash flow.

Put together, the facilities provided by Trane ComfortSite enable Trane and its distribution channel to do a better job of meeting the final customer's needs while improving their own financial performance. These two objectives are not, and cannot be, in conflict. In the customer economy, every company must achieve both.

Trane's final customer is getting better solutions at lower prices; contractors and distributors operate with less overhead and cost and are able to compete better against others who are not leveraged by their suppliers as they are by Trane; and Trane benefits through increased sales and lowered costs.

Trane is now at work extending the capabilities of this site to allow final customers access as well. Homeowners, for example, will be able to use a related site to find a Trane contractor in their area, schedule routine service visits, and check on the warranty status of their equipment. An even more extensive set of services will be available to larger customers—national accounts that buy air conditioning for several buildings, such as a chain of fast-food restaurants. Trane's site will help these national accounts manage their equipment by tracking the installations at all of their locations; it will generate a service history for each piece of equipment and offer reminders for maintenance as well as a tool for calculating when a piece of equipment has reached the end of its economic life and should be replaced. Contractors aren't positioned to offer these services, since most contractors are local, while national accounts own numerous buildings scattered throughout the country. Moreover, most contractors lack the business sophistication that solving many of these problems requires. In this area, Trane takes over, not to supplant the local distribution channel, but to augment it by offering additional customer value.

By piercing the veil that separates it from its final customers, Trane will finally have access to information about them that it can use to develop relationships with them. Its reason for desiring this information is not to wrest the customers away from the contractors who serve them. Rather, it wants to know who its final customers are, so that it can stay in close touch with their changing needs, so that it will know what to produce and when, and so that it can ensure that the customers stay customers and don't ever buy anyone else's products, whether parts or new equipment.

Even more interesting than Trane's proficient use of Internet technology is the way it has redefined its relationships with its contractors. In the past, Trane sold its products through a distributor to a contractor, who did work for the customer. Now while the product still moves down this distribution channel, the responsibility for performing the value-creating activities that the customer needs is spread throughout the system. Rather than acting as independent entities that work at arm's length and have potentially conflicting goals, Trane and the contractors now operate collaboratively to meet the customer's needs for air conditioning. Everyone benefits from this new cooperative approach.

Trane's initiatives embody two of the central themes of this book. First, the company is increasing the value it offers its customers, following the precepts of Chapter 3. Second, Trane is not doing this alone. It is dissolving the boundaries between itself and its contractors by supporting the latter's efforts in dealing with the final customer. The following two chapters will explore this theme in greater detail.

The real purpose of a distribution channel is not to get products to final customers but to solve customers' problems. Simple products, like books, may not need much in the way of a distribution channel, as Amazon has shown. But most products present their final customers with a lot of problems, and that means that the distribution channel needs to find better ways to solve them.

Few product categories are as challenging for buyers as wireless telecommunications (cell phones and pagers). These customers confront a myriad of service plans, all described in incomprehensible terms, as well as a vast number of competing phones, all with different features and capabilities. To make matters worse, all of this variety changes all the time. To help them sort through the morass, customers turn to the salespeople who work for the companies that distribute cell phones and pagers, which include operators of cellular services, such as Verizon and AT&T, and retailers, such as Best Buy and RadioShack.

Like Trane, Motorola has taken steps to transform how its wireless phones, two-way radios, and messaging devices and accessories work their way through distribution channels to the final customer. It is leveraging the capability of its intermediaries in order to make life better for the intermediary, the customer, and Motorola itself. At Motorola's Internet site, Motorola Connect, intermediaries can order accessories and marketing materials; check the status of an order, including the identity of the shipping company and the exact location of the order at the moment; and process returns and warranty claims. (Ordering of actual products is coming soon.) Before, intermediaries had to contact a company sales rep or call center to do all this, which was expensive and inconvenient for both the intermediary and Motorola. Now the intermediaries do it themselves when they want to, enabling Motorola salespeople to concentrate on selling, meeting with the intermediaries, and encouraging them to offer more Motorola products.

Perhaps most important, Motorola's intermediaries can use Motorola Connect to get current information about the company's products, saving themselves and their customers time and money. The site offers training modules about Motorola products and even provides a certification program. Via the Internet, Motorola offers its intermediaries' sales reps a formal training program. Participants have to study a set of modules and pass a series of quizzes. The site tracks which salespeople have studied which modules and who has become certified; Motorola shares that information with the intermediary's management. In other words, in the interest of increasing its own sales, Motorola is helping its intermediaries manage their sales forces.

Kawasaki Motors Corp. USA is another company that is leveraging its distribution channel. It sells its motorcycles in the United States through a network of fifteen hundred dealers. In addition to the motorcycles, the dealers also sell parts and accessories, such as helmets and jackets. Most dealers have a love-hate relationship with accessories. On the one hand, they are high-margin items, since if a motorcycle owner wants a Kawasaki jacket, there are few places that carry them. On the other hand, accessories present inventory management problems. To satisfy customers' preferences in motorcycle couture, a dealer will need to stock a number of different jackets, each in a range of colors and sizes. Fashion inventory management is not a particular strength of most motorcycle dealers.

Kawasaki has come to the rescue. The company has created two Internet sites: one for dealers to order products from the company, and the other for consumers to order accessories. Kawasaki handles and fills the accessory orders, shipping directly to the consumer. Like books, most motorcycle accessories are easy to ship and require no instructions for use. Furthermore, consumers must name a dealer with which they are (or wish to be) affiliated before the order will be processed; Kawasaki gives the designated dealer 60 percent of the difference between dealer cost and retail list price, to compensate the dealer for what he would have made had the consumer bought the accessory in the store.

Kawasaki is definitely not disintermediating its dealers. On the contrary, it rewards them for encouraging customers to buy accessories. Moreover, Kawasaki does not sell motorcycles directly to consumers. That would threaten the dealers and leave the buyer struggling to determine what bike to buy. Motorcycle accessories are a different kind of product from motorcycles themselves.

This arrangement is a win-win-win all around. The consumer gets the jacket he wants without having to roam about looking for a dealer who happens to have the right color and size in stock; the dealer gets a chunk of profit for doing almost nothing and, in addition, doesn't have to worry about inventory; and Kawasaki maintains both consumer and dealer loyalty and sells a high-margin item.

If Kawasaki distinguishes between motorcycles and accessories and has developed different distribution strategies for the two categories, one furniture manufacturer has done the same by dividing its products into furniture and furnishings. Furniture consists of large, heavy pieces, such as sofas and chairs, that require both experiential selection and support for installation and repair. Furnishings, by contrast, are smaller items, like lamps, that can be appreciated and selected online and are easier to ship and maintain.

This manufacturer has set up a Web site where consumers looking for furniture can see the sofas the manufacturer is selling and then visit a local retailer to try them out. The sofas can be ordered from the manufacturer, either electronically or via the retailer. Ordered products are shipped, not directly to the consumer, but in bulk to the retailer, who handles delivery, installation, and ongoing service. The retailer thus remains a physical intermediary but is no longer a financial one. That is, the retailer no longer buys the sofa from the manufacturer, holds it in inventory, then resells it to the consumer. As I said earlier, this process adds cost but no value. Rather, the consumer buys the sofa directly (financially) from the manufacturer and receives it (physically) from the retailer. The retailer in essence provides services to the consumer on behalf of the manufacturer—and receives from the manufacturer a commission for doing so (25 percent of the purchase price).

Furnishings, by contrast, are simple and small enough to bypass the retailer completely. The consumer can order these products directly from the manufacturer's Web site without actually seeing them, and the manufacturer ships them directly to the consumer. It would be tempting for the manufacturer to cut the retailer out of such sales, but instead it gives the retailer nearest the customer a 10 percent commission on furnishings. It does so because retailers provide value by promoting the manufacturer's brand and giving it a local presence, without which the consumer may not have accessed the manufacturer's Web site in the first place. For the manufacturer, it is worth providing the 10 percent to the retailers in order to keep them enthusiastic about its other products—the ones that many consumers prefer to buy in stores rather than in cyberspace. In short, this furniture maker has rethought its own role and the roles of its distribution partners in order to do a better job for final customers—and saves money along the way.

A similar evolution is occurring in the automobile industry. From a consumer's viewpoint, buying a car is a three-step process. First, you research the kind of vehicle you want and make a short list of brands and models to examine more closely. Next, you test-drive these brands and models and decide which one you really want to buy. Finally, you negotiate the terms, money changes hands, and you drive away. But neither the existing distribution system nor its disintermediated version adequately meets the needs of most people shopping for a new car.

In the existing distribution system, dealers buy truckloads of cars, park them on big lots, and wait for buyers. These rows and rows of unsold cars on high-rent lots drive up costs, which ultimately consumers bear. On the other hand, no one has yet figured out an Internet-based disintermediated model for automobile shopping. It is hard to imagine how the customer will virtually test-drive a car in conditions simulating actual highway driving as he or she sits comfortably at home.

As a result, a hybrid model is emerging. Before long, auto dealerships will be showrooms containing a few demonstration models. The consumer will go to the dealership for a test drive only after conducting all of his or her research online (a host of Web sites already provide car shoppers with extensive information), then go back to the Web to place the order on the manufacturer's site.

Automakers are rapidly converging on manufacturing processes that will build cars to consumer specifications at a rate that only five years ago would have seemed a pipe dream. Several have targeted ten days as the turnaround time on the order-to-delivery process. You will no longer have to wait interminably for the model you have chosen, or buy whatever the dealer has on the lot if you can't afford to wait; soon you will order exactly the car you want and drive it away, fresh from the factory, in just a few days.

Dealers won't sell in the sense that they do now. The transaction will be between the consumer and the manufacturer; the dealer will handle the car but never take possession of it. Like the furniture retailer and the Kawasaki dealer, the auto dealership will get a sales commission for each car ordered through its showroom, but it will derive most of its revenue from servicing customers' cars. In other words, the dealer will no longer be a reseller but rather a value-adder. Traditional activities that add value for the consumer will remain in the dealer's portfolio; those that add only cost will not.

Distribution channels as we know them today evolved in an environment very different from ours and were designed to solve a different set of problems from those that companies now confront. In brief, traditional distribution channels were created for the convenience of the manufacturers of products and services. Traditionally, manufacturers focused on improving product quality and lowering its cost; for them, dealing with customers was a distraction. So most manufacturers offloaded this responsibility to intermediaries, saying in effect, "Let them deal with customers; we'll take care of the product." This approach also fit in with the manufacturers' need for long production runs, which inevitably led to large inventories of finished goods awaiting customers' orders. If intermediaries held these goods, then the manufacturers did not have to; moreover, if the manufacturer produced the wrong goods, then it was the intermediaries who bore the risk of their not selling. Manufacturers were also freed of having to spend a lot of money processing a large number of small orders; they could let the intermediaries aggregate them into a small number of large ones.

Needless to say, these conditions and considerations are now long obsolete. Yet business systems frequently outlive the circumstances for which they were designed. Forecasting systems and production technology have now evolved so that manufacturers don't have to stockpile inventory; nor will customers accept passively the costs that a cumbersome distribution system imposes on them. Yet distribution systems have not kept pace with the times. The Faustian bargain that manufacturers struck with their distribution systems is now coming back to haunt them.

In the customer economy, we must stop thinking of a distribution channel as a series of independent entities that sequentially buy and sell products until they reach the final customer at a much-inflated price. This system rewards the customer with added costs, not added value. Rather, we need to see all players in the distribution channel as partners and participants in the work of satisfying the final customer's needs. We need to start with the premise that the purpose of a distribution channel is not to help the manufacturer get rid of the product but to assist the customer in acquiring and using the product. To that end, we need to consider the customer's process for acquiring and using a product. What problems does the customer have in this process, and how can a manufacturer and its distribution partners best collaborate to help solve these problems?

Thinking in this way will be a particular challenge for industries that have so capitulated to traditional distribution that they have made a virtue out of necessity. These industries have confused the distribution channels that they use to reach their customers with the customers themselves. For instance, makers of consumer products now routinely refer to grocery chains and mass merchants as their "customers," while the people who buy, ingest, apply, spray, and otherwise use their products are dismissed as "consumers." To some extent, this is a forgivable overreaction to a pendulum that had swung too far the other way. At one point, many consumer goods makers treated their retailers with contempt and arrogance. They believed that the power of their brands would bring consumers streaming into stores, loudly demanding their branded products, and that the store owners would have to do whatever the brand owners dictated. Moreover, since there were lots and lots of stores, none of them had much clout with the manufacturers. As consumers became far less brand-loyal than they used to be, and as retailers consolidated into a small number of giants with enormous clout, the consumer goods companies naturally paid more attention to their retailers than they had. But confusing them with their real customers ("consumers") is a mistake. There is only one customer for any product: the individual or enterprise that buys and does not resell it.

New relationships need new terminology. The term *distribution channel* or *distribution chain* summons up a linear picture, with manufacturer and final customer at opposite ends of a long row, invisible to each other. It also implies arm's-length connections among all the participants. Perhaps a better phrase in the age of the customer economy would be *distribution community*. Driven by a customer focus and enabled by new technology, channels are evolving into communities, groups of companies that work collaboratively to meet the final customer's needs.

This is not a small transition. Heretofore manufacturers and their intermediaries have had decidedly tense relationships. They needed each other, but each also saw the other as an adversary and as someone out of whom to squeeze the best price. Now everyone must remember that only the final customer pays anybody anything, and any friction or waste in the community penalizes everyone. Unprecedented levels of cooperation and information sharing have to become the norm, as must a willingness to redefine the roles of "manufacturer" and "distributor."

New questions will surface, such as how the final customers' payment should be distributed within the community. How much should the auto showroom (formerly a dealership) be paid for its contribution to the total value created for the car buyer? The old multiplication of cost-plus-markup will no longer apply. We are in, at best, semicharted waters that demand creative thinking to solve new problems.

Though it will be hard to turn current distribution channels into distribution communities, we have little choice but to do so. Traditional distribution is simply not up to the challenges of the customer economy. *The Communist Manifesto* ends with a call to arms: "The proletarians have nothing to lose but their chains. They have a world to win. Working men of all countries, unite." I end this chapter with a similar albeit less euphonious exhortation: "Manufacturers have nothing to lose but their antiquated distribution chains (which increase costs, drive up inventory, and prevent the delivery of the greatest possible value to the final customer). They have a competitive world to win. Manufacturers and intermediaries of the world, unite (into distribution communities)." Who says business has nothing to learn from Marx?

Distribute for, Not to, the Final Customer

- Make maximizing value and minimizing cost for the final customer your number-one priority.
- Turn your distribution channels into communities that work together for common goals.
- Use the Internet to share information and streamline transactions.
- Ensure that each community participant is doing what it does best.
- Drive out redundant work, especially the repetitive buying and reselling of product.
- Be prepared to redefine traditional roles in unconventional ways.

9

Knock Down Your Outer Walls

Collaborate Wherever You Can

I f you are like many businesspeople I know, you probably feel you have done a pretty good job at rooting out overhead and inefficiency from your company. Once upon a time, perhaps, you had let waste, duplication, and pointless activity creep into your operations, and your company suffered the inevitable consequences: delays, excess costs, errors, inflexibility, and all the other pains caused by non-value-adding work. But now you have repented and atoned for your sins. For the last decade, you have been systematically stripping out all the nonsense activity that degrades business performance. Through the application of TQM or six sigma or reengineering or some other methodology of your choice, you and your colleagues have analyzed everything you do and discarded everything that was inessential. It wasn't easy, but now you feel you are lean and mean, flexible and efficient, stripped of fat down to the bone.

Dream on.

You may in fact have done a good job at these efforts to get rid of non-value-adding work and improve efficiency. Things may in fact be a lot better than they were a decade ago. But in the larger scheme of things, you have barely started, and your company is still awash in overhead and waste. The reason is that you have not even begun to address the major sources of unproductive work in your company. You have overlooked them because these sources are not to be found within your company, but at its edges. What degrades your performance is no longer how you work internally but how you work at your boundaries with customers and suppliers and others. Getting rid of this overhead is The Next Big Thing in improving your operating performance.

The Next Big Thing, of course, is the popular Silicon Valley phrase that is used to denote the next hardware or software technology that will revolutionize the computer industry, change the world, and make billionaires of all those prescient enough to be part of it. I am using the phrase here with a broader connotation, to include any major shift in the business landscape. I have a rule of thumb for anyone hoping to identify such coming tidal waves: "The Next Big Thing" often extends "The Last Big Thing."

This idea is, in effect, a business version of Shakespeare's famous line from *The Tempest* that "what's past is prologue." Its thrust is that major developments in the business arena rarely fall from the sky unheralded. Seen through an appropriate lens, they are usually an extension of a previous innovation. In the technological sphere, for instance, the minicomputer of the 1970s was an extension of the mainframe, while the personal computer of the early 1980s was similarly an extension of the minicomputer. To understand what's going to happen next, it's necessary to understand what happened last.

When tomorrow's business histories are written, they will characterize the 1990s as the decade when the walls inside companies began to fall. Facing the imperative of improving performance, companies systematically knocked down the boundaries that separated internal functional and geographic units. As explored in Chapter 4, they did so by implementing ERP systems (integrated software systems) and by focusing on end-to-end business processes. These boundaries had been responsible for a host of performance problems that defied every previous attempt at amelioration. They led to vast amounts of non-value-adding work, because each department had to devote significant resources to interfacing with the other departments from whom it got or to whom it sent its work. Checking, logging, assigning, prioritizing, scheduling, auditing, and controlling are a few of the non-value-adding and time-consuming activities that arose as a result of intracompany walls. The consequences of so much non-value-adding work included massive delays, high error rates, excessive costs, and unresponsiveness to customer needs. These problems stubbornly persisted until companies confronted their underlying causes head-on. Fortunately, the concerted efforts in the 1990s to address these problems by bulldozing the barriers responsible for them bore remarkable fruit. By deploying the apparatus of process, companies achieved breathtaking performance improvements.

Thus, The Last Big Thing was demolishing the walls *within* enterprises. The Next Big Thing that will dominate business discourse for the coming decade is the destruction of walls *between* enterprises. However high and problematic the walls between functional and geographical units within an enterprise may be, they are dwarfed by inter-enterprise walls—especially those that separate a company from its suppliers and its customers. A company's marketing and engineering departments may view each other as "the other," but their mutual disregard is insignificant compared with that between a buyer and a seller. Though two departments in a company may seek to optimize diverse measures, they are still far more aligned than the bottom lines of distinct companies. The overhead costs that accompany a request from one unit of a company to another pale in comparison to the paperwork and non-value-adding work associated with an intercompany transaction. The reluctance of different parts of a company to share information with one another looks like eagerness next to a company's refusal to share information with a supplier or a customer.

The sharply defined boundaries behind which companies work and across which they communicate are so deeply wired into our assumptions about business that we scarcely notice them. They are the legacy of an era when company managers had their hands full keeping their own ship on course and could spare no concern for other vessels bobbing in the sea around them. The traditional company regarded everyone outside its fortress walls with profound suspicion. Enterprises treated each other as at best necessary evils—the source of a required good or service, or a means of turning production into revenue. It was a Hobbesian world of "war of everyone against everyone."

If we have become blind to these walls, we have also become inured to their high costs. Corporate walls exact a high tariff in the coin of non-value-adding overhead on everything that passes over them. The penalties are the same as in the intracompany context—costs, delays, complexity, inventories, and the rest of the familiar litany—only much magnified.

The recent experiences of one company highlight the prodigious costs of intercompany walls. Geon, a major chemical company based in Avon Lake, Ohio, is the world's largest producer of vinyl (PVC) compound. Once a part of BF Goodrich, Geon was at the time of which I write an independent company with approximately $1.3 billion in sales. (It has since merged with M.A. Hanna, and the combined entity is known as PolyOne.)

Originally, Geon was a vertically integrated business. It bought chlorine and ethylene from suppliers and used them to create VCM (vinyl chloride monomer), the business's basic raw material. VCM was transformed into resin, which in turn was converted into useful compounds by adding pigment and oils and by performing other types of engineering. In the mid-1990s, Geon initiated an effort to break down the walls within the company in order to create greater customer value, enhance customer service, and reduce costs. The company followed a program that is by now familiar: integrating and simplifying its end-to-end business processes and implementing an ERP system to support them. This work allowed information and transactions to flow seamlessly between different parts of the company, enabling them to operate in concert. As a result, the percentage of orders shipped on time soared, customer complaints almost vanished, the need to pay premium freight rates caused by schedule foul-ups shrank to nothing, inventory levels were slashed, and productivity got a boost. In financial terms, costs were reduced by tens of millions of dollars, and working capital went from over 16 percent of sales to under 14 percent. These are remarkable results indeed.

Then in 1999 Geon recognized that it did not have the sales volume necessary to produce VCM and resins in the quantities that would make it cost competitive, and so it changed its business strategy. It decided to focus entirely on the compounding side of the business, which was higher value-adding, dependent less on scale than on clever engineering to meet specific customer needs. In support of the new strategy, Geon divested its VCM and resins operations to a joint venture with Occidental Chemicals called OxyVinyls, which became its primary supplier of raw materials.

While Geon's actions were strategically sound, they were operationally disastrous. In effect, the company erected a high (intercompany) wall between itself and OxyVinyls, where it had just demolished a low (intracompany) one. VCM and resin production had just been integrated with compounding, and now they were disintegrated. What had recently merely been separate departments now became parts of separate companies. Information was no longer shared; overhead was reintroduced; and disconnection replaced synchronization.

When part of Geon's integrated production/order fulfillment process became hidden behind the walls of OxyVinyls, its smooth operation was replaced by herky-jerky, start-and-stop activity. Neither Geon nor its new supplier knew how much inventory the other had. Each was unaware of the other's shipments, and neither understood much about the other's demand. Geon's planning horizon of six to eight weeks was reduced to two to four weeks.

The higher overhead and greater formality that are necessary for conducting business with an outside party caused the time needed to process orders to jump. Expediters, schedulers, and a host of clerical personnel were required to manage the interface between Geon and OxyVinyls; a vast amount of work had to be performed twice, once on each side of the new divide. Unsurprisingly, this added work added costs. Errors multiplied as documents were hurled back and forth across battlements. Data now had to be entered twice: once at Geon and once at OxyVinyls. The result was an 8 percent error rate on orders from Geon to OxyVinyls: wrong purchase order numbers, wrong product numbers, wrong prices, wrong just about everything.

Virtually all of the benefits gleaned through the painstaking work of process integration were lost, and in many ways the situation became even worse than it had been before Geon's internal integration had begun. The net result of the split between Geon and OxyVinyls was that inventories increased by 15 percent, working capital went up by 12 percent, and Geon's order-fulfillment-cycle time tripled. Anyone who doubts the penalties of corporate walls should contemplate Geon's experience.

The 1990s taught us that internal walls are there to be broken, and we are now learning that the same is true of external walls. The new mandate for companies is to knock down their boundaries in order to integrate, simplify, and redesign their intercorporate business processes. This means recognizing that, just as corporate departments are components of larger business processes, whole enterprises are components of larger interenterprise business processes. It means understanding that even when overhead has been ground out of intra-company processes, their intercompany counterparts are still awash in it, and that the key to getting rid of it is taking a holistic end-to-end view of these processes. By taking such a view, corporate boundaries can be ignored, and ways can be found to eliminate or at least lessen overhead, redundant work, delays, and inventory. This means recognizing that, to paraphrase John Donne, no company is an island. A company cannot succeed by defeating its suppliers and customers. Ultimately, what is in the best interests of all will be in the best interests of each.

The old Washington maxim "Politics stops at the water's edge" signifies that partisan squabbling should be put aside in the realm of foreign policy. Similarly, until now, processes and the information systems that support them have stopped at the corporate edge. No longer. Now we recognize that corporate boundaries are no less artifacts than functional ones, and that processes may span them as well.

As noted in Chapter 4, virtually every company has an order fulfillment process that turns orders into deliveries. But my order fulfillment process is merely the counterpart of your procurement process, which begins when you realize you need my goods or services and ends when you receive them. If viewed and managed as two separate processes, a substantial amount of overhead and redundancy accumulate at the border between them. You enter a requisition into your computer system, print it out as an order, and then send it to me so I can enter the same data into my computer. The whole procedure is repeated when I calculate, print, and send the invoice, so you can reenter the data into your computer system in order to issue a payment. This is absurd. The route to ridding ourselves of this absurdity, and of the overhead it engenders, starts by recognizing that these two processes should in fact be seen together as just one.

This new perspective is enabled by new technology, specifically the Internet. Just as ERP systems were the fundamental technology of enterprise business integration, the Internet is the critical technology for interenterprise process integration. In fact, this represents the true significance of the Internet, which has been and remains the subject of an enormous amount of discussion and a great deal of misunderstanding. Perhaps that is not surprising, since most technologies are poorly understood in their early days. When Thomas Alva Edison invented the phonograph, he thought its purpose would be to record the "deathbed wishes of dying gentlemen." When Marconi invented the radio, he thought its purpose was to replace telegraphy—hence the name wireless. Future businesspeople, looking back on our recent obsessions with portals and dot-com retailers, will undoubtedly ask, "What were they thinking?"

In fact, the real power of the Internet lies in its capacity to integrate intercorporate business processes and the information systems that support them. This, in effect, takes a sledgehammer to the walls that separate companies from one another.

Over the last two decades, a variety of tools have been employed to streamline communications over corporate boundaries, from the fax to EDI (electronic data interchange), but all these technologies were cumbersome, expensive, and very limited. Now the Internet, combined with a set of related technologies, such as XML and higher-level protocols like RosettaNet, is enabling the integration of processes in different companies into larger units. Company boundaries will never be the same.

Geon, our poster company for the problems of intercompany walls, has become one of the leaders in demolishing those walls. It has used the Internet to connect its processes and the computer systems that support them with counterpart processes and systems at OxyVinyls and its customers. Geon's forecasting process now works collaboratively with the one at OxyVinyls; as soon as Geon uses information gleaned from customers to forecast its future demand for compounds, that forecast is transmitted to OxyVinyls and incorporated into the latter's forecast for resins and monomers. Within twenty-four hours of receiving an actual order from one of its customers, Geon translates that order into the materials it will need from OxyVinyls and automatically dispatches an order; this order goes directly into OxyVinyls's own internal order fulfillment process and system. Similarly, order acknowledgments and order confirmations, advance shipment notifications, and invoices automatically go from OxyVinyls back to Geon. Recently, Geon has gone a step further. It has put sensors into the warehouses of some of its major customers, so that now it knows how much of its compounds the customer has in stock. When that figure declines to an agreed-upon level,

Geon does not wait for the customer to order but automatically replenishes the customer's stocks. (This, of course, is a version of our old friend VMI from Chapter 3.) In other words, the processes of three enterprises—the procurement process for Geon's customer, the order fulfillment and procurement processes in Geon, and order fulfillment in OxyVinyls—have now all been integrated. They are no longer unrelated processes beset by friction and overhead. They operate as one streamlined unit in which corporate boundaries have become completely irrelevant.

The payoffs prove the point. The 8 percent error rate in orders has fallen to 0 percent; the order-fulfillment-cycle time has reversed its 200 percent increase; inventories have declined 15 percent; labor costs have gone down, as non-value-adding work has been eliminated; and people have been reassigned from piecing together the process to performing higher-level work on behalf of customers. In short, Geon has made a round trip, first building a wall, then taking it down, and finally returning to the high performance levels it had at the outset.

Some will cast this story as an illustration of the effects of interconnecting independent information systems using the Internet. While this technological description is accurate, it misses the key underlying point. In Geon's story, separate processes in separate companies have been connected and combined and now work like one. Though Geon and OxyVinyls are, in fact, separate corporate entities, they work together as smoothly and as effortlessly as they did when OxyVinyls's production units were part of Geon itself.

Much has changed as a result of this newly integrated process. For instance, the job of the production planner has been transformed. In the old days, production planners spent a lot of their time on the phone trying (often in vain) to find out what was going on in the other organization. Now that information is readily available to them, and production planners can concentrate on using it effectively. They also now have the time and information to handle complex exceptional situations—which are increasingly unexceptional. For instance, production planners at

Geon and OxyVinyls can collaborate to adapt to tight markets for raw materials, by rescheduling production runs and changing shipment plans in ways that work for both companies; one side may agree to accept a later shipment, another to reallocate plant capacity. In other words, people in the two companies work together to meet both sides' needs, instead of laboring in vacuums to solve their narrow problems.

As jobs and responsibilities change, so do measures. In the past, Geon's purchasing agents were primarily measured on the price they negotiated with suppliers, because that was about the only thing that they could control. While having enough raw material to avoid schedule breaks was important, purchasing agents were not held accountable for that because it was presumed to be beyond their control. Now that the integrated process gives Geon's people visibility of suppliers' schedules, purchasing agents are accountable for availability as well as price.

When people work in an integrated intercompany process, they also develop a better understanding of what goes on inside the other company and how they affect its performance and therefore the performance of the process as a whole. Geon's procurement and planning people now appreciate how small orders mean higher shipping costs for OxyVinyls, and they have changed their behavior accordingly; as a result, OxyVinyls's costs have gone down, as has the price that Geon pays.

Underlying and enabling all these changes has been a shift in attitude and culture. In the past, Geon, like most companies, viewed its suppliers as adversaries in a zero-sum game. One won at the other's expense, whether in terms of price, inventory, or risk. Now the two companies recognize that they are in the process together and that the goal is not to shift cost and risk from one to the other but to eliminate it from the process altogether. This new perspective is embodied in common goals and in agreed-upon principles for sharing costs and benefits.

Geon and OxyVinyls are not alone in smashing the walls that separate them. FMC's Alkali Chemicals Division (the world's largest producer of natural soda ash) has collaborated with its customer PQ Corporation (a privately held producer of inorganic chemicals) to integrate one's procurement process with the other's order fulfillment process. Adaptec, based in Milpitas, California, has done much the same. Adaptec is what is called a "fabless" semiconductor company, meaning it doesn't fabricate its products. Instead, Adaptec works with customers to identify integrated circuits that will fit into the customers' products, and then its engineers create designs for these circuits. Suppliers in Asia are sent the designs and orders. The Asian partners manufacture the chips, assemble and package them, and send them back.

This sounds simple enough, but until 1997 it was enormously difficult. When seen as one process, it involved Adaptec's California operations; the Taiwanese contractor, Taiwanese Semiconductor Manufacturing Corporation, known as TSMC, which made the chips; another company in Hong Kong that packaged them; and an Adaptec facility in Singapore that assembled the final products for shipping. Each time an order moved to the next company, so did the information, which had to be printed out of one computer system, transmitted, and reentered into the next company's computer system. In practice, it was a nightmare.

It took four to six days simply to get the information into a format that could be faxed from Adaptec to TSMC. Detailed drawings were printed out on large sheets of paper, then cut and pasted onto fax-size paper. Specification sheets had to be printed, compiled with the drawings, and integrated into an overall purchase order. More time was required at the other end. When the fabricator received the faxes, its engineers had to inspect them for transmission clarity, request retransmission of any problems, manually enter the data into their computer systems, and scan the drawings as well.

Inevitably, errors crept into each step, requiring work to be repeated and causing more delays. If TSMC's engineers had suggestions for making the design easier to manufacture, the entire process had to be repeated in reverse. Typically, it took more than thirty days just to finalize the engineering designs for production.

Given the fast-changing nature of the semiconductor business, customers sometimes insisted on a change in a chip design while it was still in production. Everything then stopped cold for days or weeks until the new drawings arrived. Often the fabricator could not hold Adaptec's place in its production queue, and the project slipped to the bottom of the list. This whole comedy of errors repeated itself at each subsequent stage in the process. Adding insult to injury, all these problems were magnified by the fifteen-hour time difference between California and Taiwan.

These problems were intolerable. Adaptec's managers calculated that it shouldn't take more than fifty-five days to turn around an order. In practice, it was taking 110.

In the world of semiconductors, where a customer's need for products can pop up literally overnight and can vanish just as quickly, doubling the minimum time needed to fill an order is a recipe for disaster. The financial consequences were also severe. All that data reentry generated extra costs, and the lethargic process created a pipeline full of work-in-process inventory that had to be financed.

Adaptec has solved these problems by integrating processes across company boundaries. Via the Internet, all the information that used to be printed, pasted, and faxed is now sent from Adaptec's systems directly to the fabricator's production systems. What used to take four to six days now takes minutes. The fabricator's engineers can review the designs and suggest revisions to Adaptec electronically. The turnaround time for finalizing a design is now ten days at most, a 66 percent improvement. Communicating with the assemblers and shippers is equally swift. Time is relentlessly squeezed out of the process at every step.

The benefits have been extraordinary. Manufacturing time is now down by 50 percent to fifty-five days—the original goal. Among other advantages, inventory carrying costs have been reduced by $9 million, and are now half the industry average. Moreover, Adaptec no longer has to spread its fabrication work across numerous suppliers to be sure that an unanticipated spike in demand can be handled. Instead of keeping six suppliers in reserve, Adaptec needs only two. Maintaining a relationship with a supplier costs about $1 million a year, so the consolidation from six to two produced an immediate saving of $4 million. All of this resulted from leveling the walls separating Adaptec from its suppliers.

Similarly, IBM has integrated its hiring process with processes at the personnel search firms it employs. IBM is increasingly a service business and, like all service organizations, finds itself having to respond to customer requests for proposals in short order. Frequently, the customer's statement of work calls for tasks that can be performed only by people with specific skills or in specific places, people whom IBM may not have available; in situations where the required skills are not available internally, the company goes to a search firm to fill the gap. In the past, it did so through a flurry of paper: position descriptions, résumés, and more. Now IBM posts position descriptions on a Web site; the search firms access it and post proposed résumés on the same site for IBM to inspect; as a result, a process that often took a week can now frequently be done in one day. Once again the Internet was the enabling technology, but the real issue was linking activities in different companies into a single boundary-spanning process.

Once we recognize our interenterprise processes, we can get to work on redesigning them and thereby improve how they perform. The most rudimentary redesign is the kind that Geon, FMC, IBM, and Adaptec have done: streamlining the connection between the parts of the process that reside in different companies. This technique slashes delays, eliminates redundant activity, and reduces costs and errors. Another way in which an interenterprise process can be redesigned is moving work across corporate boundaries. If you are in a better position to do some work that I have been doing in the past, it can make sense for you to start doing it—even if that work is "officially" my responsibility. The increased costs you incur in doing the work will be more than offset by the benefits of improving the process as a whole, benefits that will accrue to both of us. (If this sounds familiar, that is because it is a variation on the theme of customer self-service that was discussed in Chapter 2.)

For instance, IBM estimated in 1998 that it spent $233 on handling every order that it received from customers. Twenty percent of that sum went for "order management"—getting the order in, making sure that it was at the appropriate price for this particular customer, answering customer questions about payment status, and the like. Much of the order management overhead was an artifact from the time when IBM sat behind an opaque wall, screened from its customers. Thus all customer interactions had to be mediated by an IBM employee—frequently, a sales rep. By knocking down the wall between itself and its customers, IBM has integrated its fulfillment process with its customers' procurement processes and redesigned this larger process. Now customers can do for themselves much of the work that IBM had previously done for them—and do so more conveniently and at lower cost. As explained in Chapter 2, customers now can enter their own orders, check the status of these orders, and the like. IBM wins because its costs are lower; the customers win because they get the work done correctly and when they want, and they are spared the burden of interacting with IBM's personnel. There are other benefits as well. One important set of customers (value-adding resellers) has been able to reduce inventories of IBM equipment by more than 30 percent. Since they can get orders into IBM's process more quickly and can find out when the orders will actually be filled, they get by with less on hand. This makes them happier customers, which IBM knows are more loyal customers.

On the other hand, IBM is also now doing work that some customers previously had to do for themselves. IBM's large corporate customers typically standardize the computers they use throughout their organizations. Everyone in the company who orders a PC is supposed to order the standard configuration. But in practice, many people would get the specifications wrong or make other mistakes in creating the order; it was not uncommon for IBM to see an error rate in excess of 50 percent in orders from corporate customers. In effect, the customer's ordering process was defective (in not screening out inappropriate orders), and

IBM had to compensate. Now IBM has taken over the work of vetting customer orders. The customer provides IBM with a complete description of the approved configuration. IBM then presents buyers in the customer organization with the opportunity to order only this configuration. Both IBM and the customer win because they have to spend less time cleaning up the aftermath of inaccurate orders.

Coordination—allowing two companies to use exactly the same data—is a third way to improve the performance of an interenterprise process. In traditional organizations, information never gets past the corporate doorway. In part, this is because the limitations of technology have made it difficult even for companies that wanted to share information to do so. In part, it is because nobody actually wanted to. The widespread closed-door policy of "We know what we know, you know what you know, and never the twain shall meet" reflected companies' mistrust of everyone else. But this lack of information sharing has serious consequences. When companies know only about themselves and not about their customers or suppliers, they make all kinds of decisions with inadequate information. I'm not referring only to broad strategic decisions but to the day-to-day tactical and operational decisions that determine how a company works: How much should we produce? What material do we need? How many people should work in what locations? How much transportation will we need?

Making these decisions well is fundamental to any company's success. Without accurate information about the state of the world outside its boundaries, a company simply cannot do so. In the past, companies typically guessed at what their suppliers were capable of delivering, at what future demand might be, and at how much shipping space they could expect from their carriers, who in turn could only guess at the exact size of their customers' shipments.

Bad decisions are the result of guessing, and they lead to wrong schedules, wrong materials, and people with the wrong skills assigned to jobs. All this means waste—unused supplies, idle people, and goods moldering in warehouses because they are never ordered.

This situation changes when companies share information across boundaries, which is now easy to do. Imagine a world in which your company is aware of your suppliers' production plans and how much raw material they have. Imagine also knowing your customers' current supply of your products, as well as their customers' demand for those products. Imagine knowing precisely how much capacity your truckers have at any moment, and exactly where each of your incoming and outgoing shipments is right now—anywhere on earth. What's truly amazing is that all this information has always existed, carefully recorded by each of these companies. Collecting it has never been the challenge; sharing it across company boundaries has.

Matthew Arnold's poem "Dover Beach" captures how companies that haven't yet discovered collaboration through shared information operate: "And we are here as on a darkling plain / Swept with confused alarms of struggle and flight / Where ignorant armies clash by night."

Such was the darkness that enveloped a major beverage company and one of its key suppliers, a packaging manufacturer. Periodically, the beverage company forecasted its expected sales, estimated its packaging needs, and shared this information with the supplier, so that when it sent an order for packaging material, the supplier would presumably be ready to handle it. The problem was that the forecasts often changed, and the customer often didn't share these changes with the packaging supplier until much later. The beverage manufacturer might hear of a major convention to be held in Chicago that would generate a spike in sales there, and in response, it would reschedule production. Logic would suggest informing the packager, so it could update its production schedule as well. But that is not what happened. The walls between the two organizations were so high that the beverage maker's production planner did not know whom to contact at the packaging company. In short, communication and collaboration were too much trouble.

The production planner would shrug his or her shoulders and decide that the supplier would just have to cope. Eventually and inevitably, the beverage maker presented the supplier with an order for which the latter was not prepared. The supplier might then have to put on extra shifts, or hire extra people, or rob Peter to pay Paul by diverting packaging materials from another destination to Chicago, causing a shortfall in the other location and rippling consequences throughout the system.

That's no longer the case. The two companies now use the Internet to share information between their planning and production processes. As soon as the beverage maker's production planner has new information, she revises the forecast and posts it on a Web site programmed to send the new forecast to the packaging company. Now the supplier's production planner can prepare for either a surge or a cutback in orders. If the packager needs to divert materials from one location to another, this is also posted on the Web site, programmed to automatically transfer the information to the beverage company. Planners there are then in a position to adjust production schedules to the new packaging delivery schedule. In effect, by sharing information, the two companies are performing a single interenterprise planning process.

The vision that now becomes attainable is for an entire supply chain to operate in harmony and synchrony. The raw materials supplier can decide how much to produce of what, based on sales of final products on retailers' shelves. The manufacturer can decide what to ship, based on how many trucks the shipping company actually has available. It is a vision of a frictionless environment.

The term *supply chain*, like many other business terms, has been co-opted, debased, and reduced to a euphemism for procurement, much as *human resources* has become a politically correct name for personnel. In fact, however, a company's supply chain comprises all enterprises, both upstream and downstream, that contribute to creating the final product that is purchased by a final customer. Perhaps the most graphic definition of a supply chain has come from a large manufacturer of paper products, including bathroom tissue. This company says its supply chain stretches "from stump to rump."

The more extended a supply chain, the less one end of it knows about what is transpiring at the other, and the more transactions proliferate as products are repeatedly rebought and resold. The consequences can be staggering amounts of inventory and enormous, pointless costs. Hewlett-Packard is aggressively working to address these problems, harnessing the power of collaboration to synchronize the work of an extended supply chain to the benefit of all its members.

A typical purchaser of an HP computer monitor probably has no idea how many companies are involved in producing it. HP, like most computer makers, has outsourced much of its manufacturing to contract manufacturers, such as Solectron and Celestica. The contract manufacturer buys the case for the monitor from an injection molder, who in turn acquires the material used to make the case from a plastics compounder (Geon is an example), who in turn buys the resin from which the compound is formed from a resin maker. This supply chain is easy to describe and almost impossible to manage.

The suppliers at the other end of the chain from HP have no idea how many monitors HP will actually need; they may not even know that HP is the ultimate destination for their resin or compound. Consequently, each must carry a lot of inventory "just in case" an HP order comes barreling down the chain. Conversely (and perhaps inevitably), the inventory that they do carry is sometimes not what HP needs at the moment, and so when HP orders a certain kind of monitor, its upstream suppliers may have plenty of the wrong material on hand and none of the right one. As a result, HP won't have the product that its customer wants when the customer wants it, and so the customer will go elsewhere, which means that everyone in the supply chain loses revenue. Similarly, problems that arise in the commercial interactions among upstream suppliers (such as a dispute over terms or a delay in payment) can lead to delays in the delivery of material from one supplier to the next in the chain, which in turn means that HP will not have the monitors it needs when it needs them.

The disparity in scale among the participants in this supply chain has some peculiar consequences. HP and the resin supplier are giant companies, and the contract manufacturers are fairly substantial in their own right. But most injection molders are relatively small outfits, as are compounders. This means that HP's monitor case orders are likely to be split among many compounders, each of which will be buying in relatively small volume—and consequently at relatively high price—from resin makers. HP's potential purchasing clout dissipates at each step in the chain that separates it from its ultimate supplier, the resin maker. In effect, HP is insulated from its suppliers of resins and compounds by its contract manufacturers and injection molders. This means that HP does not have a big picture of the performance of its upstream suppliers, in terms of which ones are consistently providing the best terms, quality, and delivery. (Nor, it should be noted, does anyone else.) HP also does not hear about new ideas these suppliers have that might affect the design and specifications of HP monitors.

Finally, in any lengthy and complex chain like this one, it is inevitable that a lot of people will be trying to hold it together. In theory, once HP places an order, its suppliers should be ready to roll. In reality, nothing stays fixed for long. On the average, each order for a batch of computer monitors changes four times before completion, usually in response to shifts in marketplace demand. Quantity, required delivery date, and color are just a few of the things that change. In other words, exception is the rule. Problems can also crop up in the supply chain itself: Production snags occur, manpower is scarce, materials run short—all sorts of surprises can ruin the best plans. As was the case with the beverage manufacturer, these changes are not easily communicated among companies. A veritable army of people gets pressed into service to try to keep everyone on the same page, but they rarely succeed in doing so. The contractor's production systems will inevitably have different information from what its suppliers have regarding arrivals, shipments, and requested quantities. The results will be wasted effort, delays, piles of unused materials, and frantic efforts to expedite shipments at the last minute.

The fundamental issue underlying all these problems is that no one was managing the end-to-end process that began at HP and ended with the resin supplier. An army of people, dispersed among the different companies and using a host of unrelated information systems, was holding the process together on an ad hoc basis, with great cost and wasted effort, but no one was truly managing it. In 1999 HP stepped into this breach and resolved to become the active manager of the entire process. Instead of abdicating responsibility to its supply chain and pushing risk onto its suppliers, HP now acts as the coordinator of the process that links the entire plastics supply chain together. HP has assumed the responsibility of ensuring that all parties in the supply chain are working together, sharing information, and operating in a way that ensures lowest cost and highest availability for all.

The enabler of this newly integrated process is a computer system that HP set up for information sharing among all the supply chain participants. HP posts its demand forecast as well as any changes for all to use in their own forecasting. Similarly, plans and schedules of the other participants are also made visible. If any problems crop up in the supply chain's ability to meet HP's forecasts, HP learns about it early enough to make other plans. Each party also uses this facility to communicate with its neighbors; they send each other electronic orders, acknowledgments, and invoices. Thus changes to HP's orders ripple through the supply chain instantaneously, allowing everyone to react quickly.

Perhaps most important, the resin maker now gets an aggregate forecast from HP, which is the basis for a contract price that governs all the resin that it puts into HP's supply chain. After all, HP is really the party buying the resin; the compounder is merely the first link in the chain. Now HP is acting as the resin maker's customer, even though the product is delivered to various compounders. The resin maker sends HP a single bill for all the resin. This system is much better for the resin maker, because it provides the simplicity and security of dealing with one large customer rather than a host of small ones, and so it is happy to offer HP significant price reductions in exchange.

HP's procurement people now operate as the managers of this intercompany process. No longer focused narrowly on terms and conditions, their new job is to ensure the smooth functioning of the process. They monitor the performance of upstream suppliers; they intervene to resolve problems relating to the flow of funds between these suppliers; they reach out to the entire supply chain to avoid mismatches between supply and demand and to mitigate risk. It is a far cry from the traditional role of the purchasing agent.

In this situation, everyone benefits, though HP may benefit more than anyone else. In the pilot implementations of this newly integrated process, the price that HP pays for resins has gone down between 2 and 5 percent, the number of people needed to stitch together the supply chain has been reduced 50 percent, and the time it takes to fill an order for a computer monitor is down 25 percent. Perhaps best of all, HP estimates that it is increasing sales in the areas where this process has been implemented by 2 percent. These are sales that HP had previously lost because it could not get the right product at the right time. HP no longer has to commit the mortal sin of turning customers away. Knocking down intercorporate walls is a wonderful thing.

HP and its suppliers have redesigned their interenterprise process using all three mechanisms I have outlined. Connections between buyers and sellers are streamlined as transactions flow electronically; work that compounders previously did (buying resin) has been moved across corporate boundaries to HP; and all parties operate with a common database of demand and production information. The walls separating these companies from each other have become so thin, they can hardly be discerned. HP works as closely and seamlessly with its supply chain as it would were they all parts of HP—perhaps more so. They are truly operating in a collaborative fashion. Reengineering interenterprise processes to achieve tight collaboration is the way to finish the job started by the intraenterprise reengineering of the 1990s: rooting out the final vestiges of unproductive work in your company.

The consumer packaged goods industry is another that is very sensitive to losing sales because of product unavailability; yet in the past that was too often the case. Manufacturers and retailers would both develop sales forecasts for the manufacturer's products, but since they were developed independently, the forecasts were often inconsistent, leading to stock-outs in the stores or unneeded inventory in the warehouses. The manufacturer might be planning a new advertising campaign or the retailer might schedule a promotion without the other side knowing about it. The underlying problem was that the manufacturer and the retailer were each performing their own forecasting process, uncoordinated with the other's. Increasingly, they are now combining these separate forecasting processes into a single one. Kimberly-Clark and Kmart have applied such a single process to Kleenex tissue, with remarkable results: a 14 percent increase in retail in-stock, a 20 percent reduction in retail inventory, and more than a 17 percent jump in sales revenue. When companies operate in sync, everybody wins.

The power of collaboration is also being felt in the pharmaceutical industry. There as in many other industries that work through distributors, very large customers (such as major hospital systems) can negotiate special prices with the drug makers. A hospital's orders are filled by its local distributor, to whom it pays a special price, even if that price is significantly lower than the distributor's usual charges. Under an arrangement called "chargeback," the distributor can bill the manufacturer for an agreed-upon amount to compensate for its lost margin.

You don't have to be a pharmaceutical expert to recognize that this situation is ripe for chaos. Every player is likely to have different information on prices and on precisely what has been sold. There may be three different versions of how much product was delivered to the hospital; how much chargeback the distributor is entitled to; what the hospital agreed to pay in the first place; and what terms have been worked out between the manufacturer and the distributor. Even if the versions happen to coincide, that will end when the hospital renegotiates its contract with the manufacturer and the latter changes the terms of its deal with the distributor.

Two evils result. First, these discrepancies lead to lots of (mostly futile) reconciliation effort, then more work to repair the inevitable hard feelings. Each company has people whose only job it is to talk to their counterparts in the other institutions, clarify the arrangements, and correct errors. The second is that much of the time someone pays too little. Either the hospital pays the distributor too little, or the distributor expects more chargeback from the manufacturer than he gets. To maintain distributor and customer relationships and goodwill, the manufacturer is frequently the one to absorb these errors and write off significant lost revenue as the cost of doing business. It is hard to decide which of these two problems is worse.

Now at least one major pharmaceutical house has streamlined the process of which all these parties are but parts. A single version of pricing and delivery information is posted on a Web site, which everyone shares. When a contract is negotiated, it is entered into the Web site, as are records of actual deliveries to hospitals. The distributor then knows how much to bill the hospital, and the hospital knows what to pay the distributor; the distributor and the manufacturer also agree on the amount of the rebate. Sharing one database eliminates the imperfections and costs that inevitably accrue in the wake of reconciliation.

Two oil companies have worked out a similar collaborative arrangement. With the recognition that virtually all gasoline, despite various advertising claims, is indistinguishable, oil companies buy and sell a lot of product among themselves to cut transportation costs and meet spot shortages. At the end of the month, every oil company sends a bill to every other one, and payments follow the reverse path.

Given the thousands of transactions between these two companies every month, errors are inevitable. Each company has a different version of its transactions with the other, so time and energy are invested in reviewing all the transactions and determining whose information is correct. In the past, this task, which was performed manually by many people, could take as long as two months to complete.

Now the companies avoid the need for reconciliation almost entirely. Transactions between them are immediately recorded in a shared database that resides on a Web site, against which each company processes its financial transactions. As a result, more than 90 percent of the reconciliation work has been eliminated, and what still needs to be done is completed in hours rather than months. Neither company has to maintain cash to make unexpected payments to the other at the end of the month.

Most of the examples of collaboration reviewed thus far come from the area of supply chain management: harnessing a group of companies to work together to deliver what the final customer has requested. It is not surprising that the greatest progress in interenterprise process integration has taken place here. Just as the first internal process that most companies reengineered was order fulfillment, the first interenterprise process to receive similar attention has been supply chain. The pathologies besetting it are right on the surface, and addressing them yields immediate returns in terms of customer satisfaction and decreased costs.

Tantalizing opportunities in other areas are now starting to appear. The next major wave is likely to be collaborative product development. Here a company, its suppliers, and even its customers share (Web-based) information about a product as it is being created. Suppliers have the advantage of being able to begin developing the parts of the product that will be their responsibility before the overall design is complete; a supplier can also provide early feedback as to whether it thinks it can make its part within the specified cost and time constraints. Customers can review the product as it emerges and provide input that will ensure that what finally results meets their needs. Moreover, inevitable changes in customer needs, product specifications, and component designs are immediately available to all interested parties. There is no longer any reason for anyone to be out of the loop for weeks or even months, continuing to use information that is long out of date. Inter-enterprise collaborative product development is the multicompany ana-logue of concurrent engineering, which has transformed internal product development over the past fifteen years.

Building behind this wave of collaboration is an even larger wave that extends interenteprise process integration into previously uncharted territory. This wave is forcing us to find new words to describe business relationships that have heretofore been largely invisible to us.

The traditional vocabulary of business relationships is meager: If you sell me something, I am your customer, and you are my supplier; if someone else tries to sell me the same thing, he or she is your competi-tor. That's about it, because those were the only relationships that have made any difference to us. But what if you and I are both buying the same product or service from the same supplier? In the past, it was unlikely that either of us would discover that we had such a relation-ship, and if we did, the information would have been of little if any value. Consequently, we had no linguistic term to name it. Similarly, what if you and I sold different products, but to the same customer? We were not competitors, but what were we? Until today, we didn't care. Now we do.

General Mills, a giant in the business of consumer packaged goods, owns brands ranging from Cheerios to Yoplait. In this industry, margins have been steadily falling, as distribution channels consolidated and consumers became more selective. In the 1990s, General Mills led the industry in squeezing costs out of its supply chain. Remarkably, through increased purchasing effectiveness, manufacturing productiv-ity, and distribution efficiencies, General Mills's cost per case of prod-uct actually declined by 10 percent in the decade. But as the new decade dawned, the company's leaders realized that they would have to move beyond the confines of their linear supply chain in order to find new cost-savings opportunities. Just as they thought out of the box in the 1990s, they resolved to think out of the chain in the 2000s. Among their first ideas was a new approach to the distribution of their refrigerated products, like yogurt.

The refrigerator section of your supermarket is very different from the other aisles in more ways than might be obvious. In the "dry" categories of packaged goods, the top seven manufacturers (General Mills and Kraft, for example) together account for nearly 40 percent of a supermarket's sales. This means that each manufacturer is large enough to efficiently operate its own distribution network (trucks and warehouses) that moves its products from its factories to the supermarket's warehouses. In the refrigerated category, however, the top seven players represent less than 15 percent of the supermarket's sales, and all but one lacks the scale needed for a highly efficient dedicated distribution network. Nonetheless, each company has such a network, and unsurprisingly, they do not run as well as they should.

When a refrigerated truck laden with Yoplait leaves a General Mills warehouse headed for local supermarkets, it is unfortunately often not full. Even more often, the truck is carrying yogurt destined for multiple supermarkets, meaning that it will make several stops along the way. If the truck is delayed in traffic or encounters a snafu at one of its early stops, it may not make it to the final supermarket on its route that day. If that supermarket has just run an ad in the Sunday paper promoting Yoplait, it will confront angry consumers, and General Mills will face a frustrated supermarket.

General Mills realized that it could address these problems by working with another company previously outside its orbit: Land O'Lakes, the maker of butter and margarine. Instead of each operating its own less-than-optimal distribution network, the two decided to operate collaboratively. General Mills yogurt and Land O'Lakes butter now are loaded in the same warehouses and ride in the same trucks on their way to the same supermarkets. (Phrased in process terms, they have integrated their separate order fulfillment processes into a single shared one.) This means that trucks go out fuller; and since each is delivering more product to each supermarket, it has fewer stops on its route, so odds are good that it will make all of its scheduled deliveries. Significant cost savings and improved customer satisfaction for both manufacturers are the results. The two manufacturers are now working to let supermarkets order their products together and receive a single invoice.

This story echoes back to the discussion in Chapter 2 on the importance of presenting a single face to the customer. There the context was multiple parts of the same company—J&J and AlliedSignal Aerospace were among our examples. Here, I extend the concept to multiple companies. As a result of knocking down the wall that separates them and operating in a collaborative fashion, General Mills and Land O'Lakes appear to the supermarket as one company. Interestingly, one of General Mills's precepts regarding collaboration is that you can't do it with other companies until you can do it internally. The first step is for the different parts of your own company to work together; then you extend the notion outside.

General Mills and Land O'Lakes, formerly of no interest to each other, now have a deep and abiding relationship—but they lack a term to describe it. I propose the neologism *co-supplier* (*co* could stand for "complementary" or "collaborative"). They are noncompetitive suppliers to the same supermarkets, and it is to their mutual advantage (as well as that of the supermarkets) to find ways to work together.

This relationship between General Mills and Land O'Lakes has always existed, but invisibly. What is new is the companies' ability to exploit it. In the past, manually coordinating deliveries through a shared distribution network would have been a logistical nightmare. But the boundary-shattering catalyst of the Internet is making what has long been desirable into the suddenly feasible.

Co-customers is the obvious complementary term to refer to companies that purchase from a common supplier. The Internet facilitates their finding each other and enables them to deal with a supplier as though they were a single larger company with increased purchasing clout.

United Missouri Banks (UMB), a large regional bank, has recognized the power of building relationships with its co-customers.

Because of its size, UMB is able to negotiate advantageous prices with many of its suppliers (for products ranging from paper to furniture). Among its customers are many small local banks across the Midwest; UMB supplies them with a variety of financial products, as well as certain lending and back-office services. These small banks buy many of the same products from the same suppliers as UMB but at higher prices. In other words, they are both UMB's customers and its co-customers. Now the larger bank collaborates with the smaller ones for purchasing. It has created an Internet-based system through which it deals with its suppliers, and it allows its small bank customers to use it to do the same. Everyone wins here, including the suppliers. They are assured larger market share and do not have to issue bills directly to the small banks anymore. Instead, they send a consolidated invoice to UMB, which pays on its own behalf as well as for the small banks. UMB then bundles these charges with its other service fees to the small banks, not unlike the HP–resin maker relationship. UMB benefits in many ways: It receives a settlement fee for paying on behalf of the small banks; its purchasing volumes go up, and in turn its costs go down; and it holds its small bank customers even closer by providing an additional service. The small banks obviously benefit from lower prices and simplified purchasing. The next step is to broaden this collaborative to include the small banks' own customers, small retailers and manufacturers who would piggyback on the same facility, gleaning more benefits for everyone involved.

Some describe what UMB has done as creating a private e-marketplace. In contrast to the so-called public e-marketplaces that welcome all comers, only companies invited by UMB are part of this effort. But if you are intrigued by this idea and want to follow in UMB's footsteps, have a caution. Many companies have been led astray by the siren call of using e-marketplaces (private or public) to drive down supplier prices. The notion was that co-customers could use an e-marketplace to gang up on suppliers: use "price discovery" to locate the supplier offering the lowest price, then employ "demand aggregation" and "dynamic pricing" (such as reverse auctions) to drive that price down even further. Those who followed this path have been disappointed. Though the failures of e-marketplaces have not been as celebrated as the collapse of the B2C e-retailers, they have been just as devastating. The fundamental reason is that most suppliers do not in fact have a death wish; they are not willing to participate in an e-marketplace whose only rationale is to push them to the edge of bankruptcy. The fact that UMB's suppliers have benefited from this new process was not coincidental; it was essential. Only when all parties see the opportunity to realize benefits will they lower their guard and their boundaries. There is an old Wall Street saying that bears make money and bulls make money, but pigs get slaughtered. Those who try to grab all payoffs for themselves and leave nothing for others are paving their own road to the abattoir.

The more parties see an opportunity for benefit, the more benefits there are to go around. General Mills has proved this true by collaborating with both co-customers and co-suppliers in the area of collaborative logistics.

The U.S. trucking industry is enormously fragmented. There are more than 450,000 carriers, hundreds of thousands of shippers, and billions of shipments a year. In such an environment, it is not surprising that trucks end up underutilized. After all, if I hire a truck to ship goods from point A to point B, the likelihood is small that the trucker will find another shipper at point B. So the carrier moves an empty truck from B to the next destination where someone needs it. If you multiply this empty trip by millions, you can appreciate the scale of the dilemma. Approximately 20 percent of U.S. trucking capacity is moving empty at any point in time. The result, of course, is higher costs for everyone.

General Mills has played a lead role in putting together a consortium (or in our terms, a collaborative) of both shippers and carriers to address this problem. Say General Mills needs to ship goods from Cedar Rapids, Iowa, to Wells, Maine, on a certain date (or on a regular basis). It will post this information on the consortium's Web site, so that other shippers in the consortium can assess whether General Mills's need complements their own. Say Fort James Paper has a corresponding need to ship from Bangor, Maine, to Chicago, Illinois. This is a near-perfect match. This new pair of co-customers then posts its consolidated shipping requirement on the same site, where trucking companies check to see if the companies' needs coincide with their own schedules and availability. The consortium has rules regarding who gets to see whose shipping needs, which truckers get first crack at bidding, and how the cost savings that result from fewer empty trucks are to be shared among General Mills, Fort James Paper, and the carrier.

The details are too complex to explore here, but the nature of this collaboration is clear, as are the payoffs. Costs go down, because the smoothly running process means that everyone needs far fewer administrators. Furthermore, all resources, from inventory to trucks, are used more efficiently. The bottom line for General Mills has been millions of dollars in savings. In fact, the company has calculated that the internal rate of return on its investment in collaborative logistics puts it in the top 5 percent of all projects that General Mills has taken on in the last five years.

I have loosely said that "the Internet" is the enabling technology for transforming interenterprise processes, but that term is too vague. We need a more precise name for the Internet-based facility where transactions are passed and information is shared between collaborating companies, thereby enabling intercompany process integration and collaboration. A term that is starting to gain some currency and traction is *collaborative hub.* Where this hub is located, who owns and operates it, and on what technological platform it is based will all vary with the particulars of the context.

Interenterprise collaboration is terra completely incognita for most companies. If, in the last few years, some companies have made superficial nods toward "building partnerships with suppliers and customers," these have been mostly rhetorical flourishes or ad hoc projects. The notion that companies should work collaboratively with others is truly revolutionary.

I offer a few principles as guidelines for companies stepping into the uncharted waters of collaboration:

- *The (final) customer comes first.* All members of the collaborative must be aligned around meeting the needs of the customer, whom they ultimately work together to serve. Individual participants will need to submerge their narrower goals in service of this higher end. Participants in a collaborative must remember that an enterprise they have always considered a customer may in fact be merely a collaborator in serving the real customer.
- *The entire process should be designed as a unit.* Any collaborative process, be it product development, supply chain, or something else, needs to be thought through in holistic terms. Rather than each participant independently designing and implementing its own part of the larger process, everyone needs to work together on the big picture.
- *No activity should be performed more than once.* Eliminating duplication of activities across corporate boundaries is one of the slam-dunk opportunities of interenterprise process redesign.
- *Work should be done by whoever is in the best position to do it.* IBM enforces its customers' computer standards; HP buys resin for its suppliers' suppliers' suppliers. It defeats the purpose of a collaborative to attempt to be self-sufficient. Do what you do best, and let others do the same.
- *The entire collaborative should operate with one database.* When everyone shares the same version of all the information, reconciliation can be eliminated and assets can be deployed precisely and efficiently.

Companies forming collaboratives will need to find answers to questions they have never even asked before. Who should be trusted to build and own the hub? Should direct competitors be allowed into the collaborative? How do benefits get shared among collaborators? How is participation in multiple collaboratives coordinated? What are the risks associated with becoming dependent on collaborators, and how can they be ameliorated? At this point, we have barely identified these questions, much less developed the answers.

But it is already clear that the cultural shift to interenterprise collaboration will be difficult. For some managers, sharing information with other organizations, particularly those previously considered adversaries, will be very difficult. They will have to restrain impulses to capitalize on opportunities that would afford short-term advantage but sacrifice the long-term viability of the whole. Relying on others to perform the work that has long been considered part of a company's charter will also give pause to many. Collaboration requires rooting out deep-seated attitudes and practices, many of which have defined the essence of the company. The payoffs of collaboration are prodigious, but so are its challenges.

Interenterprise collaboration brings together several themes encountered earlier in this book: It builds on the notion of customer focus (Chapters 2 and 3); it extends processes (Chapter 4) across corporate boundaries; it erodes enterprise autonomy in a way analogous to the erosion of business unit autonomy (Chapter 7); and collaboratives of manufacturers and their intermediaries are, in effect, new distribution communities (Chapter 8).

Fundamentally, knocking down corporate walls requires redefining what it means to be a company. When two companies integrate their processes and operate with the same data, they are, in effect, operating as one company.

Robert Frost might have written the definitive treatise on corporate boundaries in his 1914 poem "Mending Wall." While he ironically quotes his neighbor's opinion that "good fences make good neighbors," Frost himself is of the view that "Before I built a wall I'd ask to know / What I was walling in or walling out." Frost was right. Good fences definitely do not make good corporate neighbors; they make enormous amounts of overhead. Fences wall in information and wall out cooperation. It is high time to stop mending walls and start tearing them down instead.

The consequences of doing so, however, are far-reaching. Once an enterprise breaches its external walls and begins to work closely with others, it can come to question its very identity. Does independent existence have meaning when a company is no longer self-contained, when it can do its business only by working with others? With the power of collaboration, is your company still a company, or is it part of something larger?

The answer to that metaphysical riddle is the subject of our next chapter.

Agenda Item 8

Redesign and Streamline Interenterprise Processes

- Root out the remaining sources of overhead, cost, and inventory by redesigning interenterprise processes.
- Streamline the connections between your processes and those of your customers and suppliers.
- Relocate work between companies so that it is done by whoever can do it best.
- Coordinate through open sharing of data between companies.
- Exploit the opportunity of collaborating with co-customers and co-suppliers.
- Face head-on the deep cultural challenges of intercompany cooperation and information sharing.

10

Extend Your Enterprise

Integrate Virtually, Not Vertically

I seem to spend much of my professional life in a one-sided conversation with Henry Ford. I suspect that he would not have thought much of me. He famously said, "History is more or less bunk," and as should be clear by now, I believe the best way to see where we are going is to see whence we have come. His view was that "nothing is particularly hard if you divide it into small jobs," which is a pretty complete rejection of my belief in process. Yet his presence looms so large over the course of business of the last hundred years that I find myself continually responding to his ideas and his work.

After all, although the industrial era began in eighteenth-century England, the modern corporation came of age in twentieth-century America. And while a long line of U.S. business leaders, from Alfred Sloan to Jack Welch, helped to shape and define the contemporary enterprise, no figure had more impact on how we organize and operate businesses than did Henry Ford. It is no coincidence that both *Fortune* and *The Economist* named him businessperson of the twentieth century. His ideas have dominated how people have been thinking about business for the last hundred years.

Ford might not have invented the assembly line, but he was the first to implement it on a grand scale. His Model T is the abiding symbol of mass production. His system of interchangeable parts put the final nail in the coffin of the preindustrial artisan and created the modern assembly line worker. His revolutionary five-dollar daily wage laid the foundation for a society in which workers would join the middle class and be able to buy the goods they produced. Many of his statements of business philosophy (such as "Even when I was young I suspected that much might be done in a better way," and "It is not the employer who pays wages; it is the product that pays wages") prefigured much contemporary thinking. But perhaps it was as an exponent of vertical integration that he had his longest-lasting effect on business ideas.

Henry Ford began to build the massive River Rouge complex near Detroit in 1917. Not merely an automobile assembly plant, it was an industrial complex that turned raw materials into finished goods. Freighters and railcars bearing iron ore, coal, and raw rubber from the Far East came into River Rouge, and out the other end came new Fords ready for the road.

River Rouge was a totally self-reliant operation that made nearly everything required to create the automobile that bore Henry Ford's name. At the complex, he made the steel for auto bodies and frames; parts from engines to brakes to tires; and glass for windshields. From his own forests came wood that was fashioned into paneling.

Why did Ford insist on creating such an autarky—a self-contained economic enterprise? Because he was a fervent advocate of the power of vertical integration. To Ford, verticality spelled victory. Think about the ladder of Chapter 3, on which a company's customers sit at the top and its raw materials are at the bottom. To get from the bottom to the top, a whole universe of transformations must be performed. Parts have to be made and assembled; goods must be transported; the customer must be convinced to buy the product. Under vertical integration, this entire ladder—that is, the entire value chain—is occupied by a single organization. In the first half of the twentieth century, vertical integration was the ideal toward which companies aspired.

Why?

For one thing, the more of the value chain a company controls, the more profit it keeps. Why buy parts from parts makers, who will take their own profit? Why not make the parts and keep that margin for yourself?

For another, if someone else makes your parts, your cars are hostage to that company and its mistakes. Why depend on others who might let you down? If suppliers sell you defective parts, you can't use them. If the trucking company runs late, your cars won't reach dealers on time, and you can't sell empty showrooms. In Ford's view, reliance on any company but his own posed dangers he had no interest in taking. He lived by the adage "If you want something done right, do it yourself."

If Ford had lived a few more years, he would undoubtedly have adopted as his anthem one of the show-stopper songs from Irving Berlin's hit musical *Annie Get Your Gun*—"Anything You Can Do, I Can Do Better." Ford was positive that his vertically integrated company could do anything better than anyone else.

As the twentieth century wore on, the Platonic ideal of pure vertical integration became harder to achieve. In some cases, the government's trustbusters intervened, fearing that complete control of a value chain could lead to an undue concentration of market power. For example, the early movie studios not only made movies, they also owned the theaters in which they were shown. The U.S. Supreme Court ended this practice in 1948.

The realities of scarce capital also interfered with the pursuit of complete vertical integration. In times of growth, a company may have to choose between using its limited resources either to build another plant or to expand its trucking fleet. It can't do both, and it will have to rely on someone else to do the one it doesn't. Indeed, the changing mind-set of the investment community regarding corporate performance has shifted away from trying to capture the entire margin in the value chain through vertical integration. Today companies are not measured so much on profitability as on return on assets. If, in order to capture a marginal amount of profit in the value chain, a company has to invest a large amount of capital, say, by acquiring another company, its shares will soon be beaten down by outraged investors.

Nonetheless, because of its powerful appeal, the ideal of vertical integration endured long after the practice began to decline. But over the past decade, the concept has gone into full retreat. Indeed, it is now being replaced by its polar opposite, which I call *virtual integration*.

Instead of doing everything involved in creating a product or service, a virtually integrated business focuses on doing only certain things, those that it does better than anyone else. It works in close partnership with other organizations that also focus on what they do best, thus providing the final customer with the best result that a group of collaborating companies can achieve.

Virtual integration represents the deconstruction of the traditional company. It begins with a recognition that the old Ford formula no longer makes business sense. No company does everything equally well. Those that persist with vertical integration are bound to dilute what they do best with what they do poorly. It is better to triage: Take advantage of the fact that another company does well what you do less well, and vice versa. By pooling your strengths, you become stronger than either of you could be separately.

In what is surely one of the great ironies of modern business, Henry Ford's old company is itself taking this approach to auto manufacturing on the very site of his River Rouge colossus. For many years, automakers have not turned out their own tires or steel, and over the last decade, they have been making fewer parts as well. A typical auto manufacturer today uses thousands of suppliers who provide everything from nuts and bolts to finished brakes and steering-wheel assemblies.

Until very recently, all the auto manufacturers treated their suppliers in a way that old Henry would have approved of. Though they bought the suppliers' parts, they did so reluctantly. They saw suppliers as necessary evils, as the results of an inevitable compromise, but in their hearts, the automakers were nostalgic for the good old days of vertical integration. The automakers were suspicious of and condescended to their suppliers.

Ford designed its parts when it designed its vehicles, then decided which it wanted to make itself and which it did not. For those in the latter category, the company set rigid specifications. The suppliers were told exactly how to shape each part, what materials to use, and how much to bill. When instructed, they made the parts and sent them to Ford, where Ford workers inserted them into vehicles.

This has now changed. Ford recognizes that issuing a fait accompli with regard to part designs does not make the best use of its suppliers' expertise, which ought to be reflected in the designs of the parts and even in the design of the vehicle as a whole. After all, it makes little sense to design a vehicle that depends on hard-to-make parts. When parts were simpler, Ford had enough expertise to design them, but as they have become more and more complex, Ford can no longer assume it knows all it needs to know about designing them.

Accordingly, Ford is moving to a system under which it chooses a small number of key suppliers as its partners for designing and manufacturing its vehicles. Each supplier is given primary responsibility for a key part of the vehicle—the chassis, the seats, the interior, the drive train, and so on. (In the industry vernacular, these are referred to as Tier .5 suppliers, in contrast to Tier 1 suppliers, who provide major individual parts, Tier 2 suppliers, who provide components to Tier 1, and so on.) The understanding is that all of them, as well as Ford, have to make an adequate profit and return on their investment.

Ford is responsible for the overall design of the vehicle and its positioning in the marketplace, but each supplier-partner is responsible for the actual design of a subsystem. For example, in the old days, Ford would have given Johnson Controls, a seats supplier, full detailed drawings, down to the finest detail. Under the new arrangement, it simply tells Johnson, as the partner-supplier for the interior, the characteristics of its typical customers, as well as the features (cup holders, underseat compartments, and the like) that Ford wants this vehicle to have. Johnson Controls takes it from there.

Johnson Controls works collaboratively with other suppliers to determine specifications and designs for every aspect of the car interior. It negotiates with other suppliers over who should have responsibility for which component and at what price. Ford coordinates the design of the interior with the other subsystem designs to ensure that they all mesh and that they meet overall cost targets.

In other words, Ford orchestrates, rather than performs, detailed vehicle design. And its shrinking role does not end there. A visitor to its new assembly plants, featuring what is known as modular manufacturing, will encounter far fewer Ford employees.

In modular manufacturing, the "manufacturer" (Ford, in this case) allocates a section of the plant to each key partner-supplier, where it assembles the subsystem for which it is responsible. Only at the end, when the various subsystems are ready to be put into place, do Ford's employees actually put their hands on the job. Until that point, their role is coordination and quality control.

What kind of company is Ford? Until recently, the easy answer would have been "auto manufacturer," but that label doesn't fit so well anymore. Today the description "designer and marketer of automobiles" is more accurate. Ford's primary value-added is understanding customer requirements and positioning products to accommodate those needs. Concentrating on identifying market segments and shaping vehicles to fit them, Ford leaves many details to its supplier-partners. Manufacturing still needs to be done, but Ford may not be the one to do it.

The new Ford Motor Company barely resembles the old one. Once it was one of three bright stars that shone gloriously alone in the heavens. Now it has become part of a constellation. Its role is undeniably indispensable, but so are the roles of the other members of its constellation.

Even more striking is the stylistic and cultural shift. In the old days, the stereotypical auto manufacturer was arrogant, even narcissistic. Anyone who has attended a meeting between a big car company and its suppliers would have been immediately struck, as I was, by the hostility and suspicion that dominated the proceedings.

Today Ford recognizes that its own success is intimately entwined with that of the suppliers who are now its partners. Rather than trying to control and beat them down on prices, it recognizes that cooperation and a high degree of autonomy will lead to lower costs for the total system and create profits enough for everyone to share.

In the past, information about profit margins, costs, capacities, inventories, and the like would have been a bargaining tool for one side to use in its relentless warfare with the other. Today Ford and its suppliers swap data extensively. Any party's useful information is open to all parties in the interests of the larger system.

When this new system is fully operational, an attendee at a Ford product meeting or a visitor to a Ford plant will be hard pressed to distinguish Ford employees from those working for its partner-suppliers. But one thing will be obvious: No matter who signs their checks, all of these people are working together for a common cause. In the new world of virtual integration, that is exactly as it should be.

Through virtual integration, the walls between enterprises, which were breached by the collaboration explored in Chapter 9, crumble altogether. Through virtual integration, companies stop being self-contained units that produce products or services, and become elements in a larger system.

Virtual integration represents the confluence and culmination of a wide range of themes regarding how businesses operate, some of which have already been explored in this book. The first is the concept of increasing customer value-added, which was discussed in Chapter 3. The more you do for customers, the more of their work that you undertake, the harder it is to find the line that separates you from them. Companies that perform more of their customers' work in order to differentiate themselves from their competitors and earn higher margins are, in effect, integrating themselves into their customers' operations.

The second trend, interenterprise collaboration and process integration, was explored in the previous chapter. The Internet allows companies to transform the processes that link them with their customers, suppliers, and other relevant parties. Working intimately with other companies is just one short step from ceasing to recognize distinctions from them altogether.

Virtual integration has also been given a boost by the convergence of outsourcing and core competences. Outsourcing, presented in Chapter 7 as one of the factors leading to structureless organizations, started with companies contracting out tasks that were distractions for them. The data processing industry offers a good example. EDS is one of several companies that can attribute its growth to the fact that executives in other industries wanted to wash their hands of managing the mumbo-jumbo computer world, which seemed to perform poorly no matter what they did.

Lately, however, outsourcing has acquired a new dimension by becoming intertwined with the notion of *core competence*. That term entered the management lexicon in the 1990s and referred to that relatively small number of activities that a company must perform superlatively in order to succeed. Originally, the intention behind the term was to help companies develop growth strategies by identifying and exploiting what they did best. For instance, a number of natural gas pipeline companies (such as Williams and Enron) recognized that their core competence is, in fact, network management—the ability to manage a set of "pipes" that carry things from one place to another. They have extended this expertise into new fields and are now offering network management services in areas ranging from telecommunications to water. But there is another important side to the notion of core competence.

At one time, it might have been plausible to suggest that if a company performed extraordinarily well in its core competences, it could afford to do only moderately well in other areas. This is no longer the case. In a marketplace made up of commoditized product offerings and intense competition, you cannot afford to do anything less than extremely well. Any part of your operation that adds unnecessary cost, takes longer than it should, or delivers less than outstanding levels of quality will hurt the final product or service that goes to your customer. Clearly, today's business environment has no room for mediocrity. It is no longer acceptable to be adequate; you must now be the best. A less-than-stellar performance in any area will eventually make you noncompetitive. Jack Welch's famous warning that any GE business that was not number one or number two in its market would be closed or sold is now part of business lore. I would paraphrase it to say that today, every company has to be best, or almost best, in everything it does if it is to survive. Managers today are feeling intense pressure to outsource everything except their core competences.

The new demographic realities that companies are facing further reinforce this situation. For a considerable time during the 1980s and early 1990s, many organizations faced the problem of fat payrolls. Thinking that they had more people than work, many downsized. But even in that short time, the world has changed dramatically. Birthrates have declined in much of the developed world; populations in many European countries are falling; in the United States, new technologies are increasing the already-wide gap between well- and poorly educated people; and work has become more and more complex. The result is that today capable personnel are the scarcest resource at many companies. There simply aren't enough good people for everything to be done well.

The marriage of core competence and outsourcing means that companies are doing more of what they do best and less of everything else. As one company sheds what it does suboptimally, another takes it on—and presumably casts off something else that is not its strong suit. The result is that companies are no longer whole enterprises; they contain only the areas at which they excel. In order to do the work of a complete business, they need to be virtually integrated with complementary others.

Combine increased customer value-added, interenterprise collaboration, and core competence-driven outsourcing, and the result is virtual integration: multiple companies working together to create the results normally expected from just one. From the inside, everyone can see that there are multiple enterprises at work. From the customer's point of view, however, everything meshes so seamlessly that they appear to be only one.

To meet customer needs, any business must perform a range of processes, from product development and order fulfillment to plant maintenance and personnel development. In a traditional enterprise, all of these processes are performed by employees of a single company. With virtual integration, they may be performed by different companies, though their flawless coordination gives the impression of a single corporate entity. In virtual integration, the operations of different companies are commingled and intertwined, so that none can exist independently. Each participant concentrates on those processes that it performs best, leaving the rest to others. Virtual integration achieves the same performance benefits as vertical integration without tying up capital by buying other companies.

One of the most striking illustrations of virtual integration comes from the personal computer industry, which was forced to adopt this radical approach in response to Dell Computer, itself one of the great business phenomena of the late twentieth century.

In the pre-Dell era, every player in the PC industry had a well-defined role. Parts suppliers designed and made components that were sold to PC manufacturers, who assembled them and passed them on to distributors. As in the old days of the auto industry, everyone stayed at arm's length from everyone else. This way of working might have been clean and neat, but it also had dramatic operational shortcomings.

Sharply defined boundaries and closely held information produced local efficiencies but led to terrible systemwide inefficiencies—especially in inventories. The parts supplier built parts that it placed in a finished goods warehouse, where they waited to be ordered by the PC maker. Next, the PC maker ordered them and put them in a parts warehouse. Periodically, it assembled some into full PCs, which went into a finished goods warehouse, where they sat until the distributor ordered them to place in its own warehouse.

All told, there were typically fourteen weeks of inventory sloshing around this system, which would be frightful in any industry because of the high carrying costs. But it could be fatal in the PC industry, where products and components are obsolete the day they are manufactured. In a product with less than a one-year lifetime, it is disastrous to have more than three months of inventory. The PC industry tried numerous strategies to cope with this problem. Under what was called the "price-protection system," for one, a distributor that could not sell a PC for full price, because a newer model was hard on its heels, was reimbursed by the manufacturer for its losses.

Not only was the system swimming in inventory, however; the inventory itself was largely useless. At least 40 percent of the time, when a corporate customer asked for significant numbers of a particular PC, the distributor wouldn't have what was requested in stock and would have to order it from the manufacturer, which typically took eight weeks. More than likely, the customer was unwilling to wait and bought the PCs elsewhere.

Faced with losing customers, many distributors resorted to desperate measures. They cannibalized their inventories, breaking down assembled computers to extract the parts they needed, then reassembling them into the configuration the customer wanted. Needless to say, this boosted cost and left a jumble of broken and unused components that had to be sent back to the manufacturers.

With so much inventory in the system, the distributors might have been expected to achieve high levels of customer service and high rates of filled orders. The reason they didn't was that there were too many configurations. Even though most PCs use Intel processors and Microsoft's operating system, numerous variations persist—differences in processor speeds, memory sizes, hard disks, and software. It is not uncommon for a manufacturer to be able to deliver more than three thousand configurations of a supposedly basic PC. With so many models, it is virtually impossible to make accurate forecasts of the demand for each one. Unfortunately, a corporate customer standardizes on just one model and can accept no substitutes.

This complex and wasteful system survived only so long as there was no challenge to it. But then along came Dell, with its build-to-order model.

As everyone knows, Dell sells directly to final customers. It builds computers only when it receives orders. It keeps a small inventory of parts on hand—usually less than a week's worth. It is able to get by with so little because it can quickly order parts from its suppliers and get them delivered. When an order for computers comes in, Dell builds them to customer specifications and almost always sends them out within a very few days.

As a result, Dell's costs are about 15 percent lower than the costs that conventional PC makers incur. In the commoditylike market of contemporary PCs, such a cost differential cannot be sustained. In the mid-1990s, rival PC makers found a way to survive through an approach called "channel assembly."

In channel assembly, the roles of the distributor and the manufacturer are transformed beyond recognition. The manufacturer no longer assembles PCs. After all, it doesn't know which models customers will order, so anything it assembles is a stab in the dark. Instead, it is the distributors who "manufacture" PCs.

With channel assembly, a corporate customer asks the distributor for a number of computers in a particular configuration. The distributor doesn't have them in stock, because it keeps almost no finished computers in stock. But it does have on hand the parts needed to build any combination that a customer may want. (Only a small number of different parts are needed to make many different configurations.) The distributor turns the order out in five or fewer days and delivers the computers. There is no out-of-stock problem and no cannibalization.

The distributor keeps the nominal manufacturer posted on its parts inventory and the pattern of orders that it gets. The "manufacturer," who in fact may manufacture little or nothing, decides which parts need to be restocked with the distributor and orders them from suppliers, for shipment directly to the distributor's warehouse.

Any parts destined for early obsolescence are sent out quickly, usually via overnight air. Those with longer lifetimes, such as power supplies and chassis, can go by truck. The system as a whole operates with only a few days of inventory. There is no return of unusable components back to the manufacturer. Customers have no unmet needs.

Unsurprisingly, this system compares favorably with Dell's. In fact, it is essentially the same as Dell's except that two companies—the distributor for assembly and the manufacturer for inventory management—are doing the work that Dell does on its own. Neither the manufacturer nor the distributor by itself produces a PC; it is only when they are virtually integrated that a product emerges. Together the "manufacturer" (which does not manufacture) and the "distributor" (which does not distribute in any conventional sense) form a virtual enterprise.

Channel assembly raises a number of intriguing questions.

- Why does the PC maker manage the distributor's inventory? Answer: Because it is better at the job.
- Why is the distributor suddenly capable of assembling PCs in a reliable fashion? How can the manufacturer trust it to deliver a quality product that still bears the manufacturer's logo? Answer: The manufacturer develops the assembly process, teaches it to the distributor, and inspects often to ensure that the distributor is doing it right.
- Why is the nominal manufacturer being paid? What value does it add to the final product? Answer: It adds value by performing the indispensable processes of product design, inventory management, brand building, and supplier relationship management.

Here is the deconstruction of the corporation—the end of neat defining boundaries based on turnkey products or services. Under channel assembly, product development, procurement, and inventory management are performed by the nominal manufacturer. Order acquisition, assembly, and order fulfillment are performed by the distributor. Demand creation is done by the two working together. Only when you integrate the processes of the two companies will you have what resembles a whole company.

Everyone knows that Cisco Systems makes routers, switchers, and all the other plumbing that underlies the Internet. What is less well known is that this is not true. In fact, Cisco makes almost none of its own equipment. A great majority of Cisco's orders go out without ever being touched by a Cisco employee.

Cisco's own term for virtual integration is the Single Enterprise Program (SEP). Cisco initiated this effort because it realized that it was playing in a world that changes overnight. Between 40 and 60 percent of its revenue comes from products that are less than a year old. How can Cisco stay on the leading edge of such a rapidly changing environment without losing ground to nimble start-up competitors? The answer is focus. The company's managers have decided they will do two things and two things only. They will develop cutting-edge products, and they will maintain close relationships with their customers. Everything else will be left to partners.

Jabil and Solectron are among the contract manufacturers that Cisco uses to assemble its parts. A distributor, Hamilton Avnet, coordinates the parts movements needed to assemble products and fill orders. Avnet makes sure that parts from the various suppliers show up at the contract manufacturer's plant on time, and that the finished product is shipped to Cisco's customer. Cisco shares information about expected orders with the other members of its SEP, which enables them to prepare the inventory and resources necessary for incoming orders.

Designing the product, getting the order, and billing the customer are the sum total of Cisco's responsibilities. It operates as a complete enterprise only when it merges its capabilities with those of its contract manufacturers and its distributor.

Cisco explicitly recognized the power of virtual integration and decided as a matter of business policy to pursue this strategy (under the "Single Enterprise" banner). A few other companies have done so as well, including Dell. Each has a different name for its initiative; "Extended Enterprise" is probably the most common.

More frequently, however, virtual integration is an unanticipated consequence for companies that are pursuing another set of objectives. To reduce costs and simplify its life, a company will outsource a key process to a supplier; in order to gain more revenue by adding more value, or to exploit collaboration-based opportunities for cost reduction, the supplier will encroach more and more on the customer's domain, offering more services and taking over more of the customer's activities. At the same time, the customer realizes that it can lower its supplier's costs (and thereby its own) by undertaking some work that until now had been the supplier's responsibility. Before long, the two companies are inextricably linked, and finding where one ends and the other begins is best left to philosophers.

For instance, Navistar, the truck manufacturer, has outsourced the operation of its tire warehouse to Goodyear. Goodyear keeps the inventory current and delivers the right tires in the right sequence to Navistar's manufacturing floor. Goodyear provides this service not only for its own tires but for those provided by its competitors—Bridgestone/ Firestone and Michelin.

This arrangement enables Navistar to focus on its core competences—truck design, manufacturing, and sales—without worrying about tire inventory management. Because Goodyear is proficient at the latter, Navistar gets better tire service at a lower cost than it ever did handling the job on its own.

Goodyear's initial interest in this arrangement was the opportunity to provide greater value to a key customer (as discussed in Chapter 3). Goodyear also benefited from the fee that Navistar paid for these services, as well as from access to an extraordinarily valuable lode of data. Because Goodyear now knows how many tires are in Navistar's warehouse, it can adjust its own production to minimize its inventory and lower its manufacturing costs. It also has prime data on how its competitors are doing.

This was just the beginning of Goodyear's and Navistar's journey on the road to virtual integration. Goodyear has also taken over the job of mounting tires on wheels. In a joint venture with Accuride, a wheel supplier, Goodyear and its partner supply Navistar with a steady flow of wheels with tires already mounted and balanced. Navistar just has to bolt the wheels onto its trucks.

Goodyear and Accuride are doing more of what they do best so that Navistar can do more of what it does best. To the outside world, the three companies are indistinguishable from a single well-managed enterprise. Perhaps not coincidentally, Goodyear's share of Navistar's business has doubled since these virtual integration efforts began.

The electronics contract manufacturing industry also demonstrates the evolutionary character of virtual integration. Companies like Solectron and Jabil were originally formed in the late 1970s to help electronics manufacturers take the peaks out of their loads. Rather than build plants and hire staff to handle periods of unusual demand, the manufacturers would contract out some assembly during these periods, sending the contractors boxes of parts and detailed assembly instructions. Before very long, it became apparent that the manufacturers were in fact not especially good at manufacturing; the boxes and instructions that they sent their contractors, and that they used themselves, were often incomplete or inaccurate.

Consequently, companies from HP to Nortel decided that their energies and capital were better deployed in product development and customer service than in manufacturing. They outsourced more and more of their manufacturing to the contractors, who in turn focused on developing world-class manufacturing capability. (Interestingly, Celestica, one of the industry leaders, was formed when IBM divested itself of its Canadian manufacturing operations.) The result was mete-oric growth; Solectron, for instance, grew from around $400 million in sales in 1992 to over $10 billion in 2000. As of this writing, approxi-mately 30 percent of electronics manufacturing is outsourced, and the contract manufacturing industry is growing by about 30 percent a year. Ultimately, over 75 percent of manufacturing will probably be done by these specialists.

The Solectrons and Celesticas of the world are not content to remain confined to doing relatively low-value-adding manufacturing for their customers. Instead, they are aggressively offering more services that entangle them more deeply with their customers' businesses. One such service is systems integration. Modern electronics is a rapidly moving and complex industry: Products have short lifetimes, and their specifications change frequently even in those brief periods; demand for a product will suddenly appear, then disappear virtually overnight; keeping inventory on hand is a near-capital crime; and dozens of differ-ent companies supply parts or components for making a product. In this environment, someone needs to ensure that all suppliers and suppliers' suppliers are on exactly the same page at all times: as the product is being developed, as orders for it come in, and as it is modified over its lifetime. Someone needs to tie everyone together, to ensure that all par-ties have the same version of the product specifications and knows what to do and when. This role is a long way from assembling parts according to printed instructions, yet the contract manufacturers have stepped into the breach to relieve their customers of this complex responsibility.

They are also offering procurement services; the contractors can pool buying across their customers and get better prices than even their large customers. Yet another service is product support: Since a con-tract manufacturer actually builds the product, it may be best posi-tioned to help customers solve any problems they have with it.

The emergence of RosettaNet is accelerating the virtual integra-tion of the electronics industry. RosettaNet is a set of communication standards—in effect, standardized definitions of process interfaces.

Companies that adhere to the RosettaNet standards present a familiar interface to other companies for procurement and order fulfillment processes, which enables these companies to interface and combine their processes smoothly.

Transportation is another industry in which companies are particularly eager to become integrated with their customers' operations. Doing otherwise dooms a carrier to price wars, falling profits, and all the other problems associated with selling commodities.

Like many other companies, Nike has set up a Web site, nike.com, that offers customers a new channel for ordering products. But Nike knows that it serves its customers best when it concentrates on product design and brand building and on as little else as possible. So after receiving an order on its Web site, Nike transmits it immediately to UPS, which manages the distribution center that fills these orders.

UPS no longer merely plays the role of a delivery firm, passively waiting for someone to call it to pick up a package and take it to a customer. Increasingly, UPS itself creates the package that needs to be delivered. In Nike's case, UPS takes the order and picks, packs, and ships the ordered products. It does this work at a distribution center that it manages on behalf of Nike, and that is located near its own package handling facilities. This allows UPS to provide next-day delivery on orders received as late as 8 P.M. But this is not the end of the story. UPS also handles returns processing for Nike. If a customer decides to send back a pair of shoes, UPS picks them up, returns them to its distribution center, and puts the shoes back into inventory. Because there is no handoff between Nike and UPS, returns get handled more quickly and products don't sit around, becoming obsolete, while waiting to get back into active inventory. UPS also operates Nike's call centers. When a customer calls Nike with an inquiry about product or delivery, the call is actually handled by a UPS employee—although the customer almost certainly doesn't know that. Customer orders are handled, and handled well, by a blend of Nike and UPS. It is hard to say where one leaves off and the other begins.

UPS offers similar services to a wide range of other companies, from high-technology firms to automakers. UPS's traditional capabilities had been in moving small packages; it has now extended these capabilities to managing complex distribution networks. Because it is building on related capabilities, UPS can do a better job at this kind of work than companies whose strengths lie in other areas. For instance, UPS now manages the delivery of 4.5 million vehicles a year from twenty-one Ford plants to 6,300 Ford dealers, using a mixture of rail-cars and trucks. In the year it has been doing this, UPS has reduced the time to get a Ford vehicle from factory to dealer by one-third. UPS has also rationalized three parts distribution networks that Compaq had been operating (one each for Compaq's own products and for those made by DEC and Tandem, which Compaq acquired), in the process reducing the number of field stocking locations by 60 percent.

UPS is doing even more for some customers, branching out from pure logistics activities to other work that UPS is in a better position to do for a customer than the customer is to do for itself. UPS operates repair facilities for high-technology customers, not just picking up broken parts and dispatching replacements, but also doing the actual repair work. Since UPS is already handling the part, it makes more sense for UPS to repair it than for the manufacturer to do so. UPS also does financial processing for some customers. The company has long offered a service whereby it would pick up payment for a product it delivers and send a check back to the shipper. Now, UPS will deposit such a payment into its own account and make an electronic deposit into the shipper's account the next day. This gives the shipper better funds availability and frees it from having to process a large number of receipts. In so doing, UPS and its shipper customer become ever more tightly intertwined. Payments handling is not the only financial service that UPS offers. For an Italian tie manufacturer, for instance, UPS finances the purchase of raw materials in China, provides letters of credit and export receivables financing, and handles collections in the United States. On one level, this is far removed from UPS's traditional business; on another, it is part of a natural evolution toward adding greater value and virtual integration.

In many parts of the country, Xerox copiers are delivered, installed, and demonstrated by people actually employed by Ryder Transportation Services. Like UPS, Ryder is doing more for its customers and, in so doing, is becoming hard to distinguish from them.

Bose, the manufacturer of high-end audio equipment, uses Roadway Express to deliver products to its retailers and to receive parts from its component makers. A Roadway employee, known as the Roadway in-plant representative, is assigned to each major Bose facility, where he or she is considered a full-fledged member of the Bose logistics team. A Roadway in-plant representative helps plan shipments, track status, cope with emergencies, manage inventories, and the like. This person is best described as someone who works for Bose but is paid by Roadway.

Virtual integration, like politics, makes for odd bedfellows. Chapter 7 showed how independent business units are becoming a thing of the past, as each unit leverages the capabilities of others. Virtual integration works similarly, only at the level of whole companies rather than business units. In the customer economy, companies must learn to surrender their traditional notions of autonomy, just as their internal units already have.

The advent of the virtual enterprise has vertiginous implications. As it reverses Henry Ford's vertical integration, it shatters many of our fundamental assumptions about doing business. It forces managers to make unprecedented critical decisions about what they really do: Which of our processes define us and our business? Where should we place our bets? What should we choose to do and not to do? Which processes should we dispose of, and which should we acquire?

UPS is branching out from delivery and is adding new capabilities in inventory management and financial services. Manufacturers of electronics and automobiles are easing out of their role as assemblers while upgrading their skills as marketers and brand managers.

Clearly, letting go of certain processes, especially core business processes that are fundamental to meeting customer needs, carries risks. A company may become dependent on others, captive to their capabilities, and no longer able to steer its own course. Still, holding on to certain processes carries its own costs and risks. These processes may become commoditized, obsolete, or performed better by others—in which case there is no business left at all.

Strategically, it makes sense to hold on to whatever processes add the greatest value to the final product. But determining what provides "greatest value" can be complicated.

Which is more valuable: designing, manufacturing, or delivering a product? The question is absurd. Clearly, all are essential. Merely doing one or two out of the three doesn't lead to final customer value. In the past, the relative value of the three was a theoretical question because one company performed all of them and got all the profit. Now when three parties may be involved and the profit has to be allocated among them, the question of who's doing the most for the customer becomes an enormously practical debate. It has to be answered case by case; as yet there is no formula for resolving it.

As virtual integration increases, companies will have to develop a new competence: seamlessly coordinating with suppliers, customers, co-suppliers, and co-customers. Industry standards (of which RosettaNet is only the first) will play a big role in defining how companies interface with each other. But implementing the capabilities implied by these interfaces will remain a considerable challenge.

It is hard to imagine a deeper set of cultural shifts than those touched off by the rise of virtual integration. Instead of the traditional values of haughty pride and suspicion of all outsiders, a company must now prize trust, cooperation, and partnership. It must share information with others, not reluctantly but eagerly. It must be willing to sacrifice short-term gain for the benefit of the larger virtual enterprise of which it is a part. It must recognize that success comes to every participant in a virtual enterprise or to none at all. This will be a major departure for companies who have long found their easiest victims among their closest allies, stiffing suppliers or holding up customers in order to make a bad quarter look better. Benjamin Franklin's adage "We must all hang together, or assuredly we shall all hang separately" must become every company's watchword.

Of all the ideas and principles in this book, virtual integration is by far the most radical. It does not merely call into question how companies are organized, managed, and operated; it represents a fundamental challenge to our most basic notions of what a company is. At first, I was somewhat hesitant to include this concept in this book. But then I recalled a conversation I recently had with a physician. He asked me what I thought the structure of the American health care delivery system would be in five years. I took the opportunity to unburden myself of some extreme ideas that I had been developing. After a few minutes, I took pity on him and apologized, saying, "What I'm suggesting must sound crazy to you." He replied, "So what? What we have in place today would have sounded crazy to me just two years ago." In the times in which we live, even the most extreme notions have a disturbing tendency to turn into reality before very long.

Agenda Item 9

Embrace the Radical Vision of Virtual Integration

- See your business not as a self-contained company but as part of an extended enterprise of companies that work together to create customer value.
- Define your company in terms of the processes you perform, not the products or services you create.
- Identify and strengthen the key processes at which you excel.
- Outsource everything else to someone better equipped to do it.
- Learn to work closely with others, not just on your own.
- Be prepared to rethink your company's identity and strategy in fundamental ways.

11

Make It Happen

Turn the Agenda into Action

O ver the last nine chapters, I have laid out an agenda that prescribes what companies must do to thrive in the customer economy. Here it is, in summarized form:

1. Make yourself easy to do business with. Your customers' biggest gripes aren't about your products or services per se; they center on what a royal pain your products are to order, receive, and pay for. Take a long hard look at yourself from your customers' point of view, and then redesign how you work to save them time, money, and frustration.

2. Add more value for your customers. To avoid the trap of commoditization, in which you fight for a minuscule margin against a horde of look-alike competitors, you need to do more for your customers. Don't drop your product or service at the customer's door. Go through the door, see what the customer does next, and do it for him.

3. Obsess about your processes. Customers care only about results, and results come only from end-to-end processes. Manage them, improve them, appoint owners for them, and make everyone aware of them. It's the only way to achieve the performance that customers demand.

4. Turn creative work into process work. Innovation doesn't have to be chaotic. Bring the power of discipline and structure to sales, product development, and other creative work. Make success in these areas the result of design and management, not luck; luck has a nasty habit of giving out when you need it most.

5. Use measurement for improving, not accounting. Most of your measurements are worthless; they tell you what has happened (sort of) but give you no clue as to what to do for the future. Create a model of your business that ties overall goals to things you control; measure the items that really make a difference; and embed measurement in a serious program of managed improvement.

6. Loosen up your organizational structure. The days of the proudly independent manager running a sharply defined unit are over. Collaboration and teamwork are now as necessary in the executive suite as on the front lines. Teach your managers how to work together for the good of the enterprise rather than stab each other in the back for narrow gain.

7. Sell through, not to, your distribution channels. Don't let your distribution channels blind you to your final customer, the one who pays everyone's salaries. Change distribution from a series of resellers into a community that works together to serve that final customer. Be ready to redefine the roles of everyone involved in order to achieve that end.

8. Push past your boundaries in pursuit of efficiency. The last vestiges of overhead lurk, not deep in your company, but at its edges. Exploit the real power of the Internet to streamline the processes that connect you with customers and suppliers. Collaborate with everyone you can to drive out cost and overhead.

9. Lose your identity in an extended enterprise. Get past the idea of being a self-contained company that delivers a complete product. Get used to the notion that you can achieve something only when you virtually integrate with others. Focus on what you do best, get rid of the rest, and encourage others to do the same.

VERY WELL. You now know what you need to do. All that remains is to get on with it, and that's the easy part, isn't it?

Maybe not.

Not long ago, I was discussing her company's capabilities with a senior executive of a large financial services institution. "We're pretty good at knowing what to do," she observed. "Our problem is actually getting anything done."

She and her company are not alone. Over the last decade, I have observed a great many companies undertake one or another major transformation effort, from reengineering or ERP implementation to installing a balanced scorecard measurement system or creating an e-procurement facility. They all knew what they wanted to accomplish, but while many succeeded, many did not; and even those who did eventually succeed found the experience far from smooth.

Such was the experience, for instance, of DTE Energy in the mid-1990s. DTE Energy, the parent of Detroit Edison, is a diversified electric and gas utility with over $6 billion in annual revenue. In 1994 the company undertook to turn itself into a process enterprise. While this effort did conclude successfully and led to dramatic improvements in the company's operating performance, implementing the change was difficult and painful. Employees did not understand the effort or why it was needed, and many resented it. The complex program was not always managed coherently. As a result, seeing it through took longer than was planned and left scars that took years to heal. The aftermath of the change consumed the organization for over a year, and it took many years for the recovery to be complete. And that transition involved only a few of the agenda items laid out over the past nine chapters. Similar tales could be told about hundreds of other companies.

That DTE and so many other companies have found implementing all or part of a new agenda so difficult is not surprising; the experience is almost entirely unfamiliar for them. Companies know how to do a lot of new things: They know how to find new customers, how to develop and introduce new products, and how to open new plants. They know how to do these things because they have done them all before. On the other hand, redefining themselves in customer rather than product terms, building a new generation of measurement systems, and turning a distribution channel into a community are not among the things companies know how to do, because they have never done anything like them before. When companies undertake such efforts, they are operating without a net. The destination is not entirely clear to them, and the road for reaching it is neither well marked nor lit. As a result, they are forced to improvise, to make things up as they go along. Unsurprisingly, they make mistakes, employing techniques that do not work or overlooking critical issues. Some of these mistakes may prove fatal; and even those companies that survive the transition—like the companies cited throughout this book—are left with lasting scars.

The agenda I have laid out for you is neither short nor easy. Turning it into reality will be a major challenge. Indeed, the prospect of making all these changes is probably making you very anxious. Can you really pull it off? Is this a high-stakes gamble? What are your chances of success?

You are right to be concerned. Implementing the agenda goes against the grain of everything about your company. As I have argued time and again, the great majority of companies, large and small, are organized and managed in ways that directly conflict with the principles of this agenda. The customer remains an afterthought, processes are no one's responsibility, and defending turf is everyone's first instinct. These are not abstractions. They are wired into every aspect of your business, from how people regard themselves and their jobs, to how they are trained and paid, to how the company is organized and managed. Implementing any one item on the agenda, much less all of them, will mean changing virtually everything about your company and shaking up everything in your employees' work lives.

Let's look at just one component of just one agenda item: transforming interenterprise processes in order to improve systemwide performance (discussed in Chapter 9). Instead of minimizing only your own inventory levels and driving down the price you pay your suppliers, you must focus instead on the entire amount of inventory held across the supply chain and on the total cost to the final customer.

What will this mean for your purchasing agents and your salespeople? Purchasing agents will have to think about more than extracting the lowest possible price from suppliers and will have to help them find ways to improve their operations; salespeople will have to do the analogous with customers. This will turn their worlds upside down. Traditionally, purchasing agents have been measured on and rewarded for how effectively they squeeze price concessions out of vendors, while salespeople have been exclusively focused on getting customers to buy more. Driving down inventory levels and freight costs may be good for everyone, including you, but the purchasing agent's evaluation system does not recognize or reward it. The benefits of lower freight costs will accrue to the shipping department, the warehouse will be credited with improving inventory turns, and the purchasing agent may actually be punished for having ensured these gains. Furthermore, even if you convince purchasing agents to work in this new way, they may not be prepared to do so, since they were trained at most as price negotiators, not business process reengineers. Similar changes are in store for the salespeople.

In other words, virtually every issue in the agenda entails systemic rather than narrow-gauge change. Needless to say, managing such wholesale change is mind-numbingly complex. Nor will you have the luxury of doing it with everyone cheering you on. The hard truth is that major change inevitably creates some losers in the organization, at least in the short term. The second law of thermodynamics tells us that in the world of physics you can't get something for nothing. A similar rule holds in the world of organizations. Some people always profit, and not only financially, from the status quo; for them, progress spells loss. If you elevate the significance of business processes, then the managers of functional departments inevitably lose some of their power. If you dissolve the boundaries that separate business units from one another, then executives must sacrifice some of their autonomy. If you manage sales as a deliberate, team-oriented effort, then sales reps lose some of their heroic status. In the long run, these changes may well turn out to be beneficial for all; but in the short run, they are unlikely to be perceived as such. Disturbing established patterns of power and control inevitably provokes pushback and resistance.

Feeling overwhelmed? You should be, but you have no choice but to proceed. In times of fundamental change, the riskiest strategy is not to act boldly but to continue in the old ways. That is guaranteed to lead you to failure. If you act, you at least have a chance. Moreover, it is precisely the difficulty of adopting the agenda that makes it so important. If it were easy, everyone would already have done it. Those who summon the resolve to overcome the obstacles in making the agenda reality will reap extraordinary rewards. But deciding to implement the agenda is only the first step on the road toward outperforming your competitors. You also have to follow through on that decision.

Having led you into the Slough of Despond, let me offer you a way out. As I said, even the companies that have successfully implemented parts of the agenda have found it a trying experience. They faced unfamiliar and intimidating challenges, without the benefit of an implementation toolkit. Yet these companies did manage to rise to the occasion. They developed the toolkit they needed on the fly, inventing implementation techniques just in time to put them into practice. To be sure, they made some mistakes, but they also did many things right. Remarkably, in reviewing the experiences of dozens and dozens of these companies, I came to the realization that by and large they independently developed and employed virtually identical toolkits. Whether the specific issue was implementing a new kind of computer system, reengineering a business process, or transforming distribution, and whether the company was an electronics maker, an insurance firm, or an electric utility, the same set of six tactical principles emerged. This remarkable fact should encourage you and give you hope. If this body of techniques worked for all these companies, it can work for you as well.

For many decades, the Holy Grail of physics has been the discovery of a grand unified theory that would explain all physical phenomena. I suggest the principles and guidelines that these companies have discovered are the beginnings of a grand unified theory of change implementation, a set of techniques that companies like yours can apply in realizing the agenda. In what follows, I will summarize these six keys to success.

1. Integrate and Focus Your Efforts.

This book has outlined nine issues that constitute the core of a company's agenda for adapting to the customer economy. But it would be a catastrophic error to turn these nine issues into a set of nine independent and unrelated projects: one to create a new measurement system, another to restructure the distribution system, a third to teach managers to work cooperatively and collaboratively, and so on. Such multipronged approaches are doomed to failure, because organizations have limited capacity for change initiatives.

Every student of logic learns the principle known as Occam's Razor, named for the medieval philosopher William of Occam. It says that the simplest possible explanation for any phenomenon is the best one. Put more technically, Occam's Razor urges us to "avoid the multiplication of entities." The same principle applies to change programs: The more programs a company undertakes, the less likely it is that any will succeed. When an organization pursues multiple initiatives, people grow cynical. They conclude (often correctly) that management is substituting quantity for quality; the multiplicity of programs, they feel, indicates that their leadership is not particularly serious about any one, and that, instead of investing in the success of a particular plan, the company's executives have decided to spread their bets in the vague hope that something will magically pay off. When they are presented with numerous change programs, employees inevitably become confused about the relationships and differences among the initiatives. In response, managers have to invest a lot of time in establishing relative priorities, resolving conflicts, and dealing with the fact that implementation teams will be competing for resources and executive attention.

Instead, company leadership must create an umbrella under which will fall all the efforts associated with adapting to the customer economy, a single theme to encompass all these projects. This is a matter, not of choosing a suitably exciting slogan or project name, but of identifying a compelling issue to which everyone in the company can relate and that justifies each aspect of the agenda. One consumer goods company, for instance, has established a goal of "undisputed leadership in the food business," and it uses that goal as the motivation for implementing a wide-ranging agenda, from lowering divisional boundaries to reducing finished goods inventory; a large bank accomplishes the same under the heading of generating growth by getting a larger share of its existing customers' business.

Most companies already suffer from a plethora of existing change initiatives, from the customer satisfaction task force to the innovation committee. All of these existing programs should be either folded outright or folded under the integrating theme. Not doing so results in wasted resources and ongoing distractions.

The company's leadership must be relentless in convincing employees that this umbrella effort is not a management fad of the moment that will soon give way to another program du jour. They must persuasively explain why change is necessary, and how each aspect of the plan responds to this driving cause. Their goal must be to assure that everyone in the organization understands both exactly what is happening and why. When people understand the real and unavoidable motivations behind a program of change, they are much more likely to take it seriously. Achieving this buy-in will require an unprecedented degree of openness and honesty, about the company's competitive and financial positions and the prior mistakes that leadership has made. Most corporate communications programs are as enthusiastic as a chipmunk suffering from an overdose of adrenaline. A strong measure of candor and a dose of *mea culpa* will do wonders to buy needed credibility from, and the goodwill of, the front lines.

Successfully managing this unified initiative will require very strong skills in program management, the art of coordinating a vast number of projects. Fundamentally program management represents the management of complexity. Numerous companies have experience in doing one or two projects at a time, but few, other than large aerospace and construction companies, know how to manage a large number simultaneously. Every company must turn program management into one of its core competences and put that competence to work in change implementation. Without it, realizing the agenda will degenerate into random chaos.

2. Give More Attention than You Think Is Needed to People Issues.

Many years ago, when I was still an engineering professor at MIT, a business school colleague advised me, "The technical problems are the easy problems." At first, the engineer in me was not sure what he meant; since then, I have come to value his advice highly. The real issues that determine success or failure in any important undertaking are almost never technical in nature but center instead on questions of people and culture. For instance, creating a new measurement system poses a host of technically challenging problems: identifying the phenomena that need to be monitored, crafting a set of measures that will be both useful and usable, putting in place appropriate data-capture mechanisms, and the like. But the hardest problems are not these, but getting people to let go of the measures to which they have become accustomed, teaching them how to base decision making on quantitative measures, and creating a culture that values hard measurement data over opinions and instinct. Analogous observations could be made about each of the other items on the agenda. Even if all the technical problems yield to your concentrated attention, the slippery and elusive people problems will trip you up.

Unfortunately, it is all too common for executives to consider these people issues unimportant and to develop implementation plans that address the "hard" issues only. Perhaps as a politically correct afterthought, they append to these plans activities that address human and organizational concerns. Inevitably, these activities are given low priority, are underfunded, and are the first to be cut in the face of budget pressures. Then the executives are shocked when their precious change efforts fail. I have seen this happen over and over again, in the context of ERP implementation, e-business initiatives, process redesign programs, and a host of other efforts.

One vaccine against this toxin is to follow this rule of thumb: Spend one-third of the budget on the design and implementation of the change itself, one-third on its supporting technology, and one-third on people issues. While obviously such a crude guideline will rarely be precisely accurate, it does establish a spending baseline. It makes the point that people issues are not a side show or an afterthought but are as important as any other facet of the endeavor and as deserving of first-class attention and investment. If your plans call for spending less than the normative third on these issues, you must be prepared to explain why. Training, education, communications, and change management are the major items that would fall under the people side of an implementation budget, and you are much safer to overestimate rather than underestimate their costs. You lowball them at your mortal peril.

3. Manage Different Constituencies Differently.

All people in a company do not react in the same way to major change programs. Indeed, I have found a very useful formula that I call the 20/60/20 rule.

When a major corporate initiative is announced, 20 percent or so of the population typically receives it enthusiastically. Executives are often surprised that the reaction of this significant minority in the company is not hostility or confusion but rather "What took you so long?" Somewhere between one-fifth and one-third of the population is enormously predisposed to following through on the proposed innovation. (In fact, the same people are often positive about every innovation.) Typically close to the front lines and customers, this group knows firsthand the problems that the company and its customers experience as a result of traditional ways of doing things. They intuitively recognize the power of new methods, and are frustrated when managers with the clout to change things don't. When a program for change is finally announced, this group feels vindicated and even liberated.

Their ardor should be harnessed. You need to make these enthusiasts into emissaries and evangelists for the proposed change. Find and nurture them. Make sure they are kept abreast of developments and encourage them to infect others with their positive attitude. Others will be spreading negative views, and positive front-line people are a far better counterforce than missives from remote management. This enthusiastic 20 percent do pose a risk, however. Should you back off from the proposed change, these advocates will feel not just disappointed but betrayed. Their enthusiasm will turn to cynicism, and you will find you have squandered a precious resource. Lacking Charlie Brown's endless optimism, this group will eventually stop believing that Lucy will hold the football still for them. They will conclude that you are not serious about doing things differently and that the company is beyond hope and not worth working for. They will then take their penchant for change elsewhere. A company that purges its natural constituency for change will find change much harder to effect.

It is particularly harder because another 20 percent or so will be adamantly against this change and, indeed, almost any change. In some cases, these people will be those whose oxen are being gored by the proposed innovation—their jobs will change or even disappear, their authority will be reduced, or their personal styles will have to shift. In many cases, however, the people most fervently opposed will not have any "rational" reason for their opposition. Indeed, from an "objective" point of view, they would seem to benefit. Their jobs will be easier, they will have the opportunity to make more money, and their futures will look brighter. No matter. Having deeply internalized the old ways of conducting business, they cannot imagine working or behaving differently.

What is particularly troubling is that this 20 percent is often concentrated in the management ranks, where adherence to convention has been most strongly reinforced by, among other things, the increases in income and authority that have accompanied them up the corporate ladder. Needless to say, managers are well positioned to work against a change that they perceive to be against their interests or an uncomfortable intrusion on their well-ordered lives. They can bad-mouth the idea, raise apparently well-meaning objections whose sole purpose is to delay progress, fail to follow through on commitments to support or contribute to the effort, or otherwise impede innovation's progress in ways limited only by their imaginations.

Some leaders feel that they can bring everyone along on the journey to the future. While admirably inclusive and optimistic, I have found this hope to be in vain. This 20 percent or so of the population is in fact incorrigible, so deeply opposed to new ways of doing things that they cannot be brought around. Doing something about them, however, poses two challenges. First, it is not easy to identify them. Some may keep their opposition under wraps for the time being. Others may sound the same as individuals who are raising objections, not in order to derail the change, but to resolve issues critical to its success. Second, directly removing them from the company is both traumatic and expensive.

The best way to handle them is to lead them to identify themselves, which they will do if you are scrupulously clear with everyone about what the change entails. That is, you need to be inflexible and unambiguous about the advent of the change and its implications for the company and employees. Happy talk is poisonous, and abstractions are useless. Rather, you must lay out in explicit and ruthless detail how the specifics of the business—the jobs of sales reps, the authority of executives, the structure of the compensation program, and so on—will change. You must spell out the precise repercussions of the new ways of doing business. The incorrigible 20 percent will eventually recognize that the change is in fact real and that they will not be happy in its aftermath. Many will leave before they actually have to confront it. Though you must be prepared for and welcome these departures, you should expect surprises. Some of those who leave will be among the company's best performers—best, that is, in the old ways of working. You must not flinch at this point. It is better to let a new generation of stars emerge than to hold on to the old ones at the cost of jeopardizing the agenda for change.

The 60 percent in the middle is, of course, where the battle is won or lost. This is where the full arsenal of change management techniques—communications, incentives, participation, and all the rest—must be trained. Ironically and mistakenly, many executives concentrate their efforts on the other two segments because they feel that's where the most effort is needed or will be most successful. They are wrong. The top 20 percent does not need to be convinced, and the bottom 20 percent cannot be. Save your energies for where they matter.

4. Display Committed Executive Leadership.

It is a truism that major change requires committed executive leadership. Unfortunately, it is not always clear what that actually means. For my part, I adhere to what might be called the Forrest Gump school: Leadership is as leadership does. There are five specific and concrete actions that demonstrate serious executive commitment to a program of fundamental change.

The first step for leaders is to publicly stake their own credibility on the success of the change. A transformation program has a much greater chance of success if leaders nail their reputations to it. They should commit to specific goals up front and in public, guaranteeing financial or operating results that cannot possibly be achieved without following through on the change effort. They should also adjust the reward and compensation programs to include specific financial benefits for those who operate in ways that the new strategy calls for or who contribute to making it a reality. Those in charge cannot waffle, hedge, or hesitate. A display of weakness, expressed as inadequate funding, equivocal terminology, or reluctance to remove those blocking the way, will be immediately perceived and amplified throughout the organization. When the leaders catch cold, the followers come down with pneumonia, and the change initiative quickly succumbs.

The second action is to commit the required resources and hold them sacrosanct despite the depredations of the budgeting process. While implementing the agenda is not extravagantly expensive relative to many other things companies do, from building new plants to introducing new products, it is not free. You must fund in full the up-front investment needed to get started. Underfunding a major change initiative both deprives it of necessary resources and sends a strong message to the organization that you are willing to make only symbolic gestures on its behalf. Committing the required investment and refusing to cut it back even in the face of budgetary pressures demonstrates quite the opposite.

In this vein, it is vital that you dedicate some of the organization's "best and brightest" to the effort. A lesson that I have learned innumerable times is that assigning competent but not quite excellent people, or assigning top-rate people on a less-than-full-time basis, are two certain recipes for failure. Designing and implementing new ways of doing things is extraordinarily difficult and deserves the very best talent in the company. Everyone will recognize this, and everyone will similarly recognize that if you do not assign such people, then you are not serious about the change in the first place. Trying to split the time of first-rate people between doing business and changing business is also futile. It disperses their energies, subjects them to internal conflicts, burdens them with context-switching overhead, and tells the organization that change is actually not that important.

The third way that executives can demonstrate their commitment is by becoming and staying personally engaged in it. Companies are exquisitely sensitive to the implied messages that leaders send through their own behavior, such as how they allocate their time. When those at the top spend their own time on a certain program, everyone knows it; it communicates the appropriate and desired message that the project is critical. Conversely, if you make impassioned speeches but otherwise delegate all responsibility and remain only vaguely informed, the organization will reach a very different conclusion.

Fourth, leadership must display passion for the change. *Passion* is a word that is not used in business as often as it should be. Rational arguments about improving operating performance, enhancing financial performance, and even improving the quality of work life are fine, but they do not go far enough. One CEO has told me that if you truly want change, you have to "reach deep into people's hearts." Note the use of the word *heart* rather than *head*. People have to believe that a major change is of transcendent importance, not merely economically rational. One cannot expect an enterprise's rank and file to be more enthusiastic or engaged in a change initiative than their leaders. You must not only think that what you are doing is a good idea; you must believe in it at a deep gut level. You must care so intensely that those around you cannot help but be infected with your enthusiasm.

Finally, committed leaders demand—not request—widespread participation and engagement in making the change happen, and they hold line managers accountable for achieving the results. People must understand that contributing to the change is mandatory, and that no excuses will be accepted. It is essential that you move quickly to remove any members of the senior management team who do not embrace change and whose lack of support is recognized in the company; this will quickly make believers of even the most cynical and skeptical.

5. Communicate Effectively.

To create a customer-centered company, everyone in the company will have to work extra hard, learn new skills, cope with unfamiliar problems, and in general rise to the occasion. If people do not understand, don't believe in, or don't care about what is going on, they won't do any of these things. The way to make them understand, believe, and care is by communicating with them. Yet most companies are shockingly incompetent at internal communications. Masters of shaping their customers' desires, they nonetheless seem incapable of establishing any genuine rapport with their employees. Their efforts to reach out are often tacky and naive. Many assume they can win hearts and minds by ordering everyone to watch a video of the CEO reading a cliché-laden speech at a dimly lit podium, or by distributing coffee mugs emblazoned with some hortatory logo. Such idiocies only turn people off and reinforce skepticism and cynicism throughout the company.

An entire book could and should be written about the importance of effective internal communications in support of major change. For now, I will emphasize five key principles.

There is no such thing as overcommunication. Too many senior executives assume that once they have said something, the audience has heard and understood the message. Nothing could be further from the truth. People in organizations are bombarded with so much information that they instinctively tune out most of it. You have to repeat a message endlessly if it is to penetrate the audience's defenses.

Make communications stand out. Do you really expect people to leap to attention when they receive another dreary one-page memo on one more "bold" initiative? Its very look confirms its unimportance, and into the circular file it goes, unappreciated and probably unread. People in organizations are overwhelmed with dull communications. Make yours arresting, funny, controversial, and memorable. Make it grab the eye, trigger laughs, and get tongues wagging. Use vivid colors, jokes, cartoons, stories, doggerel verse—anything to grab attention. Remember, the medium is crucial to the message. If your company can produce memorable marketing for its products, surely it can learn to sell change to its employees.

Never lie. Never. Not ever. Not even a little. It is extraordinarily tempting to blur the truth in order to make news easier to swallow—or easier to say. Sensitive issues such as the impact of a change program on jobs and pay are rarely, if ever, discussed truthfully. But a workforce nearly always knows when it is being lied to, and it reacts accordingly. Lies of omission are as bad as lies of commission; avoiding something painful merely focuses everyone's attention on it. Honesty is always the best policy. Face sensitive issues head-on, and never flinch from uttering those candid words "I don't know."

Enlist top management in communications. One chief executive has accurately described his job as chief change agent. It is the responsibility of senior leaders to personally carry the message of change throughout the company. Only by putting their own credibility on the line, and exerting their unique power, can they be sure that the message will be taken seriously.

Make communications two-way. Employees begin to internalize a message when they have to grapple with it. One-way communication is ineffective. No one likes to be addressed as though he or she were a piece of furniture, so make a point of starting a conversation and inviting ideas. Discussions, feedback sessions, and polling are some ways of getting your people engaged. Ask them how well your message is getting across. Their responses will help you determine how well you are being understood.

6. Deploy in a Series of Steps.

As I said earlier, companies know how to do certain kinds of new things: introduce new products, open new plants, expand into new markets, and so on. Their approach to doing these things entails meticulous planning. They identify everything that needs to be done to achieve the goal; they work out resource requirements and dependencies, then fashion a detailed work schedule with specific milestones that can be tracked along the way. Companies take justifiable pride in their ability to get new things done with these techniques. But if they use this approach to implement this book's agenda, they will almost certainly experience catastrophic failure.

The reason is that the "new" things for which companies use this implementation methodology are actually only semi-new. That is, the product or plant may be new, but the experience of introducing it is not. Managers know exactly what they are doing when they undertake these efforts; they have a very clear idea of their destination and can make plans accordingly.

None of these criteria apply to implementing distribution communities, creating new forms of customer value, or turning managers into collaborators. These things, like the other items on the agenda, are truly new. The enterprise has no experience with any of them, and so it lacks the basis for developing reliable plans for getting them done. The full nature of these changes cannot be appreciated in advance; unexpected problems will inevitably arise; and time frames will prove impossible to estimate. In the face of so much uncertainty, a traditional implementation strategy will assuredly go awry.

The consequences of a botched implementation are particularly severe given the high stakes. After all, these are not routine initiatives. These are high-profile, multidimensional, strategic shifts that will shape the future of the company and affect virtually everyone in it. Their announcement will be met with organizational anxiety, and the potential for widespread resistance is high. Failure to meet some milestone in an unrealistic plan will be widely interpreted as evidence that the effort is failing.

Moreover, in traditional implementations, the results are not achieved until the very end. When a computer system is installed and turned on, when a plant is ready and put online, the payoffs from the investment begin to flow. But when carrying out the kinds of changes called for by the agenda, you cannot afford to wait that long. The pressures of the customer economy and the anxieties of the organization demand early payback as well as rapid feedback so that everyone knows you are on the right track.

These conditions demand a new approach to implementation, one considerably different from the traditional one that most companies know best—the "big bang," in which everything is accomplished in one grand step. Instead, implementation must proceed in a series of smaller steps, each of which represents progress toward the ultimate destination. Each of these steps must be done relatively quickly, and it must deliver some concrete payoff (albeit less than the ultimate destination would deliver). For instance, rather than trying to completely transform its distribution channel in one step, a company might begin by providing a small set of Internet-enabled services to its intermediaries, services that are relatively easy to develop and install. Once these are successfully in place and in use, the company can follow up with another set of capabilities, then another. (This is precisely the approach that Motorola took in the work discussed in Chapter 8.) Eventually, when the full set of capabilities has been deployed, the overall relationship between manufacturer and intermediary will have been transformed. Getting to that point has been organized as a number of smaller, more manageable steps, rather than one massive, organization-paralyzing one.

THESE THEN ARE the six critical ingredients for successfully implementing the agenda: Focus your efforts under a single umbrella theme; concentrate on people issues; recognize that different people will react differently and so need to be managed differently; display committed executive leadership; learn to communicate effectively; and structure implementation to deliver early payback. If you follow these steps diligently, your success, if not guaranteed, becomes highly likely. You will be following in the footsteps of many companies that learned the hard way that these steps lead to triumph. Earlier, I referred to these six elements as a toolkit for change. Actually, there is another word that describes them, a word with which by now you should be very familiar: *process*. If you turn change implementation from the random thrashing about that it too often is into a systematic process based on these half-dozen elements, you are well on your way to success.

At this point, you, the patient reader, may be forgiven for thinking that there is no more to be said. I have reviewed the case for reinventing companies for the customer economy, presented the elements of an agenda for doing so, and outlined a process for implementing that agenda. Yet a glance at the table of contents reveals that there is one more chapter to come. What could remain? Let me merely say that implementing the agenda is not the end of the story; far from it. In many ways, it is just the beginning. To resolve that conundrum, I invite you to read on.

12

Prepare for a Future
You Cannot Predict

Institutionalize a Capacity for Change

I n a management seminar I led in early 2000, I asked the participants to list the biggest headaches that had bedeviled their
organizations over the previous twelve months. In no particular order,
here are seven of the most frequently mentioned crises that these companies had to deal with in 1999:

- *The Euro:* The new common European currency had enormous im-
  plications for how companies organized their European operations,
  to say nothing of its consequences for accounting systems.
- *Asian economic crisis:* Many U.S. exporters were devastated by the
  Pacific Rim's economic collapse in early 1999.
- *Major mergers and acquisitions:* Industry after industry was rocked
  by the coupling of its largest players—DaimlerChrysler, Exxon-
  Mobil, and AOL–Time Warner, just to name a few.
- *Deregulation:* Companies accustomed to operating under regulation
  and largely without competition found this sudden shift to a more
  competitive environment unsettling, to say the least.

- *ERP implementation:* While ERP systems offered great potential for integrating company processes and operations, they also posed enormous implementation challenges.
- *Supply chain integration:* The need to work closely with suppliers and customers in order to reduce inventories and costs across the supply chain demanded major adjustments from all parties.
- *The Internet:* Virtually every company and industry had to scramble to determine what this radical new technology meant for them.

After the group identified its issues, I turned the discussion to strategic planning, the familiar mechanism by which companies prepare themselves for the future. Usually, a company's strategic plan has at least a five-year time horizon.

I innocently asked my seminar attendees if their strategic planners had identified any of the key issues of 1999 in 1994, when they were five years away. Not a single hand was raised. I have asked this question repeatedly of many groups, and not one hand has ever gone up. In other words, every year hundreds of companies churn out long-term strategic plans that are empty exercises—virtually total failures at pinpointing and preparing for the critical issues of the future.

This picture, troubling though it is, can get even worse. At the end of 1999, a senior American Express executive reflected on the most important initiatives his company had undertaken that year. These included such innovations as the Blue Card, a credit card containing an 8K chip for Internet use, and a program entitled American Express @Work, which made it easier for businesses to manage their corporate American Express cards online.

These were among the most critical advances American Express made in 1999—yet they had not been included in the company's plan for 1999, which had been prepared just the previous year. In other words, these programs were conceived and launched within one calendar year. The need for these initiatives wasn't recognized until 1999, at which point the company had to move on them immediately. Forget about projecting the future five years hence; seeing twelve months ahead seems to be beyond anyone's capabilities.

The foregoing isn't a commentary on the inadequacy of strategic planning or on American Express. Rather, it reflects the fact that we are living in most unusual times, when the horizon has moved closer and time frames have condensed. The phrase *speed of change*, the subject of countless business books, articles, and speeches, has been so overused of late that it has been bleached of meaning. Yet change is not an abstraction, and its acceleration is not just a topic for pontificating gurus.

Consider the question of technology diffusion—the length of time it takes a new technology to reach a certain critical mass of users, say 10 million. For pagers, the time from initial market entry to 10 million users was forty-one years. Fax machines took twenty-two years, VCRs nine, CD players seven, personal computers six, and Web browsers just ten months. Napster took even less time than that. The point is that new technologies no longer have long gestation periods, during which companies and consumers can think about and adapt to their implications. They go from novel to routine practically overnight.

When I first became involved in information technology thirty-five years ago—in the mid-1960s—the expected lifetime of a new computer product was seven to ten years. The manufacturer could expect the product to remain viable in the marketplace for at least that long. Now, the viability period has been reduced to eighteen months at the outside—and more typically six to nine months. In other words, as soon as a product is announced, it is virtually obsolete.

Technology is far from the only domain of breakneck change. The context of business is constantly changing as well. Social, legal, regulatory, and political conditions shape what business can and cannot do. Legal restrictions are suddenly lifted or imposed, national boundaries dissolve, and economies boom and bust, all with virtually no warning.

I am on an e-mail distribution list for biweekly reports on major changes that affect business. One week the topic was the sharp increase in the number of women who make their families' investment decisions;

another was the sudden upswing in consumer interest in buying from companies that are socially conscious on environmental issues and third world labor. Yet another report summarized the dramatic decline in the power of fixed prices with the advent of auctions at eBay and Yahoo! It is enough to make one's head spin. Nothing can be taken for granted for more than an afternoon. Heraclitus's dictum that "all is flux" is shaping up as the greatest understatement of our age.

In my seminars, I often include a display of some contemporary headlines from the business pages:

- AOL Acquires Time Warner
- White House Increases Estimate of Surplus
- Nokia Dominates Cellular Phone Market
- California Utilities Face Default
- Hackers Halt eBay

After reviewing these headlines, I ask managers to imagine how they would have reacted if they had read them five years ago. They say that they would have found most of them ludicrous and the rest simply incomprehensible. Many of the phenomena that so preoccupy executives today were not even blips on their radar screens five years ago.

I then ask my seminar attendees to name the strongest, most invincible companies they can think of. The usual suspects are named—Intel, General Electric, Microsoft, Procter & Gamble, and the like, the bluest blue chips.

I proceed to divide the group into small teams, each of which is assigned one of the companies and the following task: Construct a plausible scenario in which your assigned company is driven to the edge of bankruptcy in five years. The operative word is *plausible*. They aren't allowed to invoke an exogenous force, such as a scientific miracle or a far-fetched intervention, divine or federal.

Despite these constraints, no one has any difficulty completing the assignment. Let's consider Microsoft. Little imagination is required to draw the outlines of a fatal plunge for the mighty king of the software hill. The free alternative operating system called Linux is now being supported through open source code by thousands of programmers around the world. If Linux catches on more, the result could be an explosion of new application software that jolts Windows out of its catbird seat. Or perhaps we will see a proliferation of so-called thin PCs— very inexpensive computers with little memory or processing power that serve mainly to connect users to the Internet. Microsoft's powerful Windows operating system isn't designed to operate on such thin platforms and the company could lose its dominant position to some upstart that had the right product at the right time.

This isn't to say that Microsoft or any of the other corporate powerhouses will actually experience any of these horrific scenarios. The point is that they could. (And according to published reports, Microsoft chairman Bill Gates spends a lot of hours worrying just about such eventualities.)

The point of this and other similar scenarios is that if they occur, the high-flier's downfall will be caused by change rather than incompetence: changes in technology, competition, customer preferences, or in some other aspect of the business environment in which it operates and competes.

Interestingly, when I started conducting this exercise with managers in the mid-1990s, some of the companies they regularly listed, such as Coca-Cola, Motorola, and Nike, were, in fact, displaced from the top just a few years later in the same ways as the scenarios had imagined. Equally interesting is that some have begun to recover and are starting to reappear on my attendees' star charts.

The reasons for this unprecedented rate of change are not hard to find. The first is the explosion of knowledge; it is an oft-repeated cliché that some 90 percent of the scientists and engineers who have ever lived in the history of humankind are at work today. Since all scientific and technological advances build on everything that preceded them, we are thus guaranteed an ever broader stream of technological innovations, which will inevitably bring business change in their wake. The second is the modern telecommunications infrastructure. Once upon a time, new ideas and techniques propagated very slowly if at all. Innovations could spread only as quickly as the speed of the horse or the train. Today innovations and ideas spread at the speed of light. What was new this morning is familiar this afternoon and old news by the evening. The third is a culture of innovation that welcomes change. Not so long ago, American culture valorized the tried and true, the well tested, the long familiar. No longer. Now people want the newest, the latest, the most up to date. Where *newfangled* once connoted unreliability and questionable quality, now *traditional* breeds suspicion if not contempt.

In short, the world is spinning faster than ever before; change is occurring on multiple fronts simultaneously and at an overwhelmingly rapid pace; and such change can be very hazardous indeed to a company's health. The implications are sobering. I opened this book by arguing that the happy days of the late 1990s are now gone and that the world of business has reverted to its normal condition of complexity and difficulty. In fact, it is worse than that. Business in the 2000s is not just as tough as it always was; it is tougher. The inexorable pace of change overlays a new level of complexity onto the challenge of creating and sustaining a winning company.

It would be tempting for me to suggest, and for you to believe, that implementing the nine items on the agenda is all that it will take for your company to succeed in the coming years. It would be tempting but wrong. Because the world is changing at a head-spinning rate, the agenda is in fact not fixed but open-ended. Before the decade is out, your company will face new imperatives that neither you nor I can now foresee. New technologies will arise that enable unprecedented ways of working and creating customer value. Customer needs will change in unpredictable ways. The sociopolitical climate will impose new requirements or restrictions. In short, you will never be finished with the agenda. Changing times will add items to it as soon as you take others off. Implementing the agenda is not a one-time effort but an ongoing responsibility.

The question, of course: How do you handle this responsibility?

Conventional wisdom would tell you to plan better; that is, to work harder at gathering data that will forecast the future and allow you to identify the new elements of the agenda far in advance, so that you may get ready to implement them. But that is precisely the approach that hundreds of companies have pursued to no avail. Even the most promising methods of prognostication, such as scenario planning popularized by Royal Dutch Shell, have very limited application. How can you possibly plan for an explosive new phenomenon like e-commerce? By the time it is tangible enough to imagine scenarios, it is too late. It moves too fast to catch up with, much less stay ahead of.

The answer is to shift the definition of planning. Traditional planning assumed that one could first predict the future and then, in response to what the predictions revealed, create detailed plans that could be reliably executed. This no longer makes sense.

Today planning must assume that the future can't be predicted— only prepared for. This sounds impossible, but it can be done if your organization has the capacity to identify and respond instantly to changes that affect it.

In other words, the way to cope with rapid change is to create a highly adaptable organization that obliterates time lags. It never looks ahead. It operates entirely in the present, only "now." It spots and reacts to significant change in practically the same breath. It does not need to anticipate what new items will be added to its agenda; instead, it will handle them the moment they appear.

Though this may sound like the kind of incomprehensible abstraction that only consultants love, it is in fact possible to create such an agile enterprise. There are three concrete steps that you can take to make your company resilient in the face of unrelenting change:

1. Create an early warning system to spot changes to which you must respond quickly.
2. Become adept at rapidly designing and installing the new ways of working that such external changes demand.
3. Create an organizational infrastructure that supports both of the first two.

Let's consider each of these in turn.

1. Create an Early Warning System.

As I have said, one major reason why companies get caught flat-footed by changes is that they don't see them even when they are staring them right in the face. A few alert people may observe what's happening, but the organization as a whole seems neither to recognize danger nor to exhibit urgency in responding to it quickly and systematically. To outsiders, such insouciance is incomprehensible. How did Montgomery Ward allow Sears to steal the suburbs, and how did Sears later allow Wal-Mart to do the same thing to it? Did Sears not see that the discounters were eating into its core market? Didn't the established booksellers see the audience that Amazon.com was preempting right before their eyes? Were they unaware of the thunderous arrival of electronic commerce? To all these baffling questions, the answer couldn't be simpler—that's right, they didn't notice.

In most organizations, change is regarded as an anomaly, an exceptional event. None of a company's sensory systems is designed to watch out for it. Inherent in the operations of most companies is the confidence that continuity and stability will prevail, and that confidence can make them almost willfully blind to what's going on around them.

In many organizations, those who first see the handwriting on the wall lack the authority to do anything about it—and those who can, don't notice it. Executives stashed away in the hushed splendor of their sixtieth-floor suites are rarely the first to recognize external threats. Critical change that really matters occurs far below, at ground level in the real world; a sudden change in customer preferences, a new competitive offering that leapfrogs yours, or an unexpected response to a new product are issues that most senior executives encounter only thirdhand. Insulated from the workaday world, they suffer the senior executive's occupational hazard: the ignorance that results from a steady diet of sanitized and virtually useless information. As one corporate leader said, "I only know what they let me know. The information I get is summarized, bleached of all important detail. It's narrow and focused primarily on financial issues. It's also painfully late. It mostly tells me about events of the last quarter, which is about as useful as telling me about the last century."

The people who do notice change first are the people on the front line—the customer service rep who hears the same new question from many different customers, or the salesperson who keeps bumping into a surprising competitor again and again, or an engineer who reads about a new technology in his or her professional publication. These should be considered announcements of change, but they are almost never heeded. The cues rarely transcend a few individuals' cubicles. It is an age-old problem: The generals who run the war are the farthest from the front and know the least about the fighting. The powerless know more than the powerful in virtually all organizations. During periods of intense change, this paradox can be fatal.

In most companies, indicators of change remain unnoticed because everyone is working busily to pursue the status quo. Routine is both a blessing and a curse for organizations. While it does get plans carried out and performance goals achieved, its comfort hinders people from straying off designated paths or challenging the front office's rosy projections.

I am talking here about more than resistance to change. I am referring to the reality that anyone who is looking for signs of change is almost certainly guilty of not keeping his or her mind clamped on the formal job—a distraction not appreciated in overworked businesses with limited resources and demanding customers. Indifference to change is less intentional than institutional. If the sales rep's job is to sell, and the engineer's is to complete the current project on time, neither will have time to recognize and to argue that the current methods for doing these things should be replaced by something entirely different. Often the companies most oblivious to change are those performing so well in the moment that no one has time to think about it.

At most companies, noticing change is not included in anyone's job description. It may come under the formal purview of the company's strategic planners, but all too often they are involved in a mindless ritual centered on budget calculations. Even when strategic planners actually plan strategies, they are usually projected so far into the unpredictable future that they are tantamount to fortune telling.

In short, the ways in which organizations are structured and operate tend to squash whatever natural inclination people have toward ringing the change alarm. In many cases, those who do so are thought of as, well, alarmists and "not team players." Even people who find change staring them in the face find it far easier to put their faces back in the sand, where their managers are already comfortably ensconced.

The information that most companies have and use also does little or nothing to encourage them to change. The most widely utilized information is internally focused, historical, and by its very inward nature unlikely to reflect external developments. We have lots of data about what our production costs were last quarter, but not about what they might be next month if we adopt new technologies. We know what our sales have been, but not those of an upstart competitor in an adjoining space. Though the most important change always emerges from places where a company least expects it, its information systems are focused on the familiar and the expected.

The only way out of this impasse is to make change watching a formal and explicit activity within the organization. In other words, make it a process. Instead of just parroting the usual platitudes about change, companies must design and implement rigorous processes through which change will be quickly detected and reported to leadership. Three elements of such a process are:

Develop Deep Insight into Your Customers.

This book has repeatedly emphasized the need for organizations to think about their customers first and themselves second. Yet even companies that make a fetish of "listening" to their customers miss their message, because the company is listening only on one frequency, that of self-interest. To appreciate nascent change, you must put aside your own point of view and adopt your customers' perspective. Walk in their shoes; experience their lives. Don't look at them just through the lens of your need to increase sales. Understand their unstated and unmet needs, and appreciate their problems, whether or not they have anything to do with what you are selling. You won't learn about their problems through formal customer satisfaction surveys. You will need to sit alongside your customers in their daily work and lives, to engage them in wide-ranging and open-ended conversation, to enter into their worlds. Your aims are to see the world through your customers' eyes and to understand them better than they understand themselves.

Analyze Potential as well as Existing Competitors.

As traditional barriers separating industries fall, and as start-ups become more common than rare, nascent competitors require serious attention. Those who don't threaten you today may well do so tomorrow. Carl von Clausewitz, the Prussian military sage, wrote that one must judge an enemy by his capabilities, not by his intentions. Companies must continuously scan the horizon looking for others that have the potential to offer competing products and services. Invite customers to be your competitive analysts—ask them what's new and interesting, who else is trying to win them over, who they think is on a roll. Track the venture-capital financing reports. Investigate adjacent and complementary industries. Attend their conventions, meet their current customers, put yourself in their shoes. Above all, follow Andy Grove's advice: "Only the paranoid survive."

Look for the Seeds of the Future in the Present.

Even the most sudden changes are heralded by early indicators that are visible to those who know how and where to look for them. The Internet, for example, was years in the making. It evolved from the government-funded Arpanet, which had been operating since the 1970s. E-commerce did not fall from the sky in 1998. Forerunners including American Airlines' Sabre reservations network and American Hospital Supply's ASAP order entry system planted its seeds years before. The key here is to inspect a lot of seeds in order to find the few that will bear fruit. It takes time and money, and it also takes creativity to avoid seeing what's new only in terms of what's old. Avoid the mistake of looking for the seeds of tomorrow in yesterday's fields. Don't ask people or companies whose expertise is the last groundbreaking development to advise you about the next one. Their investment in the status quo makes them less receptive to indications that it is about to be replaced.

THE BODY'S IMMUNE system is a biological analogy to an organization's ability to recognize change. The immune system is not a particular organ; nor is it localized in one part of the body. It is distributed throughout the body, and whenever an antigen—a foreign body—is detected, it mobilizes a response.

Every company needs its own immune system—a disciplined process for identifying, collecting, interpreting, disseminating, and sharing information that might call for a major response. To be successful, this process should be carefully and explicitly thought through; haphazard improvisation will not do. It requires a process owner who will oversee its design and execution; if detecting change is everyone's responsibility, then it will be no one's. At the same time, it can't be conducted by a single dedicated part of the company. Every individual, regardless of his or her level or area, must feel responsible for two jobs: first, his or her day-to-day work, and second, being alert to important signs of change. Finally, this process must be measured in a disciplined way, specific goals for its performance must be established, and employees' evaluations and compensation must be tied to achieving them. Otherwise the process will have no teeth.

To date, few companies have implemented a formal change recognition process, because most haven't yet realized the degree to which they need one and how much they can benefit from it. Among the companies that have seen the light and have launched early versions of this critical process are Wal-Mart and America Online. Wal-Mart dominates its industry in large part because of its rapid adaptability to change. The late Sam Walton, Wal-Mart's founder, attributed the company's success to its ability to "change faster than the other guys," not to its buying power or logistical expertise. This capability did not come about accidentally, but because of specific actions the company took and still takes. Every Saturday morning Wal-Mart leaders from all over the country gather at headquarters in Bentonville, Arkansas, to review what happened that week and in particular to share new ideas and observations. What is working well? What isn't? What are competitors up to? What shifts in customer buying behavior are we seeing? The issues are discussed, plans are made, and responses are designed.

America Online does something similar. It is difficult to imagine a company that has undergone as much turbulence as AOL. Yet it has managed to roll with the punches and stay atop a continually changing industry. One of AOL's secrets is the weekly meeting of its senior executive team, which they begin by reviewing the metrics of the business and comparing them against plan. Are subscriptions up or down? Are revenues up or down? Is connectivity up or down? Is advertising up or down? What is surprising and what is new? Changes are made to the business plan based on the answers. AOL's plan is neither sacrosanct nor set in concrete for the year. It is a living, changing guide to action.

It is also a matter of faith and policy throughout AOL that changes and issues that are not being addressed adequately at lower levels must be escalated quickly to the senior executive team. If, at other companies, people are often punished for this behavior, at AOL they are praised.

AOL's leaders spend a lot of their own time looking for possible competitive threats and uncovering new marketplace events. At too many companies, executives are the people whom others must persuade that change has arrived; at AOL, executives are the people who find change first. The leadership team at AOL sees its job as redirecting the business, not monitoring it. As one senior AOL executive puts it, "For us, managing change is the business of management. There are companies out there where managers see their jobs as keeping things the same and improving them. Our managers look at their job as pushing change through the organization all the time because that's what they're constantly exposed to."

2. Become Proficient at Responding to Change.

As Will Rogers said, "Even if you're on the right track, you'll still get run over if you're just sitting there." Noticing change is good; doing something about it is better. This is not as easy as it sounds.

Since contemporary organizations evolved in an environment devoid of broad and deep changes, they did not develop mechanisms to cope with it. If they thought about it at all, companies considered change an occasional traumatic event to be endured, after which stability would once more reign. This is no longer the case; today change is the normal state of affairs, a constant condition rather than an unusual event. Instead of long periods of equilibrium punctuated by short intervals of change, the periods of equilibrium have become shorter and shorter. For instance, in the early 1990s, IBM undertook to reengineer how it did business, to cope with the then-new environment of client-server computing. Scarcely had these efforts been finished than the company had to embark on another program of fundamental change to adjust to the e-business world.

Consequently, it is not enough to learn how to handle change—you must also remember what you learn. In the mid-1990s, facing newly intensified competition, many companies engaged in major reengineering efforts to lower costs, shorten cycle times, and minimize errors. Most of these companies had little or no experience at effecting such major changes. Through trial and error and a lot of instruction in the school of hard knocks, they managed to scrape together the required skills. They formed design and implementation teams, developed transition management strategies, learned how to deploy technology more quickly, and so on. And after these reengineering projects were concluded, everyone promptly resumed their regular jobs and forgot everything they had learned. Now that change looms again, these companies find they can't profit from their previous experiences because they didn't institutionalize the new skills and insights they developed.

The first step to such institutionalization is to develop a permanent cadre of people to assist in redirecting the company. Note the word *assist;* the worst thing a company can do is establish a "change department," thereby implying that everyone else can ignore the issue because this specialized department will take care of it. This new cadre of experts will facilitate and enable change, but they can't do it all. They will play central roles in designing and coordinating change programs, but it would be a dangerous error to position them as the only people involved.

The second step is to create a disciplined process for responding to change, analogous to the one for recognizing it. If major change were a once-in-a-lifetime event, such a process would be unnecessary. But since the time between major shifts is shrinking to almost nothing, you have to systematize your ability to deal with them.

I have already outlined such a process. Chapter 11 identified the basic elements of a process that you can use to implement the elements already on the agenda; you can also use it for the new agenda items that will appear in the future, whose outlines no one can yet perceive.

DTE Energy has successfully developed and institutionalized such a process for implementing change. Recall that in the mid-1990s DTE Energy encountered difficulties as it made the transition to a process enterprise. When it was over, instead of breathing a sigh of relief, DTE Energy's leaders took a hard look at themselves and recognized that the underlying problem was the fact that the company did not have the capacity to manage massive change. They also had the prescience to recognize that this transformation would be just the first of many they would have to undergo. Consequently, they designed and created a highly disciplined process for reinventing their company.

DTE Energy's change process consists of four primary phases. The first is to prepare the organization, by making sure that everyone understands the need for change and is committed to doing their part, and by ensuring that both the change effort and the ongoing business have the resources they need. Communication starts at the very beginning of the endeavor, building the case and educating people throughout the organization as to why change is necessary, and it never lets up thereafter. The second phase is planning, which means identifying the specific actions that must be taken to carry out the needed changes, and analyzing their impacts. Next is the execution of this plan, ensuring that all parts are carried out in an integrated way. Every transformation initiative has a governance structure and an office of program control to ensure that its large array of projects interface smoothly. The company also developed a set of computer-based management tools to assist that office. The final stage is learning, in which the lessons of this change effort are reflected back in the process, so that it may perform even better next time.

The first application of this disciplined process was in 1999, when it was used to manage DTE Energy's response to the Y2K problem. This was so successful that competitors and customers used it as a benchmark against which to compare their own programs. Now the company is applying the same process to bring about a range of innovations, most notably a major merger. Because this process is so effective, the post-merger integration is reaching its aggressive milestones; in addition, the operating decline that typically follows such a corporate marriage has been avoided. DTE Energy is also working to apply this change implementation process to programs from industry deregulation to venturing into new businesses. A company once nearly paralyzed by the new now deals with it routinely.

3. Create a Supportive Organizational Infrastructure.

In order for the processes of change recognition and implementation to succeed, they must take root in a corporate culture and structure that welcomes rather than resists them. Grafting all the change management skills in the world onto a hidebound organization will produce nothing more than the same hidebound organization that can mouth popular inanities about change.

A traditional hierarchical structure, with its fragmented network of specialized units, impedes both the recognition and the implementation of change. In traditional organizations, managers will spend their time protecting their turf, passing the buck, or arguing that everything is fine as it is, instead of getting with the program.

A group of change advocates at one major *Fortune* 100 company in the midst of a transformation effort prepared a manifesto decrying such a lack of progress. It included the following passage.

> *Each function is trying to make the minimum possible change to preserve the function and business as usual. Departments say, "We control that data," or "We don't do it this way," or "There's no place on the org chart for that." Ad hoc groups are creating new workarounds.*

We seem to be replacing one set of complex procedures with another. Managers fear change and are trying to protect their turf. The new processes are being compromised in the face of organizational resistance. There is reticence on the part of senior management to take decisive action. They are not insisting on real progress and seem not to care. They approve the familiar parts, but the least familiar parts are the most important. We grieve for the success of this program.

By contrast, the kind of company described in this book, managed by process but not locked into a rigid organizational structure, is precisely the kind ready to go with the flow, ready to move in whatever direction circumstances dictate. In such an organization, process owners are responsible for ensuring that processes continue to perform well, no matter what the circumstances. Accordingly, they look outward at changing conditions rather than inward to office politics. Of necessity, they stay tuned to evolving customer needs. Their incentive is clear: If they ignore external change, both their processes and their own performance will quickly go south.

Managers with other concerns, such as those responsible for particular customer segments or product lines, are similarly forced to search for changes that can affect their areas of responsibility. But none of these managers is looking to protect his or her turf, since none really has any. The essential teamwork that characterizes these organizations provides the environment needed to succeed with major change initiatives.

But structure (or its near absence) is not enough to assure that these change processes will take root. The dominant culture and attitudes of an organization ultimately determine how it weathers change. If people within a company view change as a distraction, as an annoyance, as a figment of overheated managerial imaginations, then they will ignore it, no matter what processes for handling it have been implemented. The company's leaders must forge a new set of attitudes: that change is an inevitable part of everyday life, that ignoring it is fatal, and that responding to it is real work, not a distraction from it.

I offer a number of quotations I have heard over the years that capture the beliefs of a change-friendly organization. They are not silver bullets, and I hope never to see them printed on T-shirts or coffee mugs, but they do suggest the spirit that leaders must inculcate in their organizations.

- "We are going to create the company that will put us out of business." I first encountered this slogan at a division of American Express that, despite the fact that it was in a market leadership position, undertook a major program in the 1990s to transform how it did business. Another way of saying this is "If we're going to be butchered, we want to hold the knife ourselves." This viewpoint implicitly recognizes that nothing lasts forever, that even the strongest position is tenable only in the short term, and that someone will come along before long and knock every leader off its perch. Better to be the perpetrator rather than the victim of such power shifts.

- "The day you believe you're successful is the day you stop being successful." This line, which has been attributed to Herb Kelleher, founder of Southwest Airlines, captures the fact that arrogance is the downfall of many great companies. Companies that believe they are successful will not feel a desperate urge to constantly guard against threats; nor will they willingly let go of the strategies that have led to their success. A variation of this observation is "The hallmark of the truly successful organization is its willingness to abandon what has long made it successful." A company guided by this sentiment knows that resting on its laurels is out of the question.

- "The best companies are always worried." This insight comes from Michael Porter, the distinguished scholar of business strategy and a professor at the Harvard Business School. My own experience confirms this dictum. The companies that continually land on their feet despite the inevitable ups and downs of business are those that never take their success for granted. The minute they achieve one success, they begin creating its successor. Hewlett-Packard is an organization that has consistently stayed strong and continued to grow in a set of high-technology industries where change occurs at a frightening pace and corporate life expectancies are low. A few years ago, one of HP's divisions recently undertook to reinvent itself because a market survey conducted by its managers demonstrated that 50 percent of its customers rated the company as worse or no better than the competition. This alarming revelation prompted massive changes in how the division was organized and operated. What is interesting is that another company could have expressed the same data very differently: 50 percent of our customers think we're best. That formulation, which would tempt a company into complacency, would never be used at HP.

- "Winners make more mistakes than losers." To a traditional organization, this phrase would seem contradictory and even incomprehensible. After all, aren't winning companies abler and smarter than losing ones? No, they are not. The real difference between winners and losers at the game of change is that the winners try things. Some of the things they try work, some don't. Losers, on the other hand, try little or nothing. They make fewer mistakes, but they also have fewer successes.

- "The best way to have lots of good ideas is to have lots of ideas and throw away the bad ones." This observation, attributed to chemist Linus Pauling, winner of two Nobel Prizes, expresses the notion that a change-friendly organization relishes debate and argument. It values the contrarian. It thrives on disagreement, discomfort, and contention. It is willing to accept that not all of its ideas will be good, and it knows that it is better to try many things rather than none at all.

- "If you wait for all the lights to turn green, you'll never get started." This advice was given me by a highly effective change leader. When responding to change, no organization can be certain of where it's going when it starts. An insistence on certainty and clarity is the absolute killer of progress.

- "When memories exceed dreams, the end is near." This chilling phrase reflects the fact that too many companies spend much of their energy fixated on their glorious histories. Companies that keep looking over their shoulders are unlikely to notice the freight trains headed straight for them. In a world of constant flux, past successes count for less than nothing. The curtain rises anew on the business stage every day. A company must take pride in its past accomplishments, but it must also remember what every prospectus states—"Past results are no guarantee of future success."

In short, a change-ready organization values ambition, humility, curiosity, inquisitiveness, risk tolerance, courage, and a focus on the future. A company that embodies these values and institutionalizes processes for recognizing and implementing change is ready for the future, no matter how hazy it may be. It is prepared to respond to tomorrow as soon as it becomes today, to cope with an agenda for change that never ends.

NOW YOU AND I have indeed reached the end of our time together. The challenge is manifest, the issues explicit, the ways to deal with them identified. If you summon the will and commitment, you can master the challenge. The fact that new issues will arise should not discourage you from addressing the ones at hand today. As the Talmud teaches, "You are not called upon to complete the work, nor are you free to evade it." Just as you build on the work of your predecessors, it is your responsibility to leave your successors a better platform on which they can build. The mission is clear, and the time is now. Your company's future is in your hands.

Index

About the Author

DR. MICHAEL HAMMER is one of the world's foremost business thinkers. He is the originator of both reengineering and the process enterprise, ideas that have transformed the modern business world. Organizations around the globe have achieved dramatic performance improvements by applying his principles to their operations and structure.

A highly sought-after lecturer, Dr. Hammer also serves as an adviser to leaders of the world's most progressive companies. His public seminars are attended by thousands of people annually. He is the author of numerous articles and three earlier books: the international bestseller *Reengineering the Corporation: A Manifesto for Business Revolution, The Reengineering Revolution: A Handbook,* and *Beyond Reengineering: How the Process-Centered Organization Is Changing Our Work and Our Lives.*

Dr. Hammer was formerly a professor of computer science at the Massachusetts Institute of Technology, and he is a founder and director of several high-technology firms. *Business Week* named him as one of the four preeminent management thinkers of the 1990s, and *Time* magazine included him in its first list of America's twenty-five most influential individuals.